God and Randomness

Thomas R. McFaul
AND
Al Brunsting

WIPF & STOCK · Eugene, Oregon

GOD AND RANDOMNESS

Copyright © 2017 Thomas R. McFaul and Al Brunsting. All rights reserved. Except for brief quotations in critical publications or reviews, no part of this book may be reproduced in any manner without prior written permission from the publisher. Write: Permissions, Wipf and Stock Publishers, 199 W. 8th Ave., Suite 3, Eugene, OR 97401.

Wipf & Stock
An Imprint of Wipf and Stock Publishers
199 W. 8th Ave., Suite 3
Eugene, OR 97401

www.wipfandstock.com

PAPERBACK ISBN: 978-1-5326-3896-1
HARDCOVER ISBN: 978-1-5326-3897-8
EBOOK ISBN: 978-1-5326-3898-5

Manufactured in the U.S.A.

"Here, the whole scenario of the creation, its future in chaotic randomness; and, the presence of God in it all, are all laid out in clear and easily understood language."

—**Emery Percell**, University of Chicago, retired pastor,
United Methodist Church

"The preface creates a sense of intrigue and a desire to discover more about the topics in succeeding chapters. I was not disappointed. I found the discussion about the possible existence of other dimensions and the further possibility that God may be operating in those dimensions to be particularly intriguing."

—**Dale Zimmerman**, Attorney and Recipient of the Milton Gordon
Award in 1989

"Here in *God and Randomness* the authors make speculations that are similar to and consistent with current research in cosmology. This provides reader with an understanding of how God might be actively at work in all that chaos and randomness that pervades our lives and our world."

—**Richard L. Schwenk**, Recipient of the Outstanding Educator
award, Philippines

"This second book by McFaul and Brunsting presents valuable new perspectives on an unusual combination of two topics, God and randomness. The authors develop clear definitions and examples of randomness of varying arenas from the universe, to nano-scale physics, to evolution and to everyday human experiences. This is a well-researched thought-provoking book."

—**James Nelson**, 18 US and many foreign patents

"The personal accounts in Chapter Two were found to be very moving."

—**Christopher T. Hill**, Fellow of the American Physical Society

"This book was found to be inspiring and profound. The inclusion of experiences in family history enhanced the authors' claim about the randomness that is a part of human life. The chapter on "Randomness, Fairness, and God" was found to be excellent as was chapter 6, where the focus was on randomness and twentieth-century history. This book speaks to the struggle to understand God and His actions that has puzzled thoughtful Christians throughout the centuries."

—**K. James Stein**, Senior Scholar in Church History at Garrett-Evangelical Theological Seminary

"*God and Randomness* is aimed for the reader who wants to know more about the Big Bang theory, the origins of life and how God fits into the scheme of things. The authors show how randomness determines this. . . This book is a natural extension of their earlier book *God Is Here to Stay Science, Evolution and Belief in God.*"

—**Howard Lange**, Physicist whose computers are helping in the search of extraterrestrial radio signals of intelligent life in the SETI project

"In *God and Randomness*, the authors present a unique investigation into the Creator's use of random events in the evolution of the universe. The reader is treated to a fascinating review of a myriad integral topics such as human choice, free will, and predictability. Finally, and most significantly—the authors introduce the concept of God's possible use of extra dimensions to understand God's mysterious influence. A great read!"

—**Gordon Leidner**, Author of *God and Dice*

God and Randomness

I dedicate this book to Sally my loving and supportive wife, soulmate, and best friend.

—Thomas R. McFaul

I dedicate this book to my dear wife, Joyce Brunsting, who is beautiful, inspiring, and helpful.

—Al Brunsting

Contents

List of Illustrations | ix

Preface | xi

Acknowledgments | xv

Chapter 1. Defining Randomness | 1

Chapter 2. Three Stories | 22

Chapter 3. Micro and Macro Sources | 35

Chapter 4. The Universe and Our Solar System | 50

Chapter 5. Conscious, Self-Aware, and Mindful Humans | 71

Chapter 6. Twentieth Century History | 91

Chapter 7. The Future | 113

Chapter 8. Fairness | 133

Chapter 9. Randomness and God | 153

Bibliography | 179

Index | 181

Illustrations

Figures

1. The principle of cause and effect results applied to an everyday example and to an example from the cosmos. | 4
2. A graphical summary of some of Lorenz's conclusions about weather patterns. This curve is not quantitative. | 7
3. The Bell Curve. "Standard deviations" is a measure of the curve's width. | 10
4. A brief summary of some size scales as they relate to where quantum physics becomes important. | 37
5. Relationships between randomness, natural law, and the physical evolution of our universe. All the randomness, R, here refers to lower left cell and lower right cell in Table 1. | 52
6. Summary of the size of our universe and various major events. The horizontal and vertical scales are not numerical. | 53
7. Difference between Fission and Fusion. | 56
8. The major evolutionary steps between the original spinning nebula and a collapsing Sun and collapsing proto-planets. | 65
9. Summary timelines of some important events in the evolution of anthropoids (higher primate mammals, including monkeys, apes, and humans). | 84
10. Joe Rosenthal's iconic photo of six US marines raising the American flag at the top of Mt. Suribachi on Iwo Jima Island. | 100
11. Alternative Scenarios and the Cone of Plausibility. | 128
12. The cone as a three dimensional object. | 157

Tables

1. Summary of Determinism and Indeterminism, Involving No Choice and Choice. | 17
2. Differences between Classical Physics and Quantum Physics show-up in the predictability of future outcomes. | 42
3. Predictability and Randomness at Micro and Macro Levels. | 48
4. Summary of requirements for explanation of the origin of the solar system. | 62
5. Summary of randomness in our universe since the Big Bang. The times in the second column from the left are approximate. | 68
6. Five basic characteristics for all life. | 73
7. Three options for when life started relative to the Late Heavy Bombardment. | 76
8. Time periods for the history of the Earth. The biological evidences are generally placed into Eras that can be compared to "Geological time period's. | 79
9. Summary of six worldwide and major mass extinctions of plants and animals. | 81
10. Intentional and Unintentional Actions and Good and Bad Outcomes. | 138
11. God's Characteristics and Evil. | 146

Preface

THIS BOOK IS A sequel to our 2014 publication *God Is Here to Stay: Science, Evolution, and Belief in God*,[1] in which we demonstrated that there is no incompatibility between modern science and belief in God. We did not try to prove or disprove the existence of God, because we do not believe this is possible using any kind of knowledge. However, after examining six specific areas of inquiry,[2] we concluded at an 80 percent confidence level that the universe is so highly structured that an Intelligent Creator brought it into existence 13.8 billion years ago through an initial Inflation called the Big Bang and guided its evolution to conscious, mindful, and self-aware life on Earth.

In *God Is Here to Stay*, we contrasted randomness with belief in God. We defined the word random to mean that the universe lacks an inherent purpose of any kind. This implies that once the cosmos came into existence, it expanded through impersonal and unguided laws of cause and effect that governed its evolution and that we humans are here purely by chance.

After examining various kinds of evidence, we came to the opposite conclusion. We believe that based on modern scientific knowledge a more compelling case can be made that the universe possesses innate purpose and that it was brought into existence by an Intelligent Creator called God who directed its evolution to the development of earthly conscious, self-aware life. While we do not claim to possess comprehensive knowledge of all of the reasons why God would design the universe this way, we are highly confident that starting 200,000 years ago we modern humans became a part of it.

---

1. McFaul and Brunsting, *God Is Here to Stay: Science, Evolution and Belief in God*.

2. These include knowledge, the anthropic principle, when life emerged from non-life elements, the brain and spirituality, the universal quest for justice, and the universal quest for morality.

Our story does not stop here. After *God Is Here to Stay* was published, we started recognizing that not everybody shares the same view of randomness. One experience in particular drove home this point in such a dramatic and unexpected way that it motivated us to re-examine this entire topic.

During July 2015, we the authors were visiting the Perot Museum of Nature and Science in Dallas, Texas. Built in 2012 by Ross Perot, the Museum includes eleven exhibit halls that are designed to be a living science lesson. The purpose of the Museum is to teach science to all age groups through hands on interactive experiences. One of the exhibits is housed in the Expanding Universe Hall that shows that the cosmos began with the Big Bang and how our knowledge of its stages of evolution has changed over time. The exhibit includes large visuals and rotating projections of our solar system and beyond. There are also displays of scientists and the technical tools they used in their quest for further understanding.

As we walked through the Hall we felt like we were travelling through time and space. Not only did it grab hold of our imaginations, it also stirred our curiosity to want to learn more. As we made our way from one set of solar system images to the next, we filled our conversation with probing questions and myriad speculations about the wonders of the universe. The Museum was packed with equally curious onlookers who shared this amazing visual experience with us. As we ended our brief trek through the Hall and were still marveling at what we had just witnessed, we heard a voice over our shoulders. "What do you mean by random?"

It came as a total surprise. Unknown to us during our time in the exhibit Hall, a young college student had been following us and had remained within hearing distance. Without being aware of it, we were using the word "random" repeatedly to describe many of the events that brought the universe into existence and that directed its development. She wanted to know what we meant by the term randomness. For a few brief moments, we shared our impressions with her, and she in turn shared hers with us. It was a teachable moment for all three of us. While we do not remember all of the details of our interaction with her, it left a lasting impression on us. Even though we did not write down her name and have not seen her since then, in that moment we knew what our next joint project would be.

This book was inspired by her through that random event.

Because of our chance encounter with a college student who remains anonymous, we began to see that the term randomness can be viewed in multiple ways. As stated above, in *God Is Here to Stay* we used it to mean that from the start the universe has lacked innate purpose. In this book, we define randomness to mean the unpredictable events that have occurred and continue to occur throughout the cosmos, on Earth, and in our daily lives. Thus, while we focus on randomness as one of the core concepts in both books, we define it differently in each one. At the same time, we view this second book as an extension of the first. Even though they are separate writings, they are meant to be read as two chapters in a single volume.

As we began preparing for this new book, we recognized quickly that we were really trying to answer a single question: Where does randomness fit into a highly structured universe that evolved through such narrow physical boundaries that even a plus or minus 1 percent deviation would have produced an entirely different world than the one that gave rise to conscious, mindful, and self-aware life of Earth? We soon discovered that randomness appears everywhere, and always has, from the time of the Big Bang down to the present day.

Furthermore, we concluded early on that in every human life random events occur over which no one has control. They just happen, and they can steer the course of individuals' lives, as well as the lives of those who surround them, in unforeseen directions. Every person's situation is filled with surprises, which means that all persons have stories to tell as they look back at the unexpected events that took them down unforeseen pathways.

Thus, from the macro level of cosmic explosion and expansion to the micro level of personal stories and subatomic particles, we are left to wonder about this key question: How does the pervasive presence of randomness relate to the Intelligent Creator called God who started it all and guided its evolution? This book and the nine chapters that comprise it is our answer to this question.

As we probed more deeply into how randomness appears at all macro and micro levels of existence, we began to realize that we humans are more inclined to view what happens to us in terms of well-known cause and effect patterns that started being instilled within us at birth and became reinforced steadily as we grew older. We suspect that this basic tendency is tied to a Darwinian survival instinct that leads us to think and act in structured ways that enhance our adaptation to the conditions of life on Earth.

Because of this, we have come to the conclusion that most of the time we remain unaware, or only vaguely aware, of the impact of randomness because we have not learned to recognize it or to differentiate it from better understood cause and effect connections. One of the purposes of this book is to broaden our understanding of the nature of randomness and how and where it appears. In the process, we will describe how breakthrough discoveries in the fields of classical and quantum physics contributed enormously to our perceptions. We begin in chapter 1 by defining what we mean by the word random. At one level, the idea of randomness is simple to grasp. At another, it is complex, as we will show by examining the diverse approaches that others have used in order to clarify our understanding and avoid later confusion.

In chapter 2, Al Brunsting gives a first person account of three important people in his life, his uncle, sister, and brother. Our purpose in starting this way is to set the stage for the next seven chapters. In many ways, his story is our story. Through the narrative of his vivid story telling style, he highlights the role that random occurrences played in each of their lives. By sharing his own unique story, he reminds all of us to remember those parallel moments that shaped our lives and led us down our own unique unforeseen pathways.

Starting in chapter 3 and continuing through chapter 8, we explore how randomness has appeared at virtually every level and stage of evolution. Chapter 3 focuses on the role that randomness plays at the micro subatomic level as well as on macro sources. This is followed in chapter 4 with a description of the random events that shaped the creation of the universe and our solar system. Chapter 5 continues with how this process contributed to the emergence of conscious, mindful, and self-aware life on Earth.

In chapter 6, we shift our attention to how randomness affected five major episodes that occurred during the history of the twentieth century and into the early twenty-first. In chapter 7, we investigate whether we will be able to improve our foresight abilities in the future. Then in chapter 8, we look carefully at how randomness affects the universal quest for fairness and various views of the relationship between God and existence of evil.

Finally, we conclude this book in chapter 9 by addressing the question of how the actions and purposes of God may work in the presence of all this randomness described it in the previous eight chapters. We are now ready for chapter 1.

Acknowledgements

MANY PEOPLE HAVE TAKEN time out of their busy lives to read and comment on *God and Randomness*. Their helpful suggestions have helped improve the book's overall development and quality. We appreciate especially the contributions of Charlie Henkle, Don Livingston, Walt Marcum, and Don Reynolds.

Also, these people were particularly helpful through discussion, review, and suggestions. Francisco Ayala and Gordon Leidner were very encouraging and supportive. Emery Percell has impressive academic credentials and a lifetime of learning not only in theology but also the sciences, especially cosmology. Ric Schwenk has over thirty years of experience teaching information technology and leading agricultural development in Malaysia and the Philippines. Jim Nelson is a good friend and greatly helped. Lately, he was the Director of Materials Research and the Director of the Asia Technology Center at ITW. Jim's wife Carol was very helpful as our initial copy editor. Besides being an attorney Dale Zimmerman is well read in theology and the physical sciences. His critical review is much appreciated. There were many others that helped us along this path.

Any and all shortcomings that appear throughout the pages of this book fall entirely on our shoulders.

1

Defining Randomness

ANYONE WHO HAS PLAYED a parlor game involving fair dice knows that the outcome of the roll cannot be predicted in advance. The odds that any preselected number will end face up on a single die at the end of the throw are 1 in 6. When the game involves two dice, the odds that the same preselected number will appear on both is 1 in 36 (1 x 6 x 6). For three dice it is 1 in 216 (1 x 6 x 6 x 6). The mathematics of throwing two or more dice and ending with different numerical combinations are well-known. The same is true for flipping coins, spinning a roulette wheel, or for playing games of chance. It is not our intent to describe the probable outcomes of these or any other forms of gambling. There are many books and internet websites that do this in great detail. Instead, our main purpose in this chapter is to define the word random in order to set the stage for the way we will use it throughout this rest of this book.[1]

On the surface, defining randomness sounds straightforward. At one level it is, especially when we think of it as being tied to the outcome of an event that cannot be known with certainty in advance, like throwing dice or flipping coins. At another level, the concept is complex and can be confusing because of the myriad ways that different writers interpret it. In the next section, we start our discussion of randomness by examining the concept of causality and then move to other terms than have been linked closely to it.

---

1. Several important books have been written of the topic of randomness. These include Bennett, *Randomness*; Mlodinow, *The Drunkard's Walk: How Randomness Rules Our Lives*; Rescher, *Luck: the Brilliant Randomness of Everyday Life*; Silver, *The Signal and the Noise: Why So Many Predictions Fail—but Some Don't*; Nassim, *Fooled by Randomness*; *The Black Swan: The Impact of the Highly Improbable*; and *Antifragile: Things that Gain from Disorder*.

Causality

We begin with the idea of causality, because we experience it in so many areas of our lives. Whenever we think or say "this makes that happen," we are referring to the idea of causality. A saying such as "no effect exists without a cause" captures well this idea. For example, if a third-grade daughter studies her lessons, does her homework, and learns from museum visits, we would probably conclude her improved grades were caused by these behaviors. As we go about the routines of life, we accept countless causal relationships without question. If we did not assume that cause and effect connections exist, we would not be able to go forward with the patterns of our daily lives and we would not be able to achieve our goals. This applies especially to behaviors that involve the natural laws of the universe that affect everyone everyday everywhere on Earth without exception.

Examples are numerous. Any child who experiences for the first time the consequences of touching a hot stove discovers one of life's most basic lessons: touching a hot stove is painful. From this experience and many others like it, all children take an essential step toward realizing that ignoring nature's laws can lead to harmful outcomes. Concerned parents everywhere hold it as a basic duty to keep their children safe by teaching them to avoid situations that put them or others in harm's way. "Look both ways before crossing the street." "Stay away from the deep end of swimming pools if you can't swim." "Don't throw stones on a crowded playground." And so on.

It is through our ongoing experiences of life's recurring patterns that we conclude by extension that the universe is structured according to stable physical laws. When we walk forward we assume that the ground will support us; unless we step onto a soft surface like quicksand and sink suddenly, we do not consciously question with every passing second whether or not the Earth will support our weight. We simply assume it will. As we learn to crawl, walk, and then run, we keep moving forward because our past experiences tell us that it is safe to do so—in both the present and the future. In short, we take causality for granted; until such time as there is convincing evidence to the contrary, we carry on with our daily routines according to the tacit assumptions we make about how the world works.

In our everyday experiences causality is straightforward and sounds simple. In reality, causality is far more complex as we will show in the following sections. Our purpose in this section is to lay the foundation for a thorough description of randomness that appears later. At this point, we are merely using ordinary examples like "a hot stove always burns fingers" to depict our everyday world that operates by cause and effect relationships that do not vary from situation to situation and that operate mechanically like gears in a machine. As one gear turns (such as touching a hot stove), it causes a second gear to move (experiencing pain). As the second one moves, it causes a third gear to turn (pulling our finger away from the hot stove), and so on, until all the gears in combination cause the machine (the final effect) to operate.

One of the major accomplishments of modern science and technology has been to uncover many of the hidden cause and effect relationships that direct the operations of nature and were not previously understood. For example, in the area of technology, we have learned that by broadcasting radio signals from cell towers (a cause) we receive messages on our cell phones (an effect). Also, as science advanced, we altered our perceptions of numerous issues about the origin, or causes, and evolution, or effects, of our cosmos. We have learned that the universe probably was caused by an unimaginably gigantic explosion called the Big Bang 13.8 billion years ago and proceeded to evolve to conscious, mindful, and self-aware life on Earth. We have learned that our galaxy was ultimately caused by gravity and the evolution of matter after the Big Bang. We have discovered that the Sun, not the Earth, is the center of our solar system, and we know that the Earth is spherical and not flat.

Sending humans to the Moon and returning them safely to Earth would not have been possible without advancements in our understanding and applying cause and effect relationships originally discovered by Galileo, Newton, and others. Successful Moon landings were byproducts of our detailed understanding of the impact of gravity and acceleration on objects in space along with technical advances in rocket science and space craft engineering and in computer innovations and control. From the simple action of walking on the surface of the Earth to the complex achievement of setting foot on the Moon, we live daily in the take it for granted world of cause and effect. These concepts are summarized in Figure 1.

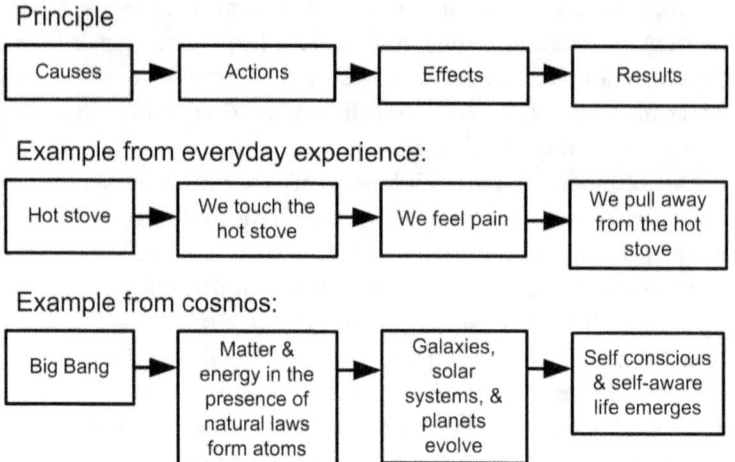

Figure 1. The principle of cause and effect results applied to an everyday example and to an example from the cosmos.

However, this is not the complete picture. It is not unusual during the routines of the day to witness the sudden eruption of incidents that defy rational explanation, that seem to challenge our understanding of how cause and effect relationships work. When something unexpected occurs that we cannot explain, we say "Where did that come from?" "It was a total surprise." Or, "It came out of nowhere." When a seemingly peaceful person commits an act of violence that leads to the tragic loss of life and has shown no prior psychological warning signs, we are baffled in addition to having other emotions. When a small minority of advanced cancer patients inexplicably go into remission while the vast majority die, we are left to wonder why.

Despite our belief that "things happen for a reason," (all effects have causes), in situations like these and others like them we are at a loss to identify the links in the causal chain. However, regardless of the appearance of many unexplainable events, scientific advancements have given us the confidence that our universe is governed by causal connections we can understand and apply to improve the conditions of life on Earth. This belief also goes by the name of determinism.

Determinism

Causality, as discussed above, is synonymous with the idea of determinism or determinacy. To demonstrate, imagine someone driving a car at eighty miles per hour, skidding off the road, and smashing into a tree. When we apply the concept of causality to this example, we are inclined to conclude that the crash was determined by a cause and effect sequence of events such as speed, friction, the trajectory of the car, and so on.

The modern understanding of the concept of determinism emerged at the start of the Western Enlightenment two centuries ago. In 1814, Pierre-Simon Laplace, one of the early advocates of a deterministic view of the universe, wrote, "We may regard the present state of the universe as the effect of its past and the cause of its future."[2] For the past two centuries, the cumulative accomplishments of science across a broad range of research areas have demonstrated the accuracy of Laplace's observation.

For example, in 1687 Isaac Newton announced the three laws of motion that operate deterministically in the universe. He also described the Universal Law of Gravitation that applies to the acceleration at which objects near the Earth's surface move through space. When someone repeatedly throws a baseball off the roof of a ten story building, the amount of time it takes before hitting the ground never varies, assuming that air currents and other physical factors are unchanged. It is always the same. After being released, the ball is pulled downward by a gravitational force. If we know the height of the building and how air resistance affects the ball, we can accurately calculate the time of the fall. The time and trajectory of this drop is caused by the dropping motion, gravity, and air resistance. We can accurately predict these details using our knowledge of the laws of motion and our knowledge of gravity.

In the mid-twentieth century, scientists working in the field of behavioral psychology applied the principle of determinism to the study of human behavior. The best known proponent of this position is B.F. Skinner who held, "Man is a machine in the sense that he is a complex system behaving in lawful ways."[3] According to Skinner, when people think they are making a decision in any given situation for which there are other possibilities, they are merely responding to "contingencies of reinforcement." In his view, a person who reinforces a given behavioral pattern in the past will continue to repeat it in the future. This happens because recurring environmental circumstances that he called contingencies strengthen the cause and effect connections.

2. Laplace, *A Philosophical Essay on Probabilities*.
3. Skinner, *Beyond Freedom and Dignity*, 22–23, 121.

Skinner's determinism is supported by J. J. C. Smart with one major difference. Smart does not focus on behavior but on the neurological and biochemical processes of the brain. Smart maintains that scientists who study the brain, as complex as it is, will one day establish that all human thought and the choices that stem from it can be reduced to natural laws. Also, feelings such as love, desire, pain, etc., as well as moral conceptions of right and wrong will eventually yield to explanations derived from scientific research.[4]

Thus, as the above examples show, a strong tradition of determinism has spanned the past 200 years. Through the cumulative discoveries of modern science, we have learned that our universe is governed by recurring patterns of cause and effect. However, this is not the whole story, as we will demonstrate in the next section.

Indeterminism

In the early twentieth century a different view of causality began to emerge. Researchers in the field of nuclear physics discovered that not all cause and effect relationships are as deterministic and predictable as those associated with Newton's laws. Through their study of subatomic particles, nuclear scientists like Werner Heisenberg, Max Planck, Niels Bohr, and others, demonstrated that it is more accurate to describe the behavior that occurs at the subatomic level as intrinsically indeterminate. Particles, such as the electron, seemed to have an uncertainty in location and an associated unpredictability in speed (described by the electron's momentum). All accepted observations, all accepted experiments, and all associated conclusions about such events led to the basic conclusion that there is a fundamental lack of certainty in our understanding of the electron's location and its speed. There seems to be a basic unpredictability here that is different from determinism.

Nuclear physicists were not able to predict with precision the position, speed, or direction that particles would take after the particles scattered from each other. The best they could do was describe their results in terms of probabilities. This is known as Heisenberg's Uncertainty Principle. It is also called the Principle of Indeterminacy that led to a shift from classical physics to quantum physics. For Heisenberg and others, the idea of uncertainty or indeterminacy does not imply that all of the laws of nature cease to follow predictable patterns of causality. It means that some of these laws should be understood in terms of probability and not certainty, that is, the potential for multiple and unpredictable outcomes.

4. Smart, *Sensations and Brain Processes*, 141–56.

Other scientists began identifying similar results in their areas of research. One perspective in particular stands out. It is called chaos theory that is also described as the butterfly effect, a colorful label that Edward Lorenz first used in the 1970s. Lorenz conducted extensive computer simulations of weather systems in order to determine how far into the future he could go in predicting emerging weather patterns. His procedure consisted of changing the mathematical numbers and relationships among the many factors that comprise weather systems to see if any given combination would increase the potential for predictive accuracy.

At the end of his numerous manipulations, he concluded that the ability to forecast accurately beyond more than two weeks was virtually impossible because weather systems are innately chaotic. There seems to be a mixture of predictability and unpredictability here.

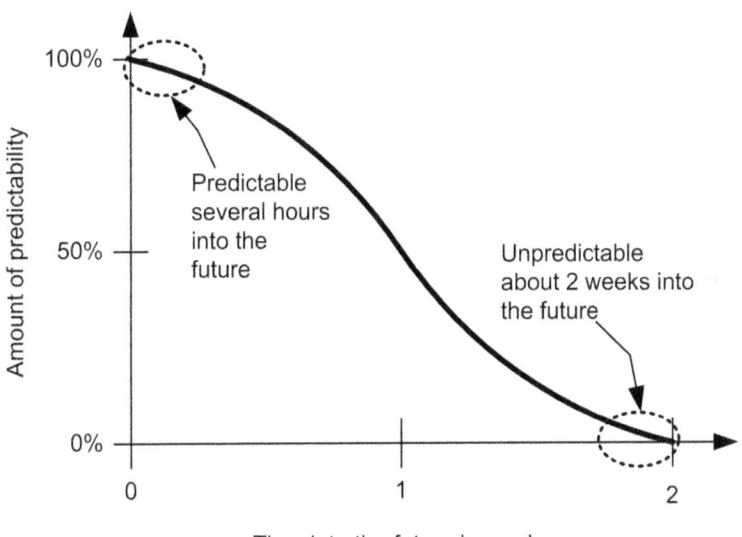

Figure 2. A graphical summary of some of Lorenz's conclusions about weather patterns. This curve is not quantitative.

As Figure 2 shows, according to Lorenz, in 1970 a person could forecast the weather one second into the future with almost completely certainty, but predicting it two weeks in advance was virtually impossible. He also observed that there was a smooth transition between predictability and unpredictability.

Lorenz did not mean that weather systems are void of any inherent order or structure. Rather, he reasoned that the Earth's atmosphere is so complex and its countless elements so fully integrated that even the smallest change in a single seemingly insignificant factor sends ripple effects that eventually change the entire system. Thus, like subatomic particles, weather systems are intrinsically unpredictable. Even his most sophisticated computer simulations could not predict where these changes would first occur and how they would correlate with other factors that in combination would produce overall weather changes. Given the integrated nature of these systems, he speculated that a butterfly flapping its wings in Brazil might release enough atmospheric energy to cause a tornado in Texas.[5]

Since the 1970s when Lorenz was experimenting with his computer simulations until the present day, meteorologists have made substantial improvements in their ability to forecast daily changes and approaching severe weather patterns, especially in areas such as hurricane development and movement and the emerging conditions that create tornadoes. Enhancements in complex weather models have made these advancements possible. In addition, we now have a better understanding of the deterministic effects of high pressure areas, jet stream patterns, and dew points. At the same time, however, given the inherently chaotic nature of weather systems, predicting long term changes that stretch over several decades involve intrinsic complexities that lead to conflicting interpretations of the extent and direction of global climate changes.[6] Thus, weather systems contain aspects of both determinism and indeterminism.

In addition to findings in the physical sciences in fields such as nuclear physics and weather patterns, researchers who study human thought and behavior began demonstrating how indeterminism applies to these areas as well. In a critique of both Skinner and Smart, Louis P. Pojman holds that no psychological or neurological research, however deterministic it may appear, supports the view that human subjectivity, that is, what goes on inside the head, is caused solely by external or internal stimuli. While neuroscience has yielded impressive results in showing how emotions activate specific brain lobes, thus far there is no scientific explanation for how a fully integrated

---

5. In the historical development of quantum physics, during the first three decades of the twentieth century, there was much discussion about the possibility of "hidden variables" that are not yet discovered but that account for quantum randomness. The modern conclusion is that there are no hidden variables and that quantum randomness is a fundamental feature of our natural world. This applies to the behavior of subatomic particles as well as weather systems.

6. For a discussion of the possibilities and limitations of forecasting short term weather and long term climate changes, see Silver, *The Signal and the Noise: Why So Many Predictions Fail—and Some Don't*.

consciousness emerges from the brain's biochemistry, how human self-consciousness emerges out of consciousness, and how self-consciousness gives rise to the human brain's ability to think, retain and recall knowledge, and make specific choices from among many possible alternatives.[7]

Thomas Nagel, a modern philosopher of note, shares Pojman's view that there is no hard empirical evidence to support the position of either Skinner or Smart. In Nagel's view, it is scientifically implausible to use Darwinian evolution to explain how the human mind emerged during the development of life or to reduce its origin to deterministic causes.[8] While there is little doubt that the human mind cannot exist apart from the brain's biochemistry, it is not at all clear how self-consciousness, rationality, and the capacity for choice emerged from it.

This is easy to demonstrate. In a deterministic universe, knowledge of the brain's functions or behavioral reinforcement patterns should increase humanity's ability to predict future actions with certainty. If people's actions were more and more predictable due to the discovery of new knowledge about deterministic effects, then eventually (after enough data is gathered) we should be able to develop software that predicts without error the behaviors of the stock market; and that would lead to enormous wealth. The fact that this has not been done, in the presence of huge financial motivations, clearly indicates that determinism is not the whole story.

As we discussed in the previous section, in various areas of science, technology, engineering, and mathematics, "causality with certainty" has direct application as in the case of repeated Moon landings; in many other fields, "causality with probability" is more applicable as shown through research in quantum physics (also termed "quantum mechanics") and forecasting weather patterns. This stands to reason because the cause and effect relationships are more indeterminate than determinate. In addition, if the countless external stimuli that affect humans and the billions of neuron networks that comprise the brain are anything like the complex dynamics of weather systems, then the ability to predict human behavior very far into the future is extremely limited.

This applies even more so to multi-level systems that are highly interactive. For example, life on Earth began at the cellular level and progressed in step like fashion to more complex systems like plants and animal species, human organizations, economic and political processes and structures, diverse cultures and subcultures, entire societies, and finally interactions

---

7. Pojman, *Who Are We? Theories of Human Nature*, 244.

8. Nagel, *Mind and Cosmos: Why the Materialist Neo–Darwinian Conception of Nature Is Almost Certainly False*.

among nations at the global level. Changes that occur at one level fan rapidly outward, upward, or downward in all directions and affect other levels in countless unforeseen and unpredictable ways.

While we possess the ability to simulate cause and effect changes that occur within some determinate systems, our capacity to do so across the layers of subsystems where widespread indeterminacies exist seems nearly, if not completely, impossible. As we will show in chapter 6, it is doubtful that anyone who was alive in the year 1900 could have predicted the coming of WWI, the Great Depression, Nazism and the Holocaust, WWII, dropping atomic bombs on Japan, the Cold War, the rise and fall of Soviet Communism, the emergence of radical Islam and terrorism, and the advent of the Internet, all of which happened before 2000.

The Bell Curve

Figure 3 shows the Bell Curve that is also called the normal distribution and is well known to anyone familiar with the study of statistical probability. This distribution curve makes it clear why indeterminism more than determinism applies to quantum physics, weather systems, a great deal of human behavior, and our inability to predict long term future events.

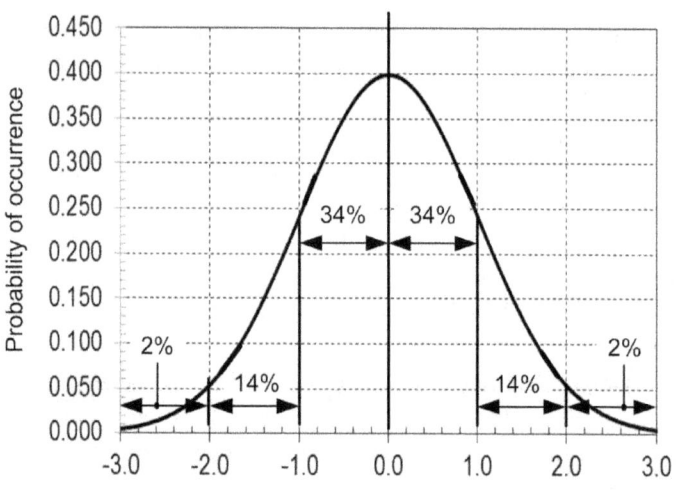

Figure 3. The Bell Curve. "Standard deviations" is a measure of the curve's width.

While both determinism and indeterminism incorporate the concept of causality and apply it to the study of nature and human behavior, the main difference between them is this: Determinism assumes that cause and effect relationships can be known in advance with certainty, whereas indeterminism implies that they can be known only in terms of probability. The Bell Curve applies mainly to indeterminism. Think of it as a template or a structured mathematical model that can be applied to many distributions in order to determine the statistical regularities and irregularities that appear within them.

Whatever the area where the Bell Curve is being applied, the overall distribution of elements within it can be divided into plus and minus three standard deviations from the mean, or average, as a standard measure for an expected random outcome. As Figure 3 shows, 68 percent of the distribution will fall within plus or minus 1 standard deviation, about 95 percent within plus or minus 2 standard deviations, and 99.7 percent within plus or minus 3 standard deviations. The Curve is useful in projecting the probability that any given event might occur, but it does not predict individual events, as the following examples show.

In the nineteenth century, an early pioneer Adolphe Quetelet applied the Bell Curve to the study of annual trends in criminal behavior, marriage and divorce rates, and other social areas.[9] Based on his study of statistical distributions, he forecast the probabilities that certain types of crime would continue to be committed without indicating who would commit them. He projected the percentage of divorces that would occur without naming specific persons.

From the start, insurance companies have used actuarial distributions of disease and death rates to determine premium and payout costs without indicating which individuals would be affected by specific illnesses. Determining the average life expectancy of any given population involves creating a distribution of the ages at which all persons die in a given period from youngest to oldest, averaging them, and comparing how they change over time. While annual distributions reveal changing life expectancy trends for whole populations, they do not identify who will die of what cause in any given year.

From the perspective of determinism and indeterminism, the Bell Curve can be used to identify statistical regularities where the specific distribution patterns are more indeterminate than determinate. It is useful for forecasting different probability levels that certain events will happen, but it cannot predict any one of them with certainty. The 1941 Japanese attack on

---

9. Pojman, *Who Are We? Theories of Human Nature*, 244.

Pearl Harbor and the 9/11/2001 Al Qaeda assault on New York's Twin Towers are cases in point. Prior to the actual occurrence of these two surprise attacks, US government agencies received countless pieces of conflicting intelligence. In the language of the Bell Curve, there was a complex distribution of information that included both pro and con probabilities.

Despite the sixty years that separate Pearl Harbor from 9/11, during the investigations that followed both, members of Congress repeatedly asked the same question: Given all the information that was available, why did not anyone see it coming? The answer is that hindsight is always better than foresight as the government committees discovered after they completed their investigations of the chain of causation that led to both attacks. In turn, the later investigation that emerged after all the facts were known fits nicely into a deterministic hindsight biased mind set as expressed in the common vernacular, someone should have "connected the dots."

However, this is a form of reasoning backwards and not forwards. From the standpoint of indeterminism, it is not possible to predict with certainty that a specific event will occur when numerous possibilities exist within a normal or Bell Curve distribution of conflicting and equal probabilities. Many potential outcomes are possible when multiple factors can be combined in different ways. It is only after the event that the most probable causal connections can be identified; even then alternative explanations are always possible. This is often called distinguishing the signal (what actually happened) from the noise (all of the possibilities of what could have happened).

The chaotic patterns of life make predicting with certainty a precarious venture at best, especially when small and unforeseen causes can lead to huge and unexpected effects. We will see three examples of this in the next chapter. Even though normal distributions can be created in anticipation of probable responses in any given situation, no single one is predictable with certainty. This is the essence of indeterminism. In chapter 7 on randomness and the future, we will examine in depth whether or not modern science and technology have helped us improve our ability to predict impending events with greater accuracy than in the past.

Permutation

In addition to understanding how indeterminacies apply to complex Bell Curve distributions and their probable outcomes, another well-known interpretation of randomness involves the concept of permutation, as biologists use it to describe the stages of evolution of life on Earth. Like the probabilities related to normal distributions, a permutation refers to how multiple factors in any situation can be combined in many different ways. For example, the modern science of genetics that Gregor Johann Mandel founded in the mid-nineteenth century examines the probable genetic combinations or permutations that comprise the blueprint of life for any given plant or animal species, including humans.

Many present day biologists hold that the sudden development of new species during the billions of years of earthly evolution resulted from natural selection in the form of genetic permutations or unforeseen combinations that enhanced the potential for species' survival. No doubt, the indeterminate nature of this long term process gave rise to the observation that new species appeared at random, that is, without any predictable connection to existing species or causes. One of the basic assumptions of the evolutionary process is that there were unforeseen mutations that were subsequently selected based on survival challenges. Even if the specific causes of a permutation remain untraceable, the randomness of these mutations might have been caused by many different factors including energy particles impinging on the Earth (for example, cosmic radiation), by toxins in the environment, or many other causes. At the same time, we know that despite the role permutations and indeterminacy have played in the evolution of new species, reproduction within any given species is deterministic because it reproduces its own kind.

This is what we mean when we say that causality is no simple concept because it includes both determinate and indeterminate relationships. When scientists conduct research across different scholarly disciplines, they discover determinacy in some areas and indeterminacy in others. The challenge in any scientific field and across fields is to identify where one leaves off and the other begins and how each affects the other. This is similar to the situation in above Figure 2 where changes in weather patterns transition from predictability to unpredictability over the course of two weeks and beyond.

Thus, based on decades of cumulative scientific evidence, when we think of randomness, we are inclined to identify it with unpredictability. Furthermore, when something happens we cannot explain, we are more likely to think of it as a random event that has no prior cause. However, indeterminacy does not mean that events occur without causes. Instead, it means that we cannot know the effects of causal relationships in advance with certainty (like gravity) but only in terms of probability (like forecasting future events related to conflicting Bell Curve distributions and genetic permutations).

Correlation

In addition, when we introduce the concept of correlation, it becomes even more apparent how randomness relates to indeterminacy. A correlation occurs in any given situation when multiple factors combine with each other and exert different degrees of influence. These factors do not exist in isolation but instead interact with each other. When their relative influences change over time, so do subsequent outcomes as shown in the following examples.

In a democratic society, politicians are keenly aware that there is no guarantee of being voted into office when changing circumstances lead to (correlate with) shifts in public attitudes that could jeopardize the probability of their election or reelection. In the game of baseball, no one can predict whether a batter will strike out, walk, or get a hit when stepping up to home plate. Batting averages merely define the chances or odds of what might happen, and this can be known only after the event. Many factors influence the outcome such as the speed of the ball and type of pitch (curve ball, fast ball, or other), the location of the ball when it crosses the plate, the batter's angle of swing, and so on.

If politics and baseball, as well as other human endeavors such as financial investment or playing chess, consisted only of determinate relationships, the effects of prior causes could be known with certainty in advance. However, they cannot, because the correlations between multiple factors change constantly; when they do, so do the results. As Heisenberg, Babe Ruth, and your local weathercaster have discovered, the elements in complex systems change in subtle, intricate, and unforeseen ways that are undetectable. In the area of human behavior, the correlations are even more complex given the interaction effects that occur across multiple levels ranging from single cells to global politics.

The Human Mind, Choice, and Free Will

Thus far we have examined randomness without discussing the human mind, choice, and free will. In this section we will describe how these are connected to both determinate and indeterminate forms of causality.

We begin by defining what we mean by the human mind and the capacity for choice. In the most basic sense, human choice entails the ability to decide on a course of action. It presupposes that we humans have minds that give us the intellectual ability to think using abstract linguistic symbols, to weigh alternatives and their potential consequences, to choose from among them, and then to act. In this regard, we are endowed with a unique ability at a highly advanced level that other non-human species do not possess.

Human choice is also called free will because as humans we have the ability to will what to do as well as what not to do; we do so repeatedly hundreds of times every day. From the moment we wake up in the morning until we go back to sleep at night, we choose what to eat, wear, buy, where to work, whom to visit, how to relate to other people, and so on. Seldom do we ever stop to analyze the act of choosing. We just do it, because it is so commonplace in our daily experiences.

While this sounds simple enough, not everyone agrees that we humans possess the capacity for choice even though we might think we do. As we described earlier, both Skinner and Smart concluded that what we call the mind, choice, and free will do not really exist. They are merely the result of determinate external and internal stimuli. This view is also called reductionism or materialism. Scholars like Skinner and Smart reduce the human mind, choice, and free will to potentially knowable natural causes. Given enough time, they held that science will uncover all of the determinate causal connections that condition how outside environmental forces and internal brain processes trigger our emotions and activities. They reason that once we possess this knowledge at some point in the future, we will be able to predict human behavior in advance with certainty.

This position is based on one of the most basic assumptions that supports modern science and classical physics: The universe is governed by determinate natural laws that we can uncover by using current rational empirical methods of investigation. In many research fields over the past 200 years, this assumption has proven to be correct. Because of modern science, we have made enormous strides in our understanding of the deterministic laws of nature that govern our universe.

At the same time, as Heisenberg and Lorenz demonstrate in their scientific findings, determinism is only part of the story. They have shown us that in some areas like the behavior of subatomic particles and changes in weather patterns, outcomes cannot be known in advance with certainty but only with probability. Furthermore, in areas such as these, whether they involve either determinate or indeterminate relationships as in the case of classical or quantum physics, human intervention and choice play no role at all.

However, two other possibilities exist: both determinism and indeterminism can be combined with human choice. As indicated above, we believe that the human mind and the capacity for choice is not an illusion. They are real. This unique capacity emerged on Earth about 200,000 years ago when anatomically modern humans first appeared in Africa. Humans chose to move out of Africa. They developed language and religion, invented tools, and sought knowledge. It is hard to see how those behaviors were determined only by nonchoice survivalist and evolutionary drivers. None of the other primates behaved in this manner. This supports the belief that as modern humans evolved they developed the capacity to think about alternative courses of action and their consequences before making a choice.

Once we accept that the human capacity for choice is real, the next step involves showing how it can be combined with both determinism and indeterminism. Imagine once again someone throwing a baseball off the roof of a ten story building. While this image comes readily to mind, complex questions about the nature of both determinism and indeterminism push to the surface. Does the person who throws the ball have the capacity to make this choice? The answer is yes. Then it is what happens next that demonstrates how choice can be combined with determinism or indeterminism. If the person decides to throw the ball, the cause (the decision to throw it) determines the effect (the falling ball). This is determinism based on choice. As human beings we do this all the time in myriad situations. We choose and we act. Our choices determine our follow up actions.

However, if the thrower reconsiders whether or not to throw the ball, then this thinking process becomes a condition of indeterminism with choice because we do not know what the outcome will be, that is, whether the thrower will finally decide one way or the other. The odds are 50/50. At the same time, once the decision is made, then the follow up action is determined by that choice even though the thrower can always change his or her mind more than once prior to the final choice to throw or not throw the ball. By using this simple illustration, we see clearly that the human capacity for choice and free will can be combined with determinism or indeterminism.

Next, if the person chooses to throw the ball off the roof (determinism with choice), then the other two alternatives of determinism or indeterminism without choice take over. We know that when the ball is thrown, the Universal Law of Gravitation will determine that it will go downward. Once it is in the air and starts to drop, it does not possess the potential to reverse itself, slow down, or speed up according to its own volition. Choice does not exist for the baseball. At the same time, differing strengths and directions of the throw along with shifting air currents and changing wind conditions means that no two or more balls will land exactly in the same spot.

Thus, as straightforward as this simple example of throwing a baseball off a ten story building appears to be, it illustrates the countless complexities that are associated with both determinism and indeterminism. When choice becomes one of many factors in situations where outcomes can be known in advance only as probabilities, the degree of unpredictability becomes more pronounced. This is well illustrated by the attacks on

Pearl Harbor and New York's Twin Towers, earnings from financial investments, chess game winners, results from rolling dice, batting averages, and long term climate change.

Thus, in light of the above discussion, we can conclude that there exist four possible combinations as identified in the four cells that appear in Table 1. They are: 1) determinism not involving choice (See upper left cell under "Determinism" and rows labeled "Choice/No.") 2) indeterminism not involving choice (See upper right cell under "Indeterminism" and rows labeled with "Choice/No."), 3) determinism involving choice (See lower left cell under "Determinism" and rows labeled "Choice/Yes."), and 4) indeterminism involving choice (See lower right cell under "Indeterminism" and rows labeled with "Choice/Yes.").

Table 1. Summary of Determinism and Indeterminism Involving No-Choice and Choice

Choice	Determinism	Indeterminism
No	No thinking and choosing or human intervention	No thinking and choosing or human intervention
	Evolutionary adaptation and survival	Evolutionary adaptation and survival
	Reductionism, certainty, and predictability	Non-reductionism, probability, and unpredictability
	Classic Newtonian physics, Universal Law of Gravitation, and burning hand on hot stove	Quantum physics, weather systems, and subatomic behavior
		Heisenberg and Lorenz
	Skinner and Smart CELL 1	CELL 2
Yes	Thinking and choosing and human intervention combined with the laws of nature	Thinking and choosing and human intervention combined with the laws of nature
	Evolutionary adaptation and survival; curiosity and invention	Evolutionary adaptation and survival; curiosity and invention
	Non-reductionism, certainty, and predictability	Non-reductionism, probability, and unpredictability
	Throwing baseballs, eating breakfast, building the large Hadron Collider, space exploration	Quantum behavior, throwing baseballs, creativity, outcome of stock market investing
	Daily human behavior CELL 3	Pojman and Nagel CELL 4

For determinists, indeterminism without choice (cell 2 of Table 1), determinism with choice (cell 4 of Table 1), and indeterminism with choice (lower right cell of Table 1) are not permanent conditions. Writers like Skinner and Smart presume that the human mind, choice, and free will are not real and that one day science will eventually discover all the deterministic cause and effect relationships that govern nature and human behavior. As stated above, this view of determinism is pure reductionism; many who accept that the capacity for choice is real, as well as those who do not, believe that many cause and effect connections contain irreducible natural laws. This means that their outcomes can be known only in terms of probability and never with complete certainty. How far science will go eventually in making discoveries that would lead to explaining currently indeterminate causal relationships into determinate ones remains to be seen.

At this point a word of caution is in order. Believing in the human capacity to think, consider alternatives, choose, and act does not preclude non-choice factors that contribute to a person's or a group's decision to select one option from among an array of possibilities. As we stated in the first section on Causality, no effect exists without a cause. Decisions are not made in a vacuum. Choices always occur within specific contexts, have particular motivators, and include certain drivers that correlate with each other to create decision options.

Before deciding, however, a conscious, mindful, and self-aware person will think beforehand about alternatives. This means that the decision making process always includes both influential non-choice factors and the human intellectual capacity to think about outcomes before willfully selecting from among them. No matter what the context, from the simple act of throwing a baseball off a ten story building to more complex circumstances like buying a house, situational drivers define the conditions and shape the alternatives from which we humans make countless daily choices.

Non-Causality

In the above sections of this chapter, we examined extensively the concept of causality that for us means that no effects exist without prior causes. At the same time, we have shown that causality is no simple idea, because it includes both determinate relationships that are predictable and indeterminate ones that can be probable as described by the Bell Curve distributions, permutations, correlations, and the human capacity for choice.

This leads us to the next question: If all of the behaviors and events that occur in the world result from either determinate or indeterminate relationships, can anything happen without a cause, even if the connections can be known only in terms of probability? That is to say, can something occur non-causally? For anyone who answers yes to this question, there are two major possibilities. The first involves one of the main proofs for the existence of God called the Cosmological argument. The second applies to the idea of God of the Gaps that is associated with Creation Science.

In the Cosmological argument, ancient Greek philosophers like Aristotle (384–322 BCE) presumed that the physical universe had to have a starting point. They rejected the idea that the cosmos is eternal. Aristotle in particular believed that there had to be a first cause that he labelled the Uncaused Cause or the Unmoved Mover that created and set in motion the natural laws by which the universe operates. In the thirteenth century of the Common Era (CE), the renowned Catholic theologian Thomas Aquinas (1225–1274) borrowed Aristotle's idea and equated it with the biblical view of God. Only God is eternal and has no cause. Everything else that God created conforms to the laws of causality.

The second view of non-causality applies to a recent formulation called God of the Gaps. Unlike the ancient Greek philosophical premise of the Uncaused Cause, God of the Gaps is a modern idea that the Creation Science movement developed starting near the middle of the twentieth century in order to dispute Darwin's theory of evolution. The Darwinian view assumes that life on Earth evolved through a process of natural selection and survival of the fittest. In order for plant and animal species to survive, including modern humans, they and we must adapt to the constantly changing environment. If not, the outcome is eventual extinction.

The goal of modern Evolutionary Science that operates by the concept of causality is to discover the biological stages of the evolutionary process. When scientists cannot explain the precise origins of permutations, that is, the indeterminate causal connections between steps on the evolutionary ladder, a gap exists. Fearing that the theory of natural selection might undermine belief in God, Creation Scientists introduced a God of the Gaps explanation. Where holes exist in our understanding of what causes what to happen during evolution, they used God to fill in the space.

Based on the creation stories in *Genesis*, they hold that by divine command God created many new species *ex nihilo* (out of nothing), including modern humans whose appearance on Earth cannot be shown to be connected to any prior chain of causality. One difficulty with God of the Gaps explanations, which we do not find useful in developing new scientific knowledge, is that as science advances, it closes many of these gaps with naturalistic explanations.

Another difficulty is that a God of the Gaps speculation is not falsifiable, that is, cannot be proven false. The reason for this is that indeterminacy is structured into the very fabric of the evolutionary process. In all likelihood new species evolved unpredictably as permutations that emerged out of existing species. Since permutations exist only as probabilities, their causes cannot be known with certainty. In turn, this opens the door for Creationists who believe in the literal interpretation of the *Genesis* account of creation to insert God as the cause for the emergence of new species.

Thus, the Cosmological and God of the Gaps arguments are two ways of understanding how an effect can be disassociated from either predictable or probable causes. Both arguments introduce the idea that an Uncaused God brought into being a physical universe that operates by cause and effect relationships (Aristotle) or that an eternally existing God created new species through divine command rather than natural evolutionary processes. In the former, God is the only Uncaused Cause in the cosmos; and in the latter, God creates something out of nothing.

As modern science advanced, it steadily uncovered the cause and effect relationships associated with a broad spectrum of disciplines ranging from astronomy to zoology. For those committed to a determinist worldview, it is only a matter of time before science completes a comprehensive inventory of the natural laws that govern the entire universe or develops a Theory of Everything. Other scientists are far less confident of this assumption. As we have shown, there are many research areas, such as quantum physics, weather systems, and human behavior, where cause and effect relationships fall under the condition of irreducible indeterminacy and can be understood only in terms of correlations and permutations. It is in domains where outcomes cannot be known with certainty in advance that we say effects occur at random.

Thus, based on the above discussion throughout the chapter, for the purpose of this book, we define randomness as unpredictability. This means that random events and behavior can be known in advance only in terms of probability and not certainty.

God, No God

One final issue remains. In this section, we shift the focus away from the scientific observation that cause and effect relationships are either determinate or indeterminate and toward the philosophical and theological question: Is randomness compatible with the existence of God? There are two possible answers to this question.

The first answer is no because randomness can be understood exclusively in terms of natural causes and conditions that brought the universe into being 13.8 billion years ago and determined its evolution. From this viewpoint, multiple species as well as conscious, mindful, and self-aware human life on Earth emerged through determinate laws of nature as well as indeterminate processes that contained unforeseen permutations (randomness).

The second answer to the above question is yes. As we have shown in our recent book, *God Is Here to Stay: Science, Evolution, and Belief in God*, the universe is so highly structured that a convincing case can be made that an Intelligent Creator started the cosmos through the Big Bang and guided the evolution to conscious, mindful, and self-aware human life on Earth. As we have demonstrated through the best scientific evidence available, we are confident of this conclusion.[10]

In the following chapters, we move to the next stage of inquiry. We will examine where randomness appears throughout the evolution of our narrowly structured universe. No doubt, much of what happened over the 13.8 billion years since the Big Bang resulted from predictable cause and effect relationships. The real challenge is to examine how indeterminacy contributed to this process. How might we best understand the role that randomness has played and continues to play in an evolutionary process that is so narrowly structured that even a plus or minus 1 percent deviation beyond its narrow boundaries would have resulted in an entirely different universe? Finally, how does the evidence for where randomness fits into the structures of our finely tuned cosmos affect belief in God? We will discuss this issue in our concluding chapter 9.

We are now ready for chapter 2.

---

10. McFaul and Brunsting, *God Is Here to Stay: Science, Evolution, and Belief in God*, 152–77.

2

Three Real Stories

IN THIS CHAPTER, AL Brunsting shares three personal stories that actually happened so that we might understand better the role of randomness not only in his life but by parallel how it plays out in our lives as well. This extended account sets the stage for the next chapters. In this chapter, Al narrates in his own words how three of the most important people in his life helped shape his personal history and the role that randomness played in each of theirs. As you read it, reflect on your own story and how life's unexpected moments molded the kind of person you have become.

The rest of the comments in this chapter are in his words: The first story is about my sister Bernace who was afflicted by polio at the age of two, leaving her permanently paralyzed in her right leg from hip to toes. She rose above this huge disadvantage to achieve many accomplishments in her life. I had the same affliction at the age of four (at the same time as Bernace), but I suffered no such lifelong dysfunction. Why was I spared and Bernace left with a lame leg?

The second story is about my uncle Al, my father's brother. I am named after him. Al was a likeable young man who lived to be only 24 years old. He entered what is now called the Air Force early in World War II. He earned his wings and commanded B-17 bombers, Flying Fortresses, from a base in England. These robust planes could carry thirty tons of men, bombs, and fuel. They had a crew of ten. For an airman a tour of duty was completed after twenty-six combat missions. On just Al's third combat mission Al was shot down by German fighter planes over the English Channel. A grateful nation bestowed its highest honor, the Congressional Medal of Honor, upon Al and those ten men of his crew. Why could not he live out his life with his newly married wife, beautiful Arlene? Why could not they have children and enjoy a full range of life's pleasures?

The third and last story is about my brother, Danny, who died just before his fifth birthday from leukemia. He brought much joy to my parents, his siblings, and others who knew him. My father, a clergyman early in his career, tried to make sense of this tragic experience that took just over a year to run its course. What purpose could possibly be served by the death of an innocent young boy? Dad and Mom actively pursued the answer to this question in discussions with other clergy, church leaders, many friends, and medical doctors. They read the popular scientific literature, the relevant news stories, and relevant religious sources. A number of possible answers are given in this story but, really, nothing was satisfactory. They continued their search for purpose throughout Danny's life and after he was gone.

Is there a purpose? Do the events in our lives happen for a reason? In our afterlife will all these questions be made clear? What is going on here? Can we better understand events such as these from other sources? Are there natural explanations? What is the role of randomness? In this book, we deal with these kinds of issues.

Sister Bernace

Here is the first story to illustrate how random events that are very small can actually have enormous life-long consequences. My father, Bernard R. Brunsting, was a B-17 bomber pilot during World War II. The B-17 had four engines mounted in its two wings. Dad and the crew he commanded flew daylight precision flights against German industrial and military targets. He completed a full complement of twenty-six combat missions over Germany. Upon the achievement of those missions he was assigned a post in the United States, awaiting deployment in the Pacific Theater of operations. On September 2, 1945, Japan surrendered after sustaining massive homeland damage from two atomic bombs. Shortly thereafter Dad was honorably discharged from the military, and he and Mom eagerly entered civilian life with their first born son, me.

Dad's first employer was Eastern Airlines and he was on track to become a passenger airline pilot. Dad's father, my grandfather Luke, was a successful pastor in the Reformed Church in Iowa. The Reformed Church is a Protestant denomination that originated in the Netherlands with a Calvinistic theology. It is similar to Presbyterianism. Dad loved Luke and highly respected him. Between Dad and Luke there were extensive, heart felt discussions about God's role in war and God's role in our lives. After much soul searching, prayer, and discernment Dad left Eastern Airlines and entered Western Theological

Seminary to become a certified pastor. During this time a second child was born to Bern and Alice, Bernace Brunsting.

For graduating seminary students, there were four awards for excellence that were much sought after by the students. Dad got two of them due to his mastery of his studies, his abilities in oratory, and his abilities to connect with people.[1] Immediately after his graduation in 1948, he was called to a major church in Western Michigan, First Reformed Church of Grand Haven. This was an unusually prominent appointment so early in a pastor's career.

So here we have this young couple just starting their chosen civilian careers. Alice (my Mom) was a college graduate and taught high school, General Science, and she was a college instructor in Physical Education. While Dad was stationed in Europe, she was a research chemist. Upon arrival in Grand Haven, Michigan, there must have been high expectations for a meaningful and fulfilling life. It was at this time that disaster struck the young couple.

In 1949 their two older children, Bernace and I, contracted polio or poliomyelitis. This is an infectious disease caused by the poliovirus. This was very serious, and there was no known cure at that time. We were transferred to the Mary Free Bed Guild Hospital in Grand Rapids, MI and placed in a ward with thirty child patients. We were two of three survivors of that ward. Bernace's case was much worse than mine and resulted in a dysfunctional right leg, while I did not suffer any such long term effects. While in my hospital bed I can remember singing this song over and over:

> *Onward Christian soldiers*
>
> *Marching as to war*
>
> *With the cross of Jesus*
>
> *Going on before.*

I am sure the nurses tired of my voice and the missionary message. My "music" also probably delayed the recovery of other nearby patients. On a related note, in my entire life no one has ever asked me to join any vocal group, ever. I think there is a message in there.

A hospital in Santa Monica, California, the Kabat-Kaiser Polio Institute specialized in convalescence of polio victims such as Bernace. Mom took her daughter there to see what rehabilitation might be possible, paid by the March of Dimes. Mom was trained to give the most effective physical therapy, customized for Bernace's case. This involved many hours of exercising. Dad took a position as lead pastor in Bellflower, California.

---

1. The two awards were for sermon delivery and systematic theology.

This allowed access to therapy, if needed, and it kept our family together. Alas, nothing seemed to work. Her right leg remained paralyzed from the hip to the toes.

So how did all this work out? Dad told Bernace when she was six that there are things in life that you cannot change. If you let those things make you unhappy, you will be sad all of your life. It would work better just to do the best you can from where you are. With such guidance and internal fortitude, Bernace developed a persistency and determination to play with the other children with little attention to her right leg. She did not make excuses. She made many friends. Mom and Dad encouraged Bernace to live and develop normally as the other children did. Amazingly, she learned to ride a two wheel bike, to roller skate with crutches, and to participate in most of the other normal activities with her childhood friends. There were many falls, many Band Aides, and many tears; but she did it. Most people did not think of Bernace in terms of her handicap but in terms of who she was and still is, of her accomplishments, her humor, and her friendship.

After graduating from Hope College in Holland, Michigan, Bernace was married. Eventually she moved to South Florida where her daughter Erin was born. When Erin was five years old, Bernace started law school full time and subsequently passed the bar exam on the first sitting. She became a practicing attorney.

Later in life Bernace developed a high level skill in the card game Contract Bridge. This is played in club, sectional, regional and national tournaments, as well as internationally. Many players take this game seriously such as Bill Gates and Warren Buffet. It takes 300 Master Points to become a life master in Bridge, a goal that many players seek but have yet to achieve. Bernace is a life master fifty times over. She is a Grand Life Master, the very highest rank awarded by the American Contract Bridge League.

Here is a communication that helps to describe where Bernace is now. It was written from Bernace to a person who helped her at the Omni Providence Hotel, Providence, Rhode Island.

To:

JoAnn
Omni Providence Hotel

From:

Bernace De Young
Monday, December 15, 2014 9:15 PM

Subject: Re: group availability

I wanted to thank you again for your help in getting me the ADA* room for the North American Bridge Championships. This allowed me to actually attend the competition. I won my first National Event, and became a Grand Life Master, which is the highest rank our organization awards. As I told you on the phone I have struggled with paralysis from polio my whole life, and now have post-polio syndrome so the logistics of moving around have increased annually. Without the efforts you made on my behalf this life time achievement event for me would not have been available to me. Thank you again. You are the best.

Bernace De Young

*Americans with Disabilities Act (ADA)

Bernace's condition, Polio/Post-Polio Syndrome, is irreversible, and consists of an advancing deterioration of mobility. This affects victims in an increasingly negative way, especially the autonomy most humans cherish. This is a motivational story that involves lifelong stress hardiness, resiliency in the face of a debilitating handicap, absence of feeling sorry for yourself, many joys, and many significant accomplishments.

So in the context of the themes we are considering in this book, I have a few comments and questions: Let us assume that when Bernace and I contracted polio that the polio virus particle moved a tiny distance to the right in my spine and not in her spine. This would mean that I was the person who would have had the dysfunctional right leg and not my sister. My life would be entirely different than the way it actually worked out. Such a small, seemingly insignificant, random event causes such a huge life-long change. Why is that? What is going on here?

Possible answers like "It is a mystery" or "We will never understand it" are not satisfying. We humans have developed a curiosity. We want to know how things work. We want to understand the underlying cause and effect. Pushing the answers off to the mysterious and the unknown is insufficient. In chapter 9, we will deal with these types of questions.

Uncle Al

Here is a true story about a young man who gave his life in the service of our country. He lived to be only twenty-four years old. He is my uncle, my father's brother. Albert Brunsting, Al, was killed in combat action during

World War II, along with his ten man B-17 bomber crew, on January 3, 1943 in the English Channel. The nation's highest honor, the Congressional Medal of Honor, was awarded to Al and those ten men of his crew. These events have strong connections with randomness and the unknowns in life and how deadly serious they can be.

Al was born on October 22, 1918, in Iowa. I am named after him, and I am proud of that. He and my father, Bern, were brothers. They were a pastor's sons and subject to higher expectations than most other children. One time there were guests in their home, the parsonage. In the living room everyone was seated in an oval and in discussion. On a platter there were pieces of cake that were being passed around the room. Each person in turn took a piece. The two boys, Al and the younger Bern, were at the end of this queue. When the plate arrived where they sat, there were only two pieces left. Everyone could see that one was larger than the other. The room went silent to see what would happen. Of course Al took the larger piece, leaving Bern with the smaller one. To the dismay of his parents, the younger and smaller Bern started to object loudly, destroying the peace of the room. Al asked Bern, "If you were the older and superior son, which piece would you have picked?"

There was only one answer for Bern in this Christian household with guests and his parents looking on. "The smaller one" was the quiet and submissive answer. Al triumphantly replied, "Well you've now got the smaller one, so why all your fuss?" There was lots of laughter in that room, and their parents smiled. Peace was restored.

In June 1940, Al graduated from Central College, Pella, Iowa. On May 8, 1941, he left for the Air Corps (later called the Air Force) and graduated from the Air Corps Basic Flying School on April 24, 1942. The next step was his completion of ten weeks of instruction on advanced flying. Upon a successful conclusion of this course, he received his pilot's wings and was commissioned a Second Lieutenant in the US Air Corps on June 23, 1942.

Al must have known that his chances of surviving this war were not good. At that time Germany had a very powerful war machine. They had many military successes across Europe, and they effectively defended their homeland. On many bombing runs at that time there was insufficient fighter support against the fast and maneuverable German fighters such as the Focke-Wulf 190 and Messerschmitt 109. While away at military training, Al's love for his high school sweetheart grew, beautiful Arlene De Moth. They were married on the day of his commissioning. Shortly thereafter Al was sent to his assigned base in England. From there he piloted a B-17, Flying Fortress. After just three missions the end came.

The young couple never got the chance to raise children. They could never make life-long friends with other young married people. They did not set life-long goals together and work toward those goals. Other than those first few days of married life, they did not laugh together; they could not enjoy each other's company, and have those romantic times together. They did not celebrate anniversaries together. All of this and much more were absent from this young couple's abbreviated time together. The partings between Al and Arlene must have been very emotional.

On a cold January 3, 1942, 3:00 am in the darkness, Al and his crew awoke and started to prepare for their duty. They knew they would be flying today because the weather allowed it. Al put on his flying outfit, which included heavy underwear, an electronically heated layer of flannel, and fleece lined leather pants. He put on his sheep skinned jacket. To the mess hall he carried heated gloves and boots in one hand, and in the other he carried his parachute and helmet.

The Flying Fortresses were not heated or pressurized. Typically the plane formations flew about 20,000 feet which made it extra cold for the crew. This is why they dressed so warmly. Also, they needed oxygen masks at those altitudes and low pressures. Large area wings and four powerful engines were required to lift the heavy load of bombs, fuel, support equipment, and crew to those heights, fly at required speeds to the target areas, and return to base.

After breakfast he walked to the briefing room with his crew. On the map for their mission they could see that they were headed for "Flak City" Saint Nazaire. In this case, flak consisted of shells that exploded at the bomber's altitude. The flak was shot at American bombers from German guns on the ground. Al sat in the front row of the briefing room with a white silk scarf draped around his neck. He listened intently.

After the briefing Al and his copilot Charlie walked to their B-17. They checked the instruments, engines, oxygen, flying controls, and bombs. At 6:00 in the morning, the entire crew climbed aboard their Fortress. Moving to position inside this plane required that an airman had to hunch over and almost crawl to his spot. Three crewmen occupied the pilot's space, and they had to move past the huge bombs placed in the bomb bay on their way to the front of the plane. Two red flares signaled the pilot to start the four engines.

At 6:27 the big ship started to taxi down the runway. During take-off the tail lifted off the ground. Further down the runway, thirty tons of bombs, plane, and men lifted from the Earth and became airborne. Other bombers proceeded in this manner, and soon there was a load roar of other Flying Fortresses as they gathered in the air to find their places in a specific formation. While gaining altitude they all flew to the east across the English Channel. Flying in formation made for more effective defenses against the German fighters. This was because 1) only the outer surfaces of those planes on the edge of the formation were exposed to enemy fire, and 2) defensive fire from multiple bombers could be directed at a single attacking German fighter. Such a formation must have seemed like a porcupine to the German attackers.

It was a clear winter day with nearly unlimited visibility over the target. For better accuracy the bombing run was made into the wind. On that day it was a strong 115 miles per hour, reducing the ground speed by more than half. For almost ten minutes they flew straight and level over the target. The flak was particularly deadly on that day. The Germans put up what amounted to a box of flak charges in the air at the point of bomb release, and the formation had to plow through it. It was a tough day.

On this mission two engines of Al's B-17 were knocked out, and much of the plane's nose was shot away over the target. Al and Charlie struggled to keep their plane with the formation. On the way back to the base, the formation flew close to the ground and later close to the water of the English Channel. This was to avoid attack from below. But Al and his copilot Charlie did not dare lose altitude, fearful that his plane could not regain that altitude when needed. About forty miles northwest of Brest, six Focke-Wulf 190 German fighters and a Messerschmitt 109 spotted the limping fortress. One after another, each German fighter made a pass at Al's plane from its rear with guns blazing. By then the other bombers were too far away to help.

Two parachutes were seen after the first attack and two more after the second one. There was hardly enough time for the chutes to open before the men hit the water. The German fighters were seen circling the drifting chutes, probably machine gunning the fliers. Al and Charlie stayed with their plane and set her down gently into the sea. After that landing, the Germans strafed them. The sea could be seen boiling under the rain of bullets. But there was something else that could be seen: The gun in the upper turret of the B-17 could be seen blazing, even as the aircraft settled and the waves closed over it. And that was the tragic end of Lieutenant Albert Brunsting and his crew.

This is at once a very sad story and a heroic story of an American lieutenant and his crew who made the ultimate sacrifice for their country. Why did not Al have the opportunity to live out his life with his beautiful bride, to give guidance to their children, and to be with his parents to the end of their lives? Why did those German fighters spot Al's Flying Fortress, shoot it down, and machine-gun members of the crew? Why was he killed before I had a chance to know him and enjoy his stories? At family reunions I am sure my pieces of cake would be smaller than his. How do we make sense of Uncle Al's story? We will come back to these questions later.

Danny

Surely there few experiences in life that are as mystifying and sorrowful as the death of an innocent, young child such as Danny. This is a real story of my brother who died two months before his fifth birthday. Danny brought great joy to his parents, his siblings, and others who knew him. He took pleasure in most experiences of his brief life and shared his enthusiasm with others around him.

Three months before Danny was four, his first symptoms appeared.[2] It became increasingly difficult for him to walk. In response, Mom and Dad bought him orthopedic shoes, and they attributed his continued difficulty in walking to those new shoes. There were no other symptoms. His appetite and spirit were healthy and normal. Danny was taken to a physician on November 14, 1958. After Danny's office examination, the doctor correctly concluded that Danny's condition was probably serious and a more thorough examination was needed. An appointment was made at a nearby children's hospital. During the office visit, Mom stayed with the rest of us children. Afterwards when they were alone Dad told Mom, "Honey, it doesn't look very good." For a moment they cried together and would do so again and again over the next few days.

A few days later, a pediatrician thoroughly examined Danny; his blood smear was examined by a medical laboratory. Within an hour the doctor called Dad with his diagnosis, "Reverend Brunsting, I want to give you the full picture—your son has leukemia." Those were the hardest words Dad ever heard. Immediately he shared that message with Mom and they wept some more. What is Leukemia? Here is a summary from the Mayo Clinic (http://www.mayoclinic.org/):

> "Leukemia is cancer of the body's blood-forming tissues, including the bone marrow and the lymphatic system. Many types of leukemia exist. Some forms of leukemia are more common in children. Other forms of leukemia occur mostly in adults."
>
> "Leukemia usually involves the white blood cells. Your white blood cells are potent infection fighters-they normally grow and divide in an orderly way, as your body needs them.

---

2. Brunsting, *He Is Not Gone*, 9–13.

But in people with leukemia, the bone marrow produces abnormal white blood cells, which don't function properly." [3]

At that time, childhood leukemia was a universally fatal disease. There was no cure. It was a death sentence for Danny. There were three drugs that were effective in forestalling the inevitable. Each had a useful period of about three months. During this period, called remission, there would be the normal production of blood cells in the bone marrow. Danny would return to his normal active life during these three periods. These three drugs extended Danny's life by a little more than a year, but it was clear that the final result would be Danny's death.

At this point Mom and Dad started to ask the inevitable question: Why? Later Dad said to Mom, "It seems to me it would be far better if Danny were never born than to have him a few years and lose him." Dad reasoned that if Danny had never come into this world, there would never be pain for him or sorrow for his parents. If God brought him into the world only as a plaything for us and then snatched him away again after a brief time, it would be a cruel and senseless thing. Dad then reasoned that God is neither cruel nor senseless and that there must be a purpose for Danny's terminal illness. Not only that but this purpose must come to light and have definition. In their prayers, Mom and Dad asked that God show them this purpose.

News of Danny's condition spread throughout Dad's church and his denomination of churches in Southern California where they lived. Many letters and calls of sympathy, compassion, and kindness were received by my parents. One of the first notes came from Rev. Herman Rosenberg and his wife, Flora, "We want you to know that we join the thousands who reach out to you with loving thought and tender hand to try to help you bear this burden." These expressed communications of love from dear friends were received as valued blessings. Mom and Dad were part of a large, highly valued community of faith and support.

Through all these notes, calls, and face to face discussions, Mom and Dad started to discern some purposes for this family tragedy. One man, studying to be a pastor, and his wife, John and Elaine Rex, shared their story of their young daughter's death from a rare type of cancer. John concluded, "Now when I become a pastor I'll be able to bring a comfort to others, which I could not have done if I had not myself experienced God's comfort when Sally died." Dad indicated that at this point he and Mom were starting to recognize the design God had in mind. Call this purpose number 1.

---

3. http://www.mayoclinic.org/.

Another purpose involved the death of a five year old boy and his terminal illness as told by his mother in her letter to Mom and Dad. After four surgeries her little son died. The mother concluded "I would, of course, have preferred to keep our precious Donny here. But just think how far better for him to have been in the Lord's presence already for nearly five years now. Call this purpose number 2. Shortly after Donny died, one of Dad's parishioners told him, "Donny taught Bethel how to pray.[4] So this is the third purpose as discerned by my parents. Here is the forth purpose: This life is just a prelude to the adventure of eternity.

I have no doubt that these four purposes were authentic to my parents, but we are left to wonder if the death of an innocent little one is an awfully high price to pay for these assumed results. For purpose number 1, does this imply that for all (or most) situations in which a pastor is seeking to provide some level of comfort for a specific distress that the pastor must have that specific experience? What about suicide? What about drug addiction? The other three purposes depend on a specific belief system, in this case Christianity. However, what if the person to be comforted had another belief system such as reincarnation? Can atheists or agnostics be comforted, using purposes number 2 through 4? As Danny's life approached its end, Dad and Mom kept searching for a purpose. For Dad, Danny was not only a very dear, sweet son to be enjoyed but also his life had real worth.

In some ways, Dad and Mom actually looked forward to the special year they would have with Danny before he departed this world. They did more heartfelt living during that time than many parents do with their children during all of childhood. One special moment came just after a bedtime story. Danny and Dad had just prayed before Danny went to sleep. He told Dad without coaching, "Jesus and I are friends."

In his journal Dad wrote, "This uncertainty of life has a great lesson to teach us that we saw again and again in connection with Danny . . . We belong to a race of dying people—this is universally true. Should not every association, then, be mellowed with the kindness and tenderness and affection we show for the one whose dying has become more real because of a medical prediction? . . . Knowing Danny had just a year or so of life certainly made us appreciate him in a way which would never have been done under ordinary circumstances."

Dad was of the opinion that scientists have an obligation to society to use their skills in medical research that lead to cures in diseases like leukemia. He also believed that Christians have obligations to use their skills in prayer. He wrote, "Surely prayer is the most dynamic resource available to

---

4. Bethel Reformed Church in Bellflower, California.

the human being." He was intent on developing the partnership between scientific progress and constructive results from prayer to find a cure. But, alas, in spite of much effort and discipline by Dad and Mom and their prayer groups, no such results were found and verified. All of this prayer notwithstanding, Dad continually felt "the gnawing agony that my son had an incurable disease . . . It was there, always there."

Except for Danny's disease, which was in remission much of the time, he had a happy childhood. Most days were filled with play. He had the ability to turn the everyday world into a magic kingdom of make believe. He enjoyed telling and hearing jokes. For example, instead of saying the customary "hot-diggidy-dog" he might say "hot-diggidy-cat" and then giggle with delight. Danny especially liked the swimming pool, and he swam like a fish. He loved life and he loved others. At bed time, he would sink into untroubled sleep. Next morning he would be grinning, bouncing, and ready for another happy day of play.

Toward the end of Danny's life, he experienced more and more pain. After an evening family meal, we had a Bible story as was our custom. This story was about a brass serpent found in the book of *Numbers*. While wandering in the Sinai Wilderness, the Children of Israel were afflicted by poisonous serpents. God sent this punishment because of their complaining. Their leader, Moses, was instructed by God to make a brass serpent and place it on a pole. All who were bitten by those snakes and looked upon the pole lived. Danny was asked to say the dismissal prayer for our family. After thanking God for several things, he said, "And thank you there was a brass snake, so the people could look at it and their aches and pains would be gone." Then after a thoughtful pause, he added, "Sure wish we could have a brass snake, too. Amen."

The end for Danny came on December 14, 1959, at home in the presence of Mom and Dad. During his last hour, Danny repeated a sentence three times. That whole sentence was unintelligible except for one word, which was heard distinctly. It was the word "home." What was on his mind? Was it his present home in the arms of his parents? Or was it another home to which he was going? Danny was buried in Sioux Center, Iowa, my father's home town. Dad's last words in his journal were these:

> "O God, how I wished I still had that little boy! I do have him;
> I would always have him—in my heart where I also have Jesus.
> Danny and Jesus, my son and God's son."

Throughout this ordeal Dad consistently looked to answer the "why" question. Many friends, including many clergy, offered words of comfort and offered some possible ways to answer the "why" question. Dad did much reading in the news media, in some of the popular scientific literature, and in the Christian literature. He discussed Danny's medical condition with medical specialists and general practitioners. Ways to effectively merge scientific research with prayer were explored. He wanted to know the purpose of Danny's life and premature death.

Conclusion

To conclude this chapter, the story of Al's journey lays the foundation for many of the questions that we are addressing in this book. What role did randomness play in Danny's life as well as in the lives of Bernace and Uncle Al? How are we to understand the place of randomness in all of our lives? We will be addressing these and other questions that apply to the many topics that we examine in the following chapters. Then, in our final chapter 9, we will pull together what we have learned in order to more fully understand where random events fit into our highly structured universe that we believe God created. We are now ready for chapter 3.

3

Micro and Macro Sources

IN THE PREVIOUS TWO chapters, we defined the nature of randomness and described how it affected the lives of three members of Al Brunsting's family. In this chapter we describe how randomness applies to both the micro and macro levels of our lives. First, we will focus on that random, fuzzy, and unpredictable nature of matter and energy that exists at really tiny sizes. Then we will shift to a discussion of how this applies to the larger patterns and experiences that occur all around us. In effect, we will be discussing changes that have occurred within the field of physics during the past 100 years and more. We need a few key concepts to get started.

Randomness at the Micro Level

From about 1900 through 1930, small groups of physicists developed quantum physics. Eventually, they realized that this new theory totally redefined how we interpret much of our physical world, especially at the smallest sizes. This new understanding turned out to be very important. "The quantum physics world seemed to require descriptors such as fuzzy, uncertain, and spooky action-at-a-distance."[1] This development in physics was a really remarkable accomplishment that has been found to work in all applicable situations involving validated experiments and observations. In short, quantum physics appears to describe reality and has many applications.

For example, it has become essential to apply quantum physics in designing and engineering many of the electronic devices we commonly use today. As we will show in later chapters, it is necessary to use quantum physics to better understand the evolution of our universe from the Big Bang to the present, why the sun shines, and why supernovas produce the heavier atoms that comprise our bodies, our clothes, and our shelter. Quantum physics

---

1. Lederman and Hill, *Quantum Physics for Poets*, 20.

and its commercial applications ultimately account for a significant part of the US gross domestic product. It is the beginning of most known laws of physics and is the indispensable key to revealing a deeper comprehension of matter and the universe as a whole. It is hard to overstate the importance of quantum-based effects and how we understand them.

At the same time, when we focus on the size of objects that we normally encounter in our everyday world, quantum effects are hidden. See Figure 4. To illustrate, the typical height of an adult is less than 2 meters or 2 m. 1 m is slightly longer than a yard. When we go smaller, the size (diameter) of a typical basketball is a quarter of a meter, 0.25m. Smaller still, we come to 1 mm, which is a meter divided by a thousand, usually abbreviated at "mm."

At sizes smaller than about a human hair width, we cannot see with our unaided eyes. These are sizes of slightly less than 100 μm and smaller. 100 μm is 1 mm divided by 10 or 100 micrometers (100 μm). Going smaller than anything we can see brings us to the smallest size that a research grade light microscope can resolve, about 200 nm. One (1) μm (10^{-6}m) divided by 1,000 is 1 nm or 10^{-9}m. One (1) nm is 1 meter, divided by 1 billion (1,000,000,000), exceedingly small. Here is the pattern: (1m, 1mm, 1μm, 1nm) are (1m, 10^{-3}m, 10^{-6}m, 10^{-9}m), respectively.

In the size range larger than 1 nm, classical rather than quantum physics becomes important and explains events in our world, such as how airplanes take off and land, why eclipses happen when they do, and how pinball machines work. In this size range, effects apparently have precise causes that are completely determined with no uncertainties. We think of things as being clean, neat, intuitive, and perfectly predictable. Pool balls collide with each other and the results are very certain.

As we shrink our size scale to below 1 nm, quantum effects start to become apparent. In this size region we have most atoms, some molecules, and subatomic particles (such as electrons, photons, protons, mesons, neutrons, neutrinos, and quarks). Our common experiences with chairs, toothpaste, and a single human hair are of a much larger size scale than this region of quantum physics. So our direct experience with nature at these extremely small sizes is nonexistent. We have not hopped with atoms or molecules, watched a package of light being absorbed by an atom's electron shell, and watched directly two atoms come together and form a molecule.

Therefore, our intuition about how nature behaves smaller than 1 nm is missing. Our intuition, formed at classical physics sizes, is misleading at these quantum physics sizes. It is at these dimensions where spooky, counter intuitive quantum effects start to become important. Here is where randomness, fuzziness, undetermined, and unpredictable behaviors become important. Despite these completely unexpected behaviors, quantum physics is the only way we have to accurately understand how matter behaves at these sizes.

MICRO AND MACRO SOURCES

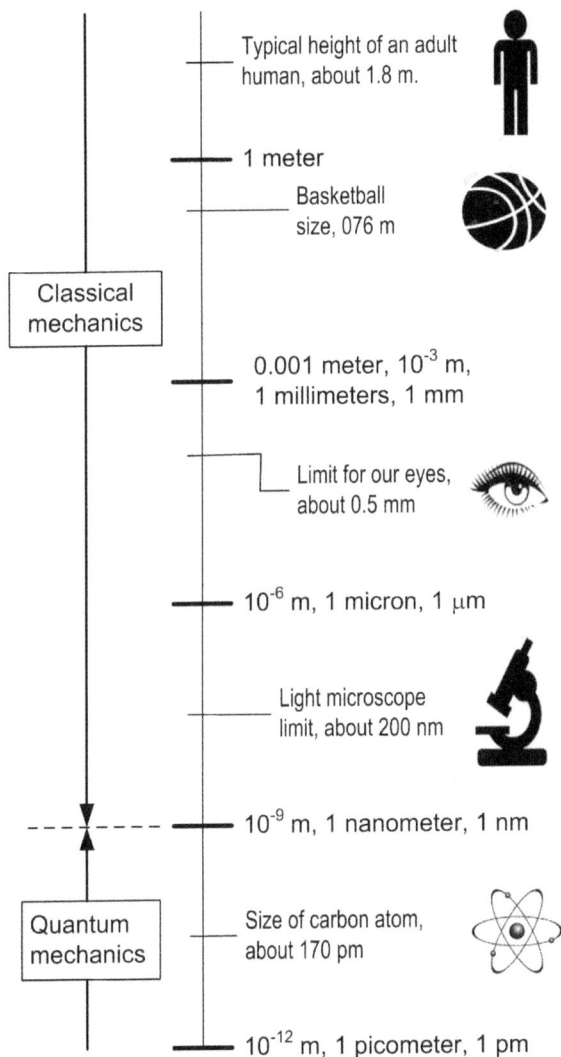

Figure 4. A brief summary of some size scales as they relate to where quantum physics becomes important.

Quantum Effects in Our Everyday Lives

These quantum insights have been so commercially successful and have led to so many insights about how the world works that we now accept our understandings based on quantum physics. For example, our smart phones, tablets, televisions, and GPS navigation systems are connected to ever advancing technology. Many of the electronics in these devices ultimately depend on quantum physics and associated randomness. How does this work? Nearly all our electronics (based on semiconductors), such as our lasers at the heart of many of our printers, DVD players, and Blue Ray players, all depend on this ultimate randomness. Also our magnetic resonance image scanners that allow our physicians to examine the soft tissues inside our bodies, all fundamentally depend on this randomness, which is a consequence of the quantum nature of light and matter. It turns out that the matter that makes up our bodies, our food, and our smart phones display a certain randomness at extremely small sizes.

To understand this more completely we must go to those really small size scales which is where this randomness, related to quantum physics, starts to become important. If we imagine shrinking ourselves to really small sizes such as a carbon atom, which is smaller than 0.2 nm as Figure 4 above shows, we can visualize the really tiny sizes that are required to get into the quantum domains based on the Heisenberg Uncertainty Principle. At sizes smaller than individual atoms, the behavior of matter has random and fuzzy behaviors. Such quantum behavior is not intuitive to us.

If this sounds strange, it is. When we shift to the scale of every day sizes of the world in which we live, all our expectations of how matter behaves are found there, such as the sizes of pebbles, pencils, and pianos. Thrown baseballs are caught in baseball gloves. Rockets blast off from a launching pad to deliver satellites into orbit around the Earth. A book drops from our hand to the floor. This is the realm of classical physics. At these size scales if we know the location, mass, and velocity of all particles and objects in the past, we can accurately predict all future locations and velocities. That predictability in the absence of randomness is called determinism. As summarized in chapter 1, Table 1, outcomes are predictable.

As our size scale shrinks to smaller than the size of a carbon atom, the behavior of the matter we observe transforms into something very different. Here matter behaves unexpectedly. We have reached the realm of quantum physics, and it took scientists over three decades to arrive at workable explanations for what happens at these sizes. It is here that determinism does not work.

In addition to electronic devices that we routinely use in our everyday world, the quantum world is important for other key reasons as we will see later. It helps us to better understand how nature works. Consider the sun as an example. Nearly all life in the bio-sphere of the Earth has the sun to thank for its ultimate energy source. This includes nearly all our food, nearly all plant-life and crops, trees, and flowers. Without the sun there would be no grass, no rain forests, and no orchids. Sunlight provided the power that sustained previous life such as the dinosaurs and the plants and animals that eventually became the fossil fuels that now provide most of the power for our cars, trucks, and ships. Since plants started using photosynthetic chemistry about 2.7 billion years ago, the sun has been our principle power source without which we would not exist.

In order to grasp how the sun produces all this solar power, we must turn to quantum physics for an explanation. The sun is essentially a fusion nuclear reactor. This means that deep inside the sun lighter atoms are fused together to form heavier atoms and release energy in the process. The most important nuclear reaction occurs where the sun fuses hydrogen gas nuclei (the lightest atom), atom by atom, into helium gas nuclei, atom by atom, releasing power from those reactions.

This is the power that starts in the sun's core and eventually comes to us as sunlight on which we are so dependent. Two hydrogen nuclei must get very close together for the necessary fusion reaction to occur. But there is a problem for this to happen. As the hydrogen atoms come closer together, a repulsive force between them becomes really strong because each nucleus is positively charged. This force tends to push the two atoms apart. This is the electromagnetic force. Think of it this way: For fusion to occur the two hydrogen nuclei must essentially pass through a thick, seemingly impenetrable wall, at quantum sizes. Think of a baseball being thrown so fast that it passes through the Great Wall of China. That would never happen in our experience but at quantum mechanical sizes it does happen inside the sun.

These atoms obey quantum rules, not the classical rules that we experience every day of our lives. The hydrogen nuclei use a process called "quantum tunneling" to get close enough to fuse and form a helium nucleus plus energy. It is as if a hydrogen nucleus digs a tunnel through the Great Wall of China (at their size scales), passes through, and appears on the other side where that nucleus can now fuse with another hydrogen nucleus. This is the currently accepted explanation for power production by the sun, and it is based on quantum rules, not on classical rules. There are other nuclear reactions in the sun, but this one is for us the most important one. Despite its apparent ambiguity and uncertainty, quantum physics provides the only way for us to understand atomic configuration, quantum tunneling, molecular construction, and emission of sunlight.

This being so, why do we not experience random, fuzzy, unpredictable quantum behaviors in our everyday lives where activities (like the speed and direction of baseballs) are very predictable, distinct, and deterministic? Here is why: Large classical physics objects, like baseballs consist of approximately 10^{23} atoms and molecules (one followed by twenty-three zeros, an exceedingly large number). Each of these atoms and molecules exhibits quantum behaviors, but the overall result in the whole baseball is for all those 10^{23} quantum effects to average out to the precisely predictable flight of that baseball from the bat to the fielder's glove. The randomness, the fuzziness, and the uncertainties of the much smaller quantum world average together statistically at the size of baseballs. This is an example of the correspondence principle, which states that the behavior of matter described by quantum physics reduces to classical physics in the limit of large numbers of atoms.

Those 10^{23} atoms and molecules that are located in our baseball all vibrate erratically and are in a constant state of random motion due to heat energy. The atoms and molecules in that baseball, each exhibiting quantum behavior, together combine to precise, predictable, classical behavior. The random quantum behaviors average out. The sum total of these quantum effects is what we see at a baseball game. We do not see baseballs tunneling through gloves and bats. We do not see players missing the baseball thrown to them because of the baseball's unpredictable trajectory in the air.

Our experiences are very limited when we consider the grand scheme of things. We have not experienced the heat of the center of the sun. We have not looked atoms in the eye and directly observed their behavior. We have not directly seen the randomness that exists at sizes smaller than about 1 nm. Yet scientific experiments and observations have unambiguously led to the conclusion that at very small sizes there really is this fuzziness, this uncertainty. It is really there; it really exists.

When compared to classical physics, here is how the random effects that appears in quantum physics differ. In classical physics all events are theoretically predictable. Picture billiard balls on a billiard table, one of which is a cue ball. Let us assume that we know the exact speed, spin, and direction of the cue ball as it heads for a cluster of stationary balls all in the configuration of a nice, neat triangle. We can further assume that we know the exact location of those other balls. Knowing these facts and a few others such as the interaction between moving balls and the table's surface and air resistance, by classical physics we should be able to predict the final location of all the billiard balls and the cue ball after the collisions. Similarly, in theory, we can predict (or determine) a precise outcome for almost all other events in the classical world.

However, this is not the whole story. In the world of quantum physics, we are not able to predict precise outcomes. We can only predict a probability for outcomes and not certainty as in the case of classical physics. In quantum physics the well-accepted Heisenberg Uncertainty Principle says that our inability to predict the exact behavior of matter is a fundamental property of all matter not just a consequence of the inability of our measuring devices to make accurate measurements.

For example, picture a baseball being thrown by a big league pitcher. A radar gun measures the baseball's speed at ninety miles per hour when it is halfway from the pitcher to the batter at home plate. Well accepted quantum rules say that the speed and location of that baseball, scaled down to the size of an atom, can only be known to certain fuzzy limits. Those limits are a fundamental property of nature and do not depend at all on which radar gun is being used or how it is being used. It turns out that those quantum limits are so small that it makes no difference whatsoever in actual baseball games. However, unlike baseballs, those hydrogen nuclei inside the sun are of critical importance as are other quantum rules.

From these considerations of the quantum world, we can begin to understand that all matter (at subatomic levels) involves a fundamental randomness, a fundamental unpredictability, a fundamental changeability. Our bodies, our children, our spouses, everyone is comprised of matter that ultimately, at small enough sizes, is founded on random behaviors. All the objects we contact in our daily lives are similarly based on random behaviors, such as our food, clothing, and shelter. In fact our planet, our solar system, our galaxy, and our universe are all connected to this fundamental randomness at these small sizes. Normally, we are not conscious of this quantum randomness because it is so different from our common experiences. Nonetheless, it affects everything we do.

For example, the digitally integrated circuits that are found in our iPhones depend on quantum mechanical tunneling to work and produce that image on the touch screen. The DVD player that is the source of a movie uses a focused laser beam (a quantum device) to read the ones and zeros embedded in the disc. That digital information is processed and displayed on a monitor for us to watch. In modern electronic devices, semiconductor components are used, and the understanding of how these components work and making them work well requires a rigorous knowledge of quantum physics.

These conclusions are summarized in Table 2. In our world of classical physics, we can predict the flight of baseballs while in the air; and the outfielder can run to where the baseball will come down. This means that if we could know enough about the past, we would be able to make precise predictions about events that would occur in the future. In quantum physics, however, the inherent fuzz in nature means that we would not be able to predict the future with complete accuracy no matter how much we would know about the past. We will say more about this in chapter 7, where we discuss randomness and the future.

Table 2. Differences between Classical Physics and Quantum Physics show-up in the predictability of future outcomes.

Name	Size range	Outcomes
Classical Physics	Larger than about 1 nm	Deterministic. Future can be precisely predicted if enough is known about the past. (mostly not random)
Quantum Physics	Smaller than about 1 nm	Not deterministic. The future cannot be precisely predicted no matter how much is known about the past. (mostly random)

Random Effects at the Human Level

If quantum effects are important in most of our electronic devices, might there also be a connection between the randomness that appears at the quantum physics level and the randomness that occurs in the events of our everyday lives, which we experience at the classical physics level? The answer is yes, which we can show by referring back to the three personal stories that Al Brunsting described in chapter 2.

To restate, Al's sister Bernace was afflicted by polio at the age of two, leaving her right leg paralyzed permanently from hip to toes. Al had the same affliction at the age of four (at the same time as Bernace), but he suffered no such lifelong dysfunction. Why was he spared while Bernace was left with a lame leg? Polio is an infectious disease caused by a virus. To initiate infection the virus attaches itself to a cell surface receptor of a motor nerve cell (neuron). The RNA[2] of the polio virus is then delivered inside that nerve cell where it fools the cell's normal actions and within hours makes thousands of copies of itself. This viral invasion probably occurred in

---

2. RNA or ribonucleic acid is one of the four major macromolecules needed for heredity in biological cells. RNA is critical for all known forms of life.

the spinal cord in the area responsible for the movement of muscles such as Bernace's right leg.

The subsequent destruction of the nerve cells in the area of infection led to the eventual lifetime paralysis of her right leg. This invasion of the virus and damage to nerve cells likely occurred due to the attachment between a surface area of a nerve cell and the invading virus. This would have happened at a molecular level on the surfaces of the viruses and nerve cells where receptors matched for such invasions. This would be in the size ranges where quantum randomness occurs and might have been partly responsible for a specific nerve cell being destroyed. That same randomness apparently did not occur in Al's spinal cord. This implies that Bernace's polio possibly could have been the consequence of quantum randomness that affected her life-long physical condition.

The second story recaps the events of Al Brunsting's Uncle, also named Al. On Uncle Al's third combat mission over Germany during World War II, he and his crew were shot down by German fighter planes over the English Channel. Everyone on that plane perished. We can speculate about the role that randomness played in this event by focusing on the behavior of the pilots of those fighter planes. Almost certainly they were motivated by a desire to defend their homeland from the bombs that were being dropped. They obeyed orders given by their commanders.

No doubt, there was a moment when they saw and recognized a tiny spec in the distance and above the horizon. It was the bomber formation of planes flying back to their base in England. Because of this recognition the fighter pilots approached the formation. They saw and recognized that one bomber was damaged and separated from the other bombers. Those fighter pilots attacked the weakened bomber, and the result was that Uncle Al who piloted the B-17 bomber and his crew perished from that attack.

The necessary signals in the brains of those attacking pilots are of an electrochemical nature, which occurs at molecular, atomic, and subatomic levels.[3] At the moment when they first identified the bomber formation, we can suppose that there was randomness at work in the neurons of their brains at the molecular level. This could have translated into missing the identification of that formation, which would have spared the lives of Uncle Al and his crew. However, this is not what happened. Looking back on that tragic event, we are left to speculate about the role that randomness played in the neurology of the brains of the pilots who attacked and destroyed the bomber instead of failing to see it.

---

3. McFallen and Al-Khalili, *Life on the Edge*, 241–48.

The third and last story involves Danny, Al's younger brother, who died from leukemia just before his fifth birthday. As the parents searched for a causal explanation for why this happened, they realized that Danny's premature death was caused in part by genetic origins. In one type of a genetic mutation, a single DNA base pair might change permanently[4]. This type of genetic change could have led to the continual formation of dysfunctional white blood cells in Danny's system, which in turn could have caused his fatal leukemia. Because of quantum randomness, genetic changes of this type occur at molecular and atomic levels and are understood to be the basis for genetic evolution.[5] Such a hugely important consequence like terminal leukemia that took Danny's life could have originated from such a small and seemingly insignificant random event in a tiny, seemingly insignificant region of a DNA molecule.

While we do not know for certain, in all three of these personal stories at the micro level, quantum randomness could have been an important cause of the heartbreaking outcomes that occurred at the classical physics level. In addition, there are many examples of how random quantum effects apply to events that occur at a macro level.

Random Effects at the Macro Level

As we show in this section, there are other unpredictable events that occur at the macro classical physics level, but their specific causes and origins are not completely known to us. Examples include tornados, tsunamis, earthquakes, hailstorms, and avalanches, to name a few. We tend to interpret those kinds of natural occurrences in terms of randomness. In what follows, we take a closer look at six specific examples taken from a wide variety of circumstances in order to show that random effects are not confined to only a set number of circumstances. Instead, they show up everywhere and more often than not when we least expect them.

Our first instance occurred on August 28, 1990, an F5 tornado powered through Plainfield, Illinois, which is located about forty miles southwest of downtown Chicago. Homes, stores, and factory buildings were not able to withstand the strong and powerful winds of this tornado. There were boards,

---

4. DNA or deoxyribonucleic acid is a molecule that carries genetic instructions in the nucleus of a cell. Base pairs within the DNA molecule encode genetic instructions that are used for cellular growth and reproduction. All known living organisms and many types of viruses rely on DNA to carry genetic information from one generation to the next. DNA is critical for all known forms of life.

5. Ibid., 196–230.

parts of roofs, and tree limbs flying through the air at speeds in excess of 200 mph. This debris smashed into other buildings. In this area, 1,500 structures were damaged or destroyed. Three hundred people were injured, and twenty-nine people died because of this huge and mighty storm.

Tornados are ranked on a scale of F-0 to F-5 with F-5 being the most powerful, having wind speeds over 200 mph. Tornados are not completely understood and certainly originate from turbulent and severe weather systems. The extreme circular motion of a tornado is partly due to updrafts and downdrafts in the associated thunderstorm, which is itself caused by unstable and turbulent air. Interactions occur with wind shear, which tilts to form an upright tornado vortex. On this day in Plainfield such a seemingly innocent development of storm clouds turned into a disastrous, life changing event for hundreds of people. Tornados are one kind of natural event that appears to originate, at least in part, from random and unpredictable causes.

This second example originated under the sea. On December 26, 2004, one of the worst natural disasters in modern history happened. On the seabed of the Indian Ocean, just off the coast of Sumatra, a 9.1 magnitude earthquake occurred. (The world's largest earthquake happened on May 22, 1960, in southern Chile. It had a magnitude of 9.5.) The movement in the Earth's crust disturbed enough ocean water to cause a tsunami that killed almost a quarter of a million people in that part of the world. A full passenger train in Sri Lanka was swept off its tracks and 2,000 people died. A patrol boat in the waters near Thailand was carried swiftly more than a mile inland. In that country 8,212 people died. In Indonesia, more than 170,000 perished while helpless in the tsunami caused river flooding that quickly and powerfully flowed into the cities and towns.

The sequence of events seems to be this: There was a sudden movement of a large volume of the Earth's crust. This resulted in a strong underwater earthquake. Large volumes of seawater were then suddenly displaced from their normal positions and currents due to the earthquake. The displaced sea water, now moving more quickly, caused such a large and devastating tsunami that people were killed around the Indian Ocean. A tsunami is a series of waves in a water body, such as the Indian Ocean, caused by the displacement of a large volume of water, generally in an ocean. The sudden shift of a portion of the Earth's crust appears to be caused by the random motion of the Earth's crust. While how this happens is not understood completely, the result is that it causes much death and devastation.

In this next example, the randomness occurred above the sea in the atmosphere. On August 24, 2005, a tropical depression intensified and became Tropical Storm Katrina in the Atlantic Ocean east of the Florida coast. On August 25 after heading westward, Katrina became a hurricane briefly as it passed over southern Florida and entered the Gulf of Mexico where it strengthened and enlarged. On August 29, it made landfall a second time in southeast Louisiana. Overall this storm was responsible for the deaths of 1,245 people and approximately $108 billion in total property damage.

The damage was extensive in the areas of central Florida, southern Alabama, southern Mississippi, Louisiana, and Texas. Eighty percent of New Orleans was flooded. The formation of tropical depressions, their interactions with other weather patterns, and their paths over land and warm waters are all not very predictable. The turbulences of these severe planetary weather systems clearly have a strong randomness component to them, and they cause extensive property damage and loss of life.

Our fourth example occurred in ancient history during the time of the Romans. On August 24, 79 CE, Mount Vesuvius in Italy erupted. As a result, the nearby ancient Roman city of Pompeii was completely destroyed by being buried in the resulting hot volcanic ash. Its location was on the western side of the Italian Peninsula and had a 700 year history as a Roman colony when the eruption occurred. At that time the city had a population 11,000. It had a port, amphitheater, four public baths, and gymnasium. Pompeii was fortunate to have fertile volcanic soils so that the residents could harvest a variety of crops. Life appeared to be pretty good for most of the citizens compared to many other places in the Roman Empire.

On that day, everything changed. Recent studies show that the dominant cause of death from the eruption was heat due to the hot gases from the volcano. The people baked to death. The volcanic ash rained down on the city for six hours to a depth of about twenty-five meters (about twenty-seven yards). At that time, the motion of the Earth's magma under the external crust went undetected. Randomness affected how the molten lava moved upward through the crust, when and how much it moved, how the crust responded to it along with the explosive force from the volcano, and the direction of the wind at the time of the explosion. While this combination of events was unpredictable, nonetheless it resulted in the deaths of thousands of people.

Our fifth example comes from Ireland where randomness is associated with the biology of plants. Between 1845 and 1852 there occurred a massively devastating event called the Irish Potato Famine. Approximately 1,000,000 people in Ireland died as a result. Another 1,000,000 people left Ireland to escape the famine. The island's population declined by at least 20 percent as a consequence. Potato crops throughout Europe were ruined, but the impact on Ireland was more substantial than in other places. This disaster happened because of a potato disease known as potato blight. At that time, one-third of those living in Ireland were supported by potatoes.

Also, there was little genetic variability in the types of potatoes grown there, which meant they were more susceptible to biological attack by algae and fungi that could break through the potatoes' defenses. These and other factors only amplified human death, misery, and emigration from Ireland. The details of exactly why the blight happened when it did, why it happened where it did, the dependencies on agricultural and weather conditions, and the severity of the blight are not completely known. Ultimately this was a blight caused by parasitic, non-photosynthetic algae (not a fungus) that attacked the potatoes. These small, seemingly insignificant, algae multiplied without limit and became the cause of so much human death, misery, and relocation.

Example six refers to one of the most widely known catastrophes in human history. On April 15, 1912, more than 1,500 people died when the Titanic sank in the North Atlantic Ocean. This ship was on her maiden voyage with 2,224 passengers and crew. This peacetime disaster was one of the deadliest in seafaring history. At about midnight that morning, the ship struck an iceberg. There were not enough spaces in the lifeboats for all the passengers. Those not in life boats were plunged into lethally cold water of about 32 degrees Fahrenheit (0 degrees Celsius) where nearly everyone died within thirty minutes of cardiac arrest due to the temperature of the water. Broadly, these are the conclusions from the following inquiries: 1) the number of lifeboats on board was inadequate due to faulty regulations, and 2) the ship's captain erred by not recognizing the danger of icebergs and taking proper actions. Another inquiry by Americans concluded that this disaster was an act of God.

Here are some additional questions in the context of our randomness theme. What caused that lethal iceberg to apparently separate from its parent glacier? Why did it wander into the path of the Titanic just at the time the ship passed through that area of the ocean? Why was that iceberg detected too late by the crew such that there was a disastrous collision with the Titanic? Why was not that collision a glancing blow such that the ship did not sink? Why was not the ocean a little warmer so that the iceberg was smaller, resulting in no loss of life? These types of questions all seem to point to a randomness, based on the turbulence related to iceberg formation, wanderings, and sizes. Of course, there were human factors too, but here we have focused on the natural causes and their relationship to random outcomes.

In the following Table 3, we summarize the differences between micro and macro sizes as described throughout this chapter. The Table shows that both predictable and random events can occur at both size levels. Predictable events have understandable causes, and random event do not.

However, randomness happens in situations that involve a high degree of predictability, and predictable outcomes occur in areas where behavior is predominantly random.

Predictability and Randomness in Micro and Macro Area

What we observe in the above discussion is that in terms of both classical and quantum physics, both predictability and randomness occur at all size levels. From micro to macro, neither level is purely predictable or random. Instead, they are inseparable although they appear together in varying degrees. In some situations, predictability dominates, whereas in others randomness does. Thus, as we stated earlier, while we typically view our interpretations of what happens in the world through the lens of predictability, we are beginning to understand that randomness plays a much larger role from all micro to macro areas than we previously thought.

Table 3. Predictability and Randomness at Micro and Macro Levels

Area	Micro	Macro
Size range	Approximately less than 1-nm	Approximately greater than 1-nm
Name of area	Quantum Physics	Classical Physics
Can predictable events occur?	Yes	Yes
Can random events occur?	Yes	Yes
Does each predictable event have an understandable cause?	Yes	Yes
Does each random event have an understandable cause?	No	No

Conclusion

We began this chapter with a discussion of the differences between quantum and classical physics and of how discoveries in quantum physics altered the classical view. Starting at the tiniest level, we are now keenly aware that randomness pervades all areas of life from the micro level to the macro. From the behavior of subatomic particles to personal stories of family events, randomness is ubiquitous. As we have shown, this also applies to the many powerful acts of nature that we see all around us, including tornados, tsunamis, hurricanes, volcanic explosions, famines, and the sinking of mighty ships. In drawing this chapter to a close, we have set the stage for the next chapter where we will focus on the largest macro structure of all: our universe and solar system and the role that randomness played in their origin and evolution.

4

The Universe and Our Solar System

How did our universe begin? Imagine a small little speck of matter, so small we cannot see it through the most powerful light microscope in the world. The speck is way smaller than our imagination's ability to consider the tiniest of objects. Now think of a time in the distant past that is 13.8 billion years ago. No one can envision this immense time span. If we presume that this time, 13.8 billion years, is compressed into one condensed year, then 434 of our normal years are equivalent to one second of condensed time. 434 normal years are equal to about six lifetimes and six lifetimes are equivalent to just one compressed second. As every second passes in our everyday experience it is equivalent to six lifetimes on the 13.8 billion year scale. This little exercise shows us how unimaginably long is 13.8 billion years ago. It is way beyond our comprehension. The current best explanation for the beginning of our universe starts with that small spec of matter 13.8 billion years ago. There is absolutely no way we can rely on our intuition to give us any guidance in thinking about the Big Bang.

The currently accepted idea is that the entire universe, all the stars and planets we see on a clear night, plus all the additional stars and galaxies seen by the Hubble Space Telescope, plus all other matter and energy, and all of space and time were compressed into that little unimaginably small speck 13.8 billion years ago. The weight of this speck, more accurately all its mass and energy, would equal the mass and energy of our current universe plus its energy. To say that this picture is beyond our understanding would be one of the greatest understatements we could make. Such a picture is way, way, way beyond our understanding in the sense of time, so long ago; in the sense of space, so unimaginably small; and in the sense of matter and energy density all packed into such a small space, essentially infinite density. This speck is sometimes called a singularity, which really means we have no explanation or theories for it, and our understanding of natural law is useless there. We can guess that there was substantial randomness within this cauldron or singularity, which seems reasonable.

This is only the beginning of the story. A vast expansion occurred, called the Big Bang 13.8 billion years ago. All matter and energy and all of space and time originated from this event. Before the Big Bang there was . . . well we do not know. It is not possible to begin to comprehend this event. What triggered this sudden expansion of all matter and energy and all of space and time? That also is a mystery and remains unexplained in our current understanding.

Immediately after the initial expansion there was a runaway process called cosmic inflation in which a peculiar type of energy was suddenly mobilized. This inflationary expansion ended only when this inflationary energy was transformed into more familiar forms of matter and energy. During the inconceivably short inflationary time the universe underwent this accelerated expansion from infinitesimally small to the size of about a golf ball. During this instant, the universe doubled in size at least ninety times and undoubtedly the mass and energy experienced random mixing.

For the sake of our discussion here, let us assume that cosmic inflation provides an accurate explanation, even though not all specialists today accept this view. Notice a kind of balance here: The Big Bang occurred 13.8 billion years ago, a totally unfathomably long period of time, while cosmic inflation started just 10^{-34} seconds (0.00 . . . [plus thirty zeros here] . . . 001 seconds) after the Big Bang, an incomprehensibly short period of time. Common sense and our intuition offer us no guidance at all when we consider these events and their long time scales and their short time scales.

The Big Bang and cosmic inflation are the first steps in a physical evolution that eventually takes us to where we are now, including conscious, mindful, and self-aware life (humans). These and some of the main intervening steps are summarized in Figure 5, which shows that randomness and non-randomness have been with us since the Big Bang.

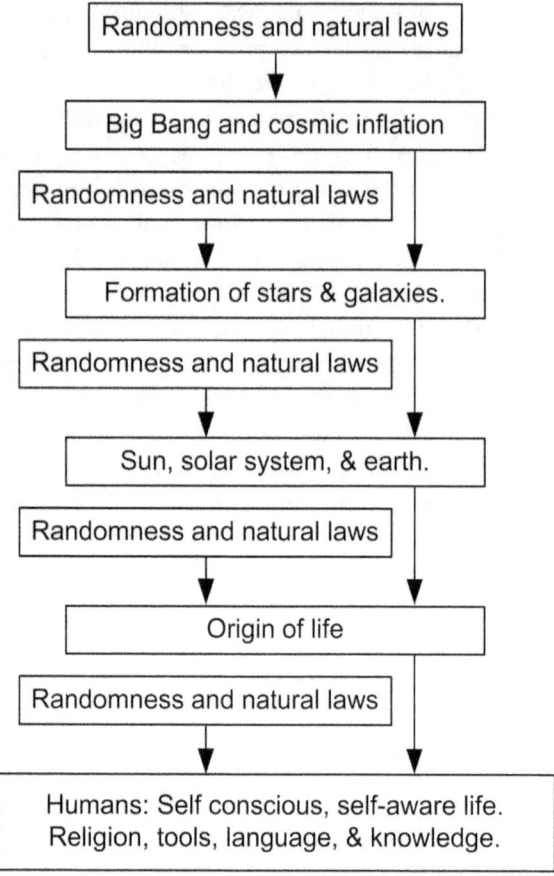

Figure 5. Relationships between randomness, natural law, and the physical evolution of our universe. All the randomness, R, here refers to lower left cell and lower right cell in Table 1.

Each step from the Big Bang to humans is controlled by natural laws as shown near the top of this figure. For example, consider gravity, conservation of energy (first law of thermodynamics), and the amount of disorder in a closed system always increases or stays the same (second law of thermodynamics). Based on certain observations, it is commonly held today that these laws were unchanged throughout these 13.8 billion years. In addition, each step has randomness injected into it, such as scattering of debris that eventually formed our Sun and solar system and the random distribution of energy due to various stellar and galactic instabilities throughout their lifetimes.

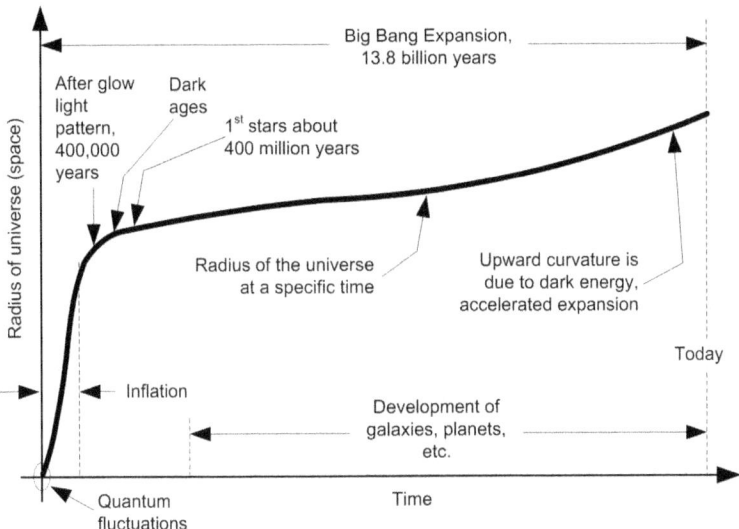

Figure 6. Summary of the size of our universe and various major events. The horizontal and vertical scales are not numerical.[1]

Figure 6 summarizes a few of the major events between the Big Bang (shown as Quantum fluctuations) and today. It also shows the radius plotted as space of the universe from the time of the Big Bang to today. We are now ready to describe these major events and indicate how randomness likely played a role.

Big Bang and the Cosmic Inflation

Today our understanding of the Big Bang comes from two basic sources: 1) rigorously tested mathematical simulations that use known natural laws and their mathematical descriptions, and 2) observations from both Earth and space with instruments such as the Hubble Space Telescope and the Keck telescopes in Hawaii. Concepts from which mathematical simulations can be developed include theories of subatomic particles, the force fields that work at these dimensions, and Albert Einstein's general theory of relativity.[2] Initially quantum fluctuations get the universe started, including warped and twisted space and time. A quantum fluctuation is

1. http://science.nasa.gov/media/medialibrary/2011/04/13/WMAP_320.jpg.
2. http://science.nasa. gov/astrophysics/focus–areas/what-powered-the-big-bang/.

a temporary change in the amount of energy within a small volume of space, allowed by the Uncertainty Principle. Fundamental limits to how accurately we can measure the location and momentum (related to speed) of a particle such as an electron, are set by the Uncertainty Principle. Immediately, at the first instant, the start of the universe involves randomness in those first quantum fluctuations.

The most elementary components of matter were furiously moving within the unimaginably small dot that contained all the mass and energy that would become our universe. The environment included the most extreme temperatures and pressures but was still controlled by natural laws that we understand today. These conditions included elements of both determinacy and indeterminacy Also, time and space were unimaginatively warped and twisted, way beyond our imagination.

Cosmic inflation (or just inflation) comes just after quantum fluctuations in Figure 6. From the perspective of life on Earth, cosmic history started with inflation, a celestial reboot that wiped out whatever came before and left the cosmos a featureless place. As the universe expanded as a result of inflation, its temperature dropped. The universe cooled. Time and space were stretching. Inflation then filled the expanding universe with an almost completely uniform brew of radiation (light, xrays, radio waves, etc.). Time and space were also compressed. Energy varied from place to place in a random fashion. This is our current understating of how it all got started and is based on verified observations that all support these associated scientific theories.

Formation of Stars and Galaxies

When inflation slowed, the universe was filled with hot, dense subatomic particles such as electrons, quarks, pions, protons, neutrinos, and neutrons. This is called an ionized gas. These particles had not combined yet to form atoms because they were so energetic. In this condition, the gas is opaque; light cannot make its way through the gas. The light particles, the photons, scatter from one particle to another within this ionized gas. As time continues, the gas becomes cooler and less dense; the energy content within the gas goes down.

Eventually, as the environment cools, the subatomic particles combine into atoms, complete with atomic nuclei and electrons. Under these conditions, the gas becomes transparent. Light and radiation can now shine through it. This happened about 380,000 years after the Big Bang. If we could see that far back in time, the light would be the earliest light from our universe's formation, at 0.002 percent of its current age. In fact, we can indirectly see that far back in time. The detected radiation, called the cosmic microwave background (CMB), gives us information about the structure of the universe at that time, assuming natural laws operated then as they do today.

Randomness played an important role during this time. Before the subatomic particles joined, they were in close contact and randomly scattering off each other. After each scattering event, the particles would quickly move off in random directions at random speeds. If we could observe these events (which we, of course, cannot) at an atomic scale, we would see chaos, pretty much an absence of any structures or patterns. 380,000 years after the Big Bang there also would have been much randomness as the atomic gas particles scattered off each other. The light and radiation energy passes mostly through the gas now giving some structure and pattern to the whole picture.

For the next ten million years or so, the universe was filled with a thin haze, made up of mostly hydrogen and some helium, the lightest atomic elements. The dim radiation within this haze would probably remind us of a bed of glowing charcoals just after an outdoor bar-b-que and after the Sun has gone down. The universe appeared to be dying.[3] Not nearly enough materials of the right type were available to form the planets of our solar system, let alone for life to develop. There is no gold, no silver, no carbon, and no oxygen. Earth certainly could not have formed then. Something else must have happened after this time so that the right materials were eventually available to form our solar system, including Earth. What happened?

It seems as though small clumps of particles formed randomly. Think of driving through a fog as droplets of water randomly form on your windshield. You cannot predict where the next water droplet will settle on your windshield, but water droplets continue to form as you drive through the fog. It may have been something like that in the beginning when the clumps were small and their associated gravitational forces were weak and not important. As the clumps grew in size, gravity became more important. The larger the clump, the larger the gravitational field, and the more influence gravity had. This all happened about 13.8 billion years ago. Could the natural law of gravity have changed during this time span? We have no evidence for such a change. The best assumption we can make is that gravity did not change during this time; this implies that we are safe to conclude that the clumps grew under the influence of gravity, as it exists today.

Next, there occurred an apparent death of the universe, which we call the Dark Ages. See Figure 6. It started 380,000 years after the Big Bang and lasted until about 300 million years. The size of the universe grew from 0.1 percent to about 10 percent of its present size. Slowly, rather formless groupings of clumps randomly came together, influenced by gravity, to form what eventually became galaxies. Within these primitive galaxies, smaller clumps randomly came together and formed what eventually became stars. Our

---

3. Lederman and Hill, *Symmetry and the Beautiful Universe*, 51.

current understanding of natural laws predicts most of what is observed in support of our understanding of the Dark Ages.

When a future star clump gathered enough mass and the clump was dense enough, nuclear fusion started. The clump became a star, and it started to light up and emit energy. Under large pressures and high temperatures, nuclear fusion is where two or more light atomic nuclei collide at high speed and merge together to form one resulting nucleus where there were two nuclei before. This process releases energy for lighter nuclei such as hydrogen and helium. It is easy to confuse nuclear fusion with nuclear fission. The primary difference is illustrated in Figure 7.

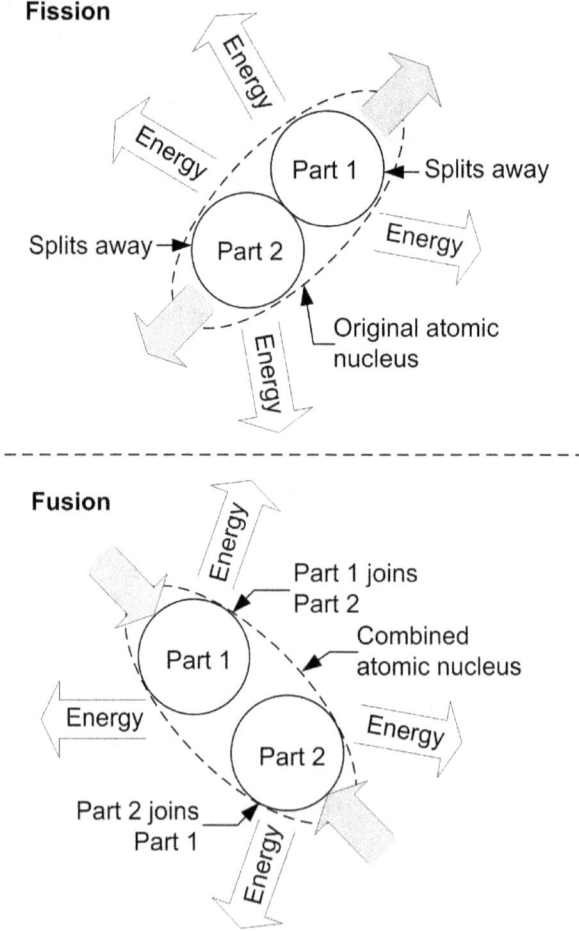

Figure 7. Difference between Fission and Fusion.

As Figure 7 shows, in fission, the original atomic nucleus splits apart releasing energy. In fusion, which is our focus here, the two atomic nuclei repel each other before they combine. This repulsion is especially strong as the two nuclei get closer to each other. Also, the individual nuclei are moving fast and in random directions, because the interior of the star (where fusion occurs) the temperature is very hot. Due to the random motions of the nuclei and the gravitational forces due to the star's mass (natural law), every once in a while two nuclei randomly fuse together. When they fuse, much energy is liberated from the new nucleus, which releases heat into the star and also releases light and radiation into the star. Such fusions are occurring throughout the interior of the star, and the combined release of fusion energy tends to push the star outward, enlarging it.

For example, think of blowing up a balloon. Your breath entering the balloon is analogous to the combined release of energy due to all the fusion events. The stretchiness of the balloon is analogous to the star's gravitational attraction, which contains the star's fusion. These two forces are balanced in a stable star.

Role of Giant Stars

Pretty soon (100 million years or so) the universe changed into a space containing these young, energetic stars, each lighting up a region of its galaxy. These stars are first generation stars, the first ones to appear after the Dark Ages. However, our Sun has yet to be born because it came from the remnants of these first generation stars. Random collisions of lighter atoms, mainly hydrogen and helium, ignited the fusion events that eventually became these first stars. Natural laws, as we currently understand them, control the fusion deep within the interior of those stars.

Some stars are considerably larger than what our Sun eventually will turn out to be. Near the centers of these large first generation stars, atoms heavier than hydrogen and helium were formed from nuclear fusion. Think of diving into the deep end of a swimming pool and swimming to the pool's bottom where you sense more pressure on your eardrums than at the water's surface. Similarly, in the star's interior the pressure is greater than at the star's surface. Also, the temperature increases as you move toward the star's center. This increase in temperature and pressure yields more nuclear fusion events per cubic meter. For example, when two helium nuclei collide with enough energy, they fused and combined to form a beryllium nucleus. Other fusion events occurred in the star's interior to produce lithium, boron, carbon, nitrogen, oxygen, and other heavier elements. Carbon and oxygen in this early stage were especially important for the eventual evolution of conscious, mindful, and self-aware humans on Earth.

These fusion events occurred as a result of randomly directed nuclei (some move up, some move down, and some move at an assumed angle of 137 degrees). There was no pattern or predictability for the direction of a given nucleus. Some nuclei moved fast, near the speed of light with high kinetic energy, which is the energy of motion. Some nuclei moved at a more pedestrian pace, say only at 90 percent of the speed of light with somewhat less kinetic energy. Again, there was no pattern or predictability for the kinetic energy of a given nucleus. Recall that we have evidence that natural laws were the same then as now. For example, electromagnetic repulsion of the atomic nuclei and the nuclear strong forces, which hold atomic nuclei together in spite of the electromagnetic repulsion, applied then as they do now.

Each fusion event of the lighter elements produced more energy than it consumed. Much of that extra energy was converted into light and radiation so that the star shone brightly. Many other stars produced such light from all that fusion so that the Dark Ages came to an end. The fusion process produced heavier and heavier elements 1) hydrogen, 2) helium, 3) lithium, 4) beryllium, 5) boron, 6) carbon, 7) nitrogen, 8) oxygen, and so forth until we got to 26, iron. What happened then? Iron was the end of the road for fusion in a star and the end of life for a star. At this point, the smaller stars stopped shining forever and did not contribute to the subsequent evolution of the physical world.

The story was different for the larger stars, the giants, which exploded as supernovas. These explosions were the source of many of the atoms that make up our bodies, homes, and cities. Also, these stars were the source of the atoms that make up our planet, Sun, and solar system. The explosions of these giant stars were critical for our subsequent existence. But if iron was the end of a star's life, how do we have heavier elements such as copper, silver, gold, and uranium? When iron was eventually formed in the cores of these giant stars, the source of fusion energy effectively dropped to zero. Recall the balloon analogy where the breath we use to blow up the balloon is like the outward pressure of fusion energy that tends to enlarge the balloon while the stretchy material of the balloon is like gravity that pushes back against our breath (fusion pressure). When the air inside the balloon is allowed to escape, the stretchy material collapses back toward its original shape while the balloon flies randomly around the room and then drops to the floor.

The escaping air inside the balloon is now analogous to the nuclear fuel that is being expended and no longer can support the outward pressures on the star, leaving only gravity to pull the star's material into its center. The outer layers of the large star now fall inward under the force of gravity toward what is now the iron core. Because the star is so big and the gravitational forces are so large, these outer layers chaotically speed toward the star's center. Imagine a video of a firecracker exploding. Next, imagine that video playing in reverse, which gives us some idea of all that confused mass and energy imploding. The mass consists of elements lighter than iron. The push back on all this inrush of matter and energy is the iron core, but it cannot withstand this disintegration. This process is of special interest to us because it is where most of the atoms that make up our bodies originate.

At this point, when the iron gives out deep inside the star, we must look at the nuclear effects to understand what happens next, the weak interactions. Protons and neutrons were found within atomic nuclei, while electrons spent their time outside the atomic nuclei. The protons and electrons that came from what were the iron atoms were squeezed into neutrons and something else, neutrinos. Neutrinos are not well understood. They are similar to the electrons that carry a negative electrical charge. But a neutrino does not carry an electric charge. Due to the weak interactions in this situation, the giant star was compressed into a volume of neutrons. This matter was not composed of atoms, complete with electrons. In this case, the neutrons had now become extremely dense, only about ten miles in diameter. The mass of this volume exceeded our Sun, yet it was so small and so dense.

Meanwhile the neutrinos burst outward from the center of the giant star driving a huge, bright, very intense explosion. These explosions were some of the brightest explosions in our universe, except for the Big Bang. There was enough energy in these explosions to distribute throughout the neighboring space the elements heavier than helium through iron. These supernova explosions outshone their host galaxy for a brief time. They radiated more energy than our Sun radiates over its life time of about ten billion years. The supernova spreads its material outward into its galaxy.

Our Everyday Experiences

Let us think about our everyday lives for a moment, our homes and possessions, families, donations to worthy causes, country, and so forth. Let us think about our everyday objects such as our chairs, tables, buildings, and our technology. All of it is nothing at all like this story about the Big Bang, cosmic inflation, and nuclear fusion. The events, the forces, and the time and space that have produced the atoms of our body and made it possible for the evolution of life on Earth belong to a different time and space compared to our everyday lives. It is like there are two completely different spaces: One for the causes and origins that eventually led to us and others. The first is highly incomprehensible and not at all intuitive, and the second is comprehensible and intuitive, at least most of the time. Why this difference? There are at least three fundamental reasons for difficulties here.

1) Time. The events that happen in our lives typically occur over a few seconds at the shortest to several decades at the longest. The Big Bang occurred 13.8 billion years ago. How can we possibly think of that time span in a realistic way? To be comprehensible, we need to compare that length of time to things that are familiar to us. Our lifetimes are only seventy to eighty years or so. The time period from our grandparents, parents, ourselves, children, and grandchildren is about 125 years from start to finish. A billion years? While we can write down the number and think about it, we cannot really get a feeling, an appreciation, or a common sense understanding of what a billion years is like. In addition, there are events in this story that happen so quickly that we do not have a chance to appreciate those time scales. For example, Cosmic Inflation occurred just 0.000 (thirty-one more zeros) 1 after the Big Bang. A Big League pitcher, throwing a fast ball ninety miles per hour from the pitching mound to home plate occurs in a little less than half a second. Again the shortness of the time between the Big Bang and the start of Cosmic Inflation is really incomprehensible for us. In a similar way, the length of time from the Big Bang to now is much too long for us. The subatomic events in these processes also happen on such short time scales that we cannot begin to comprehend them.

2) Space. In our perception of space, parallel lines go off into infinity and never meet; our house has a specific location (using GPS coordinates); and an American football field is 100 yards from one goal line to the other. Using our technology, we can navigate across town from our starting point to our favorite restaurant. When we fly from Chicago, IL to Dallas, TX, we can determine the miles and flying time and we can locate our flight path on a map. All of these types of experiences are nothing like what happened after the Big Bang when time and space were extremely contorted in that first fraction of a second. The universe is approximately ninety billion light years across, and a light year is about 5.88 trillion miles or about 9.5 trillion km. Needless to say, these distances are way, way, way beyond any sizes in our humble, tiny experiences. On the other hand, the size scales of subatomic particles, which play important roles in our physical evolution, are way, way, way smaller than any sizes in our experiences.

3) Intuitions. In our ordinary lives when we drop a baseball from shoulder height it falls to the ground as if it were pulled there by the Earth. When we throw a water balloon at a loved one on a hot Texas day because they so desperately deserve it, that balloon follows an arc from our hand

to the intended target. When we step on the brake pedal to avoid hitting the car ahead of us, our car comes to a stop. These are all examples of how we expect our physical world to behave, based on our past experiences. In our everyday lives we depend on our intuition to help anticipate what happens next, what we can expect in that next business meeting, how those chocolate cookies will come out of the oven, and how that baby will respond when we smile.

Based on accepted conclusions about the evolution of our physical universe, all of our intuitions are pretty much useless. We have to rely on our understanding of strong and weak subatomic forces, strange warpage of space and time at the beginning, and of gravity that is associated with the curvature of space. The associated mathematics also guides us. There is nothing we can do, we have to let go of our intuitions here, of our experiences, and of what we have learned. In many ways we have to trust the specialists, the cosmologists, the mathematicians, and the physicists and their conclusions. However, the specialists have not always been right. In the mid-sixties the Steady State Universe[4] appeared to be the preferred understanding of our cosmos. Today that conclusion has been substantially discarded. It appears that prevailing theories of the universe can be supplanted from time to time by other competing theories with more observational support and/or a more complete theory.

Start of Our Solar System

Until recently the prevailing theory was that heavy elements (heavier than lead) are distributed around a host galaxy due to the explosions of supernovas. This picture is currently being updated.

Among these heavy elements are gold, platinum, and rare Earth elements. There are basically two explanations for the production of these heavier elements. One involves the explosive collapse of a large star (greater than ten times the mass of the Sun), a supernova after it burns its fusion material. This type of star forms a neutron star. Recent studies have shown that matter ejected from these neutron stars does not contain enough neutrons

---

4. The Steady State theory was proposed in opposition to the Big Bang model for how the universe got started and how the universe evolved to its present condition. In the Steady State theory, the expanding universe results from a continuous creation of matter. The result is that the observable universe is basically the same for any time throughout its history and any place within the universe. While the steady state explanation enjoyed much popularity in the mid–twentieth century, it is now discarded by nearly all cosmologists and astrophysicists. This is because the observational evidence overwhelmingly supports the Big Bang.

to synthesize those heavy elements. The other explanation is a neutron star merger, which seems to be the preferred explanation today.

Think of two heavy stars that experience catastrophic supernova explosions and become neutron stars such that they orbit each other as a pair of neutron stars. Over time, they slowly fall toward one another due to gravity, taking at least ten million years or so to finally merge. Results of studies show that this merger is extremely explosive and produces heavy elements and ejects them.[5] It has been estimated that one merger event ejected an amount of gold equal to seventy times the mass of the Earth.

The debris from previous super-nova and from neutron star mergers seemed to have collected in our regions of the Milky Way Galaxy in some kind of overlapping configuration. This region was a wispy cloud of stellar dust, a nebula. This process originated from the proximity of those parent stars, the influence of gravity, especially from nearby stars in our galaxy, and random effects of particles, molecules, and atoms scattering off each other to form a region of space with higher densities of these seed materials. A shockwave from a nearby exploding star may have played a role in our nebula becoming more concentrated and forming a disk of material. Our solar system was now ready to be formed about 4.5 billion years ago from the material from those parent stars. Table 4 gives a partial summary of requirements for an explanation for how this happened.

Table 4. Summary of requirements for explanation of the origin of the solar system.[6]

No.	Characteristic	Comments
1	Motion of planets	All planets move around the Sun in the same direction that the Sun rotates and close to the equatorial plane of the Sun.
2	Angular momentum	The Sun has 99.9 percent of the mass in the solar system; the planets have 99.7 percent of the system's angular momentum (rotational motion).
3	Rocky & giant planets	The inner planets are smaller and denser than the outer planets, and are made of silicates and metals. In contrast, the outer planets are dominated by hydrogen (close to cosmic composition) and have many satellites that are rich in water ice and other volatiles.

5. See http://www.nao.ac.jp/en/news/science/2014/20141014-neutronstar.html.

6. See http://lasp.colorado.edu/~bagenal/1010/SESSIONS/11.Formation.html, accessed Nov. 4, 2015.

No.	Characteristic	Comments
4	Asteroids	The asteroids have compositions intermediate between the rock & metal rich inner planets and the volatile-rich outer solar system, and are located between the orbits of Mars and Jupiter.
5	Meteorites	The oldest and most primitive meteorites contain grains of compounds that are expected to have formed in a cooling cloud of cosmic abundance at temperatures of a few hundred degrees.
6	Comets	Comets, like the surface of some outer planet satellites, appear to be composed primarily of water ice, with significant quantities of trapped or frozen gases like carbon dioxide, plus silicate dust.
8	Retrograde planets	Despite the general regularity of planetary orbital and spin motion, Venus and Uranus all spin in a retrograde direction.
9	Regular satellites	All of the giant planets have systems of regular satellites orbiting in their equatorial planes, rather like miniature versions of the solar system.
10	Irregular satellites	Except Uranus, the giant planets have one or more irregular satellites (which have orbits that are either retrograde or have high inclinations and/or eccentricities).
11	Galilean satellites	The Galilean satellites of Jupiter exhibit a decrease in density with increasing distance from Jupiter

A disk shaped cloud or nebula of gas and fine dust grains were rotating as shown in Figure 8. The size of our current solar system is about a million times smaller than that original cloud. The material in the cloud spins faster as the cloud becomes smaller due to gravity, similar to an ice skater pulling her arms into her body while spinning, making her spin faster. The cloud also starts to flatten and become more like a pancake. In the center of this cloud a dense mass forms, which will eventually become the Sun, called the proto-Sun. The shape of this cloud explains why the planets all orbit the Sun in the same direction today and why they are close to being in the same plane. See number 1 in Table 4. Densities of hydrogen grow as do the temperatures in the proto-Sun due to gravity. At some point nuclear fusion starts in this new star (see Figure 7 and associated text), our Sun, generating lots of heat, which is radiated outward. Some of this heat warms the Earth. The Sun's heat generates higher temperatures in the flattened disk, especially closer to the Sun.

Many of the materials that make up our Earth and the other rocky planets (Mercury, Venus, and Mars) tend to melt at higher temperatures compared to the materials that comprise the outer planets (Jupiter, Saturn, Uranus, and Neptune). At higher temperatures, closer to the proto-Sun, these rocky type materials tend to migrate toward the center of the solar system and toward the proto-Sun. This partly explains why the inner planets are made of rocky type materials such as silicates and metals while the outer planets where it is cooler are dominated by hydrogen (number 3 in Table 4). Also, the abundance of these elements also needs to be taken into account during planet formation. Dust particles collide with and stick to each other although this process is not well understood. Larger grains form.

This process continued until the particles were big enough to sustain at least some gravity to attract other, smaller particles. Thus the planets started to form within the flattened disk, called proto-planets. This process involved turbulent environments that included collisions, heating and cooling cycles, and melting and condensing. Heat was generated in the proto-planets from these collisions. The solid materials melted due to this heat and the denser liquids moved to the center of the proto-planets because of gravity. This further heated the proto-planets. After this period of bombardment the disk and proto-planets within it radiated away some of the thermal energy, which as a result cooled the proto-planets.

At approximately one million years after the nebula cooled the proto-Sun, generating energy by nuclear fusion started to produce a solar wind. This has been observed in newly formed stars similar to the Sun. The solar wind consists of energetic, charged particles (plasma), mostly electrons and protons, that stream away from the proto-Sun at high speed and high temperature. At this time the solar wind pushes most of the gas in the flattened nebula outward. The size of the developing proto-planet, where it is located in the developing solar system, and when it develops relative to the proto-Sun's development will determine if the proto-planet can hold onto its atmosphere and whether or not the proto-planet becomes a gas giant.

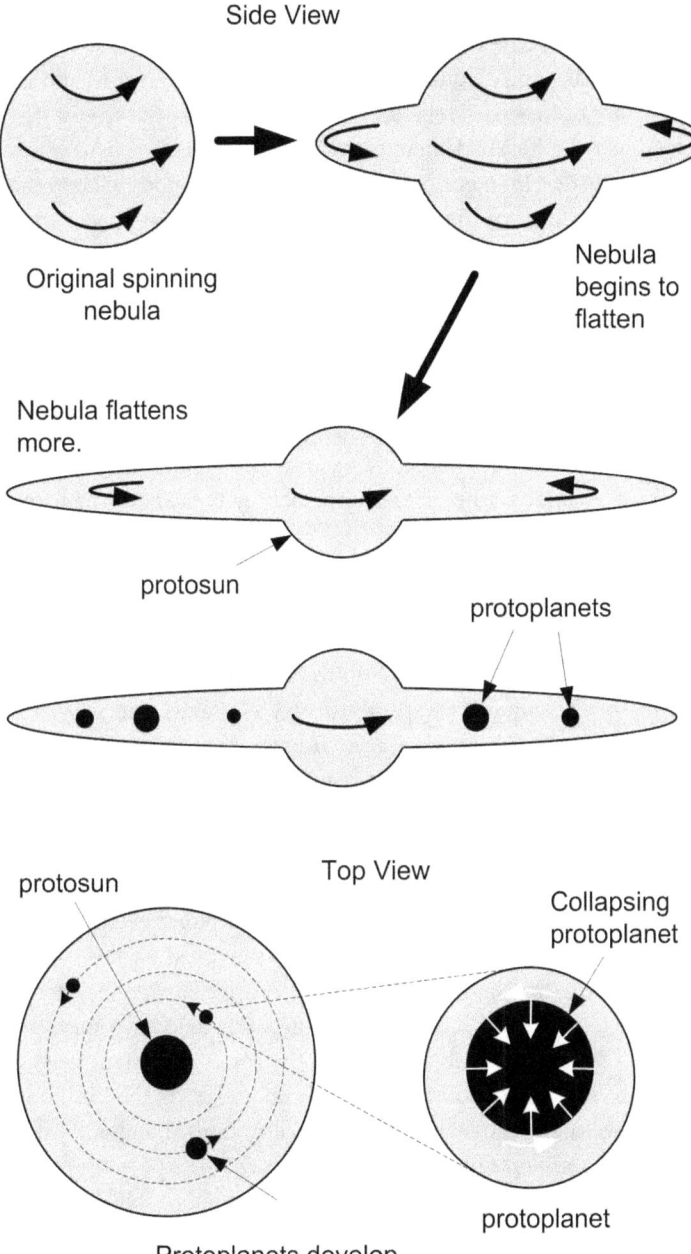

Figure 8. The major evolutionary steps between the original spinning nebula and a collapsing Sun and collapsing proto-planets.[7]

7. http://csep10.phys.utk.edu/astr161/lect/solarsys/nebular.html.

There are two regions in our solar system where debris and smaller bodies are located. One is the asteroid belt between Mars and Jupiter. The other region is beyond Neptune, called the Kuiper belt. Planets did not develop in either of these two regions, most likely because the closest gas giant planets (mostly Jupiter) had enough gravity to perturb those two regions and frustrate planet development. Some objects in these regions fell into the Sun, some were ejected from the solar system into interstellar space, and some collided with a planet such as Earth.[8] Most of these fragments were about the size of sand grains; when they approached the Earth, they burned up in the Earth's atmosphere, causing them to glow.

After fifty to 100 million years or so, eight planets became installed into substantially stable orbits. This is a brief summary of our current understanding of how our solar system formed. In addition, the eventual planets and their surfaces may have become heavily modified by big collisions. There are many other, lesser important details about the formation of the solar system.

What about the comets (number 6 in Table 4)? The original nebula (see upper left, "Original spinning nebula" in Figure 8) in the space outside Neptune a large number of comets or ice balls were formed. They all did not become absorbed into planets but remained a long distance from the Sun. Some of these comets were perturbed by gravity and moved inside the orbit of Mars. This happened more frequently in the early solar system history. Collisions of these comets may be the source of atmospheres of the rocky planets.

The Earth sustained major disfiguring impacts from asteroids, small planets, and other rocky bodies until about 3.5 billion years ago. This is called the Late Heavy Bombardment. For each of these larger events, the Earth's surface substantially melted. No liquid water remained on the Earth for at least 3,000 years. No solid rocks remained on the Earth after each event. Also, no life forms or pre-life forms or molecules could have survived after each event. The Earth's Moon was likely the result of a Mars sized object crashing into the Earth at that time. Major upheavals on the Earth's surface occurred due to earthquakes and volcanic eruptions. By about 3.0 billion years ago, the continents became more permanent.

As soon as the Earth was able to sustain life, about 3.8 billion years ago, the earliest life forms appeared. Around 2.0 billion years ago the Earth's bacterial organisms invented photosynthesis and started to convert the abundant carbon dioxide and abundant water into atmospheric oxygen (O_2). This was probably the most important, single innovation by bacteria in the history

---

8. Chambers and Milton, *From Dust to Life*, 263–73.

of our planet, because it was required for the eventual development of self-conscious, mindful, and self-aware humans.

This summary does not explain everything, however. For example, how did the small dust grains stick together and form bodies large enough for gravity to start playing a role in a planet's evolution? Extra-solar planets, exoplanets, have been recently discovered orbiting other stars. Their sizes and locations relative to their parent star (or stars) are not well understood with this model. Also, why are the current planets sized the way they are? Why are Earth and Venus larger than Mercury and Mars, their neighbors? Why is Jupiter three times larger than Saturn, its neighbor?

The Role Randomness Played

Randomness played a major role in the formation of our solar system. Consider a pebble sized rock that orbited the proto-Sun in the early stages of the evolution of our solar system. That rock collided with a larger boulder. The resulting heat allowed the rock to be embedded in the boulder. There were unknown details about this collision, such as the speed of the rock, its shape, its direction, the rock's orientation at the time of collision, the location of where the rock struck the boulder, the boulder's shape, the amount of heat generated due to the collision, how much debris flew off the boulder, what happened to the debris after the collision, exactly where the rock was embedded into the boulder after the collision, and whether the boulder grew larger after the collision.

The absence of these kinds of specifics means that for this collision the exact outcomes were not predictable. For example, for the new boulder, we do not know its increased size, its new shape, the new orbital path, and its location relative to other nearby objects. We cannot predict the specific outcomes of this collision. We conclude that this event was a random event, that is, unpredictable. Generally, even though we can see how these types of collisions contributed to the growth of proto-planets, we cannot exactly characterize them.

These types of random events occurred throughout the evolution of the structures and processes that eventually gave rise to the proto-Sun and our solar system. Also, these types of random events occurred before the solar system and proto-Sun began to form. It is our contention that random events occurred through the entire physical evolution from Big Bang to the eventual development of the Earth and the origin of life on our planet. Both determinate and indeterminate interactions occurred during this process. An abbreviated list of some of the most important of these random events is given in Table 5.

Table 5: Summary of randomness in our universe since the Big Bang.
The times in the second column from the left are approximate.

	Billions of years after the Big Bang	What was random?	Effects of randomness	Comments
1	0.0004	Small density differences in mass & energy in the universe	Regions of higher density eventually evolved into galaxies	Evidence comes from cosmic microwave background.
2	0.15 to 0.80	Energies & the directions of individual atoms	Gravitational attraction eventually formed the 1st proto-stars	During the dark ages before nuclear fusion occurred. See Figure 6.
3	0.8	Distribution of heavy elements due to 1st stars that ignited, due to nuclear fusion. The larger stars died in super novae, randomly distributing these elements.	Distribution of heavy elements within galaxies to places where solar systems might form.	Our solar system evolved where heavier elements were located.
4	0.8	Distribution of even heavier elements due to locations of neutron star encounters, which distributed these elements.	Distribution of even heavier elements to other places within galaxies.	Our solar system evolved where these elements were also located. There was an overlap.
5	9	Energies & directions of individual atoms & molecules that formed our proto-Sun.	Evolutionary path of our Sun's development that led to nuclear fusion.	Energy from our Sun drove most of the evolution of life on Earth.
6	9.5	Energies & directions of individual atoms, molecules, and larger objects that formed our proto-planets, especially Earth.	Evolutionary path of our Earth's development, the platform for life.	Development of our planetary home. One of the main reasons we are here.

	Billions of years after the Big Bang	What was random?	Effects of randomness	Comments
7	10	Size, location of development, & time of development of early Earth.	Earth retains its atmosphere.	Originally there was no oxygen. Eventually oxygen appears due to photosynthesis, using the early atmosphere.
8	9.0–13.8	Energies & directions of large objects, asteroids, & small planet-type objects with Earth.	Possible delivery of water & organic molecules to Earth. Delivery of some heavier elements. Mass extinctions. Stabilizer for Earth's orbiting & rotation, the moon.	All the ingredients for life to start & evolve. Elements necessary to support our modern technologies. Earth's seasons are stabilized. Some life forms go extinct while others thrive in their absence.

From this Table we can see that much of the randomness seems to come from subatomic particles, atoms, and irregularly shaped rocks and asteroids (for example, see number 6 and number 8). Larger objects such as planets, our Sun, and our galaxy seem to be more predictable and not so random. The reason for this is that the number of subatomic particles, atoms, and irregularly shaped rocks and asteroids is so overwhelmingly large that the application of natural laws, using computer-based simulations, is beyond our reach. This means that to understand their general behaviors requires us, using statistically based simulations, to predict the consequences of their motions, collisions, temperatures, and scatterings. The application of natural law to regularly shaped objects, like spheres such as our Sun, is more tractable.

In the future it is likely that we will be able to more accurately simulate some of these random type events and thereby better understand this evolutionary process. There are some roadblocks to our complete understanding because we cannot place each type of randomness in a laboratory and do controlled experiments. Even if this were possible, this would require that we have an accurate knowledge of those conditions that existed 13 billion years ago or so. We would need to know the distributions of matter and energy at that time.

There would be many specific details to get right before careful, well controlled experiments could be run. Assuming such laboratory experiments were possible, it would still be impossible to compare those specific results with the naturally occurring results (the real results) because we do not know exactly what the real results were. This is because we are separated by such great distances in space and such early times. In a certain way we can think of some of the events, summarized in Table 5, as becoming less random as we learn more and as the technology supporting our experimentation advances. But there are processes, especially at the subatomic and quantum physics level, where randomness is fundamental to our understanding of nature; no amount of technology will overcome that.

Conclusion

Some of the most important events that eventually led to the formation of the Earth were described in this chapter. The main purpose was to identify some of the random physical events in the eventual evolution of the Earth. Recall that randomness refers to the absence of predictability in outcomes. We saw that randomness played a huge role in the eventual formation of our solar system and the Earth.

An interesting pair of opposites seemed to come into play during the evolution of our universe. We focused on the role of randomness in this chapter with an absence of predictability such as the collision of atoms during the dark ages, random distribution of heavy elements after a larger star's death, and the energies and directions of asteroids during the Late Heavy Bombardment. In opposition to this unpredictability there was structure and predictability in the natural laws such as the formation of the first proto-stars due to gravitational attraction, radiation from the cosmic microwave background, and nuclear strong forces. See Table 5 for some other examples.

We have seen how the universe evolved from the Big Bang to a time when the Earth formed and became life friendly. The origin of life remains an unsolved problem. Even considering the start of life and subsequent evolution, how did modern humans emerge on the scene? We are now ready for the next chapter, which focuses on the evolution of conscious, mindful, and self-aware life on Earth.

5

Conscious, Self-Aware, and Mindful Humans

IN THE LAST CHAPTER, we took a look at how the universe got started from the Big Bang. We examined how stars started to shine and how solar systems were formed. The time and space scales of those events greatly exceed our everyday experiences. For example, the Big Bang occurred 13.8 billion years ago and the Earth began to form 4.6 billion years ago. See Table 5, the Cosmic Year. Other time and space scales at the start of the Big Bang were infinitesimally smaller than our everyday experiences.

For example, all of the mass and energy of what is now the whole universe was compressed into a tiny space, called a singularity, which was smaller than an atomic nucleus. The atomic and subatomic reactions occur on time scales that are far shorter than the quickest events we ever experience. Therefore, to appreciate those events, we must completely release ourselves from our own common experiences and rely on our understanding of physical laws. This, of course, is impossible but we must at least know about these time scales and these space scales both large and small. We also saw the important roles that random processes play in the evolution of our highly structured universe as summarized in Table 5.

Let us now look at the origin of life, which is similar to the origin and evolution of the universe and the role that randomness played. This will turn out to be an important relationship that is often not yet fully appreciated.

Origin of Life and Randomness

About 3.85 billion years ago, a strange and amazing event occurred on the surface of our planet. Where once there was lifeless, inanimate matter in one instant, in the next instant there was a life form. This life form was able to reproduce itself. It did not die. This new life was sustainable.[1] Before we look at the origins of life in the context of randomness, we need to define what we mean by life.

Let us assume that you are a parent responsible for a teenage son that has trouble keeping his room tidy. This is likely to be quite believable and not much of a stretch for many parents to imagine. To live up to the parents' requirements for neatness, the child must spend physical and mental energy to decide to clean up the room and not suffer the consequences. He needs to survey the room and to decide which items need to be stowed in an acceptable place. Some new place assignments might need to be made. He has to decide if his action plan will pass his parents' inspection. If yes, he needs to spend the energy to tidy up his space. In a way, this situation is similar to a life form. Life also has small compartments called cells, analogous to the teenager's room that separate the exterior environment from internal workings.

We can compare a cell to a teenager's room that separates the child from the outside world. In the cell, energy is required to process its biochemicals. The teen needs food in order to have the energy it takes to bring order to his clutter. The processing of chemicals and metabolism brings internal order to the cell and is like the teen who brings order to the previously cluttered room. Some environments provide sources of energy where life flourishes, such as the geothermal pools in Yellowstone National Park (thermal energy), a rain forest on the Olympic Peninsula of Washington State (solar energy), or a coral reef off the east coast of Australia (also solar energy).

In Table 6, five basic characteristics of all life are given. Life reproduces itself. The life forms stay pretty much the same from generation to generation. See number 1 in Table 6. Life not only needs to reproduce itself, it needs to reproduce the cellular structures that allow the progeny to reproduce subsequent generations. Life continues to change after a copy is made of itself. This can be called development and is part of the evolutionary process.

---

1. McFaul and Brunsting, *God Is Here to Stay*, 67–88.

Table 6. Five basic characteristics for all life.

	Characteristic	Comments
1	Reproduction	Life self assembles itself (reproduces) and brings order in the presence of an energy source (usually the Sun). Without an energy source, nature's general tendency is toward disorder or higher levels of entropy. From generation to generation, life forms typically reproduce themselves. All life on Earth uses the stable molecule DNA as an instruction book (genetic code) to pass along instructions for reproduction to succeeding generations.
2	Dependencies	Life survives on available food and energy. Life does not require large molecules that are generally not available. Typically, small, simpler molecules are assembled in the living cells into more complex structures.
3	Needs	Photosynthesis is used by plants that exploit the energy source of sunlight to make sugars. Our bodies have cells with mitochondria that convert food energy into ATP, a molecule that provides energy for most of the cells' functions.
4	Evolution	Life has the ability to evolve over time in response to environmental conditions.
5	Containment	Life needs a container such as your skin or cell membrane to distinguish life from its environment, to contain cellular components, and to protect it from the outside.

One of the most fundamental properties of life is that it evolves or changes over many generations. Even though life copies itself in reproduction, it must change so that it can adapt to its environment and survive. This changeableness comes from mutations of the cell's genes. This process can be compared to putting together a 500 piece jigsaw puzzle. Let us say that you assemble all the jigsaw pieces that form the bottom border from the left corner to the right corner. In the pile of the remaining puzzle pieces, there are other pieces that fit with the assembled pieces of that bottom border.

This analogy is something like how a piece of genetic information, a puzzle piece, is replicated on the molecular level and fitted with its complementary puzzle piece. Every once in a while there is a random change in the genetic information, a different puzzle piece, which can lead to a change in the cell and ultimately a change in the cell's organism. This process is called a mutation. See number 4 in the Table.

All life processes chemicals. In that activity, life needs energy to digest and use the food. See number 3 in Table 6. Not all of the incoming energy is used and needs to be expelled by the cell. This processing and ejecting of the waste energy is called metabolism. In addition to processing the chemicals, the energy is used to maintain internal order and structure.

A cell needs to be contained. See number 5. There needs to be a separation between all that activity inside the cell and the cell's environment in the same way that teenage boy needs a separation between what is going on in his room and what is going on in the rest of the house. The cell's energy, the chemicals it is processing, and the cell's maintenance of orderliness all need to be contained and protected from the outside world to prevent disorder from ruining the cellular structures and reactions. Some kind of wall or a membrane is required. Without such containment, the cells energy and orderliness would all dissipate into the surrounding environment and that cell would die.

Life needs only a few elements: carbon, hydrogen, oxygen, nitrogen, sulfur, and phosphorus. Only a few other trace elements are required for life to exist. Carbon is used the most. The reason for this is that the number of types of carbon based molecules is much greater than for any other element. There are many more evolutionary pathways for life to develop with carbon compared to any other element. Because the number of pathways is so large, randomness plays a much greater role in evolution compared to what would have happened with any other element besides carbon. Based on evolutionary considerations, carbon is the basic element of choice for life.

Liquid water is a fundamental solvent for life. Living cells require water for their metabolism, and water is required to transport nutrients within the cell and from cell to cell. Also, water is very useful as a solvent for the raw materials and energy. It has a wide temperature range that varies from freezing to boiling, which helps life to sustain itself over a wide range of environments. It is difficult, if not impossible, to imagine life without water. Randomness plays an important role inside the cell. Some of the molecules dissolve in the water, forming a solvent inside the cell and move in random directions. Their speed of movement is random. There is a random distribution of speed where some molecules move faster than others, and this depends on temperature and random collisions with other molecules.

While there is widespread consensus about which elements are essential to sustain life, the focal question of this chapter remains to be answered: How does a diverse collection of nonliving molecules randomly and without guidance come together and start to function in order to morph into the first living cells? Life is self-regulating and a delicately complex set of very small machine type structures of a high order. Today there is no comprehensive explanation that describes how life could have appeared spontaneously and undirected. The short answer is that we really do not know.

One of today's experts Andrew Knoll speculates that there might have been some kind of molecule that balanced as much simplicity as possible with enough complexity that it began reproducing in those primitive conditions. When that happened, lifeless matter, molecules, may have morphed into the earliest primitive life forms. This means that the complex molecular structures and biochemistry we see today are almost certainly unlike beginning life forms. This becomes clear when we reflect on what the Earth and atmosphere were like at the time of life's origins.

Earth's Environment When Life Started

From the last chapter, we see how the early Earth sustained impacts from asteroids, comets, and meteorites from about 4.1 to about 3.8 billion years ago. This period is called the Late Heavy Bombardment. Each impact can be considered a random event in that the path and energy of the impactor were not predictable. The sources of the impactors that bombarded the Earth were from the asteroid belt, the Kuiper belt, and other locations in and around the young solar system. Those impactors took trajectories that were altered, slowed down, and speeded up and were influenced by the gravitational forces from the other planets and bodies in the solar system.

We can imagine a pinball machine where the ball zig and zags down the play field as it hits various obstacles. Lights from the pinball machine are flashing and its bells are ringing. That pinball is kind of like an impactor that zig and zags on its path in the solar system and eventually strikes the earth. Each deflection on its path depends on the location, mass, and energy of motion of the object that defects the impactor from its original path. Also, as these objects are themselves influenced by the impactor, the object moves and influences still other objects. This is called the many body problem: each object is influenced by all the other nearby objects.

Let us assume that we had a super computer to keep track of all objects that might influence the potential impactor, all the potential impactors, all the cross interactions (many body problem), all the other factors that would determine the impactor's crash site on the Earth's surface, and the amount of energy deposited in the crash. Let us assume further that we could do this throughout the Late Heavy Bombardment, some 300 million years. We suspect that the description of all these collisions would easily overwhelm any super computer. Because of the large number of deflections and influences on each impactor, we can safely conclude that each impact on the Earth's surface during the Late Heavy Bombardment is a random event. We also can assume that all the impacts sustained by the Earth during this period were mostly caused by random influences, that is to say, unpredictable influences.

Table 7. Three options for when life started relative to the Late Heavy Bombardment.

Option	When did life start?	How many starts?	Consequences.
1	Life started before and/or during the Late Heavy Bombardment. Life was restarted just after the Late Heavy Bombardment.	multiple	Life was wiped out after each large impact. Life was restarted after it was temporally wiped out.
2	Life started before or during the Late Heavy Bombardment	one	Life struggled and somehow survived after each impact. It flourished after the bombardment ceased.
3	Life started just after the Late Heavy Bombardment.	one	Earth's environment was too harsh during the Late Heavy Bombardment but it flourished afterwards.

We can think of when life started relative to the Late Heavy Bombardment using Table 7. For option 1, there are multiple starts for life throughout the Late Heavy Bombardment and at various locations on the Earth's surface. The average temperatures, the temperatures during and just after each impact were very high. It is also generally suspected that the very earliest life forms were more fragile than life forms today, especially at the molecular level. The early atmosphere contained high concentrations of water and carbon dioxide and possibly methane, ammonia, and nitrogen. Volcanoes erupted releasing gases, including water vapor. This built up in the atmosphere. At that time there was no oxygen. Some of those gases were poisonous for today's life. It is difficult to identify accurately the atmosphere's components. All the direct evidences, such as rocks, have long since disappeared.

We do not know exactly how life started at the molecular level. It is likely that it was more delicate than today, which means that options 1 and 2 seem to be ruled out and that life somehow started after the Late Heavy

Bombardment was completed some 3.85 billion years ago. This early atmosphere is much different than what we breathe today. This is one important reason why the very first life forms must have been different from today's life. Other reasons include these: There were no predators, and there was no other competition by other life forms for food. The impacts during the Late Heavy Bombardment, the details of volcanic eruptions (frequency, intensity distributions, gas emissions, and locations), and the energy output from the Sun all seem to have unknown and random origins. Yet these effects must have affected how life got started.

Evolution and Life's Adaptations

Each species of life (type of life) has a lifetime from when it first appears on Earth's surface until the last individual dies. At that time the species is said to be extinct. Consider the Irish elk, which had large antlers. This may have been due to the females sexually selecting those males with the largest antlers. Of course as time passed, the males grew even larger antlers. Over the land, there was a plant species on which the elk grazed in order to grow its antlers. When those plants gradually disappeared after the last ice age, it became more difficult for the males to grow their antlers in order to attract females. As a result, approximately 10,000 years ago the Irish elk became extinct.

Over long periods of time (for example, 100,000 years), species slowly change in order to better adapt to their environment, which is also likely to be changing. Species change or evolve so that they are able to survive, grow in numbers, and prosper. Evidence for evolution is plentiful. We have a nearly infinite number of clues in support of evolution from fossils to genes (DNA, the genetic material for all life). The sum total of all of these clues shows that all forms of life are related to each other. Also, it shows that many species became extinct long before modern humans appeared on the Earth. Most scientists around the world accept evolution as a fundamental explanation for biology, and this is documented in many references.[2]

However it happened, life started on Earth 3.85 billion years ago. Life is self-regulating and a delicately complex set of nano machinery (small machinery) of a high order. Biological materials might have been delivered to the Earth's surface from space and then life might have started. Life might have started near deep sea vents where temperature might have been an energy source. Or life might have started on the surfaces of clays or similar materials. Today we do not have a comprehensive explanation that describes

---

2. For example, see Fairbanks, *Evolving*, 15–192

how life could have appeared spontaneously and undirected. The short answer is that we really do not know.

Earliest life forms were likely tiny, single cells called prokaryotes. Such cells do not have an interior nucleus with a membrane or other specialized internal structures. More developed species with nuclei and organelles are called eukaryotes and probably appeared more than three billion years ago.[3] Inside the prokaryote, all the intracellular components that can be dissolved in water (such as proteins, DNA and metabolites) are enclosed by the cell membrane rather than into separate cellular compartments. Bacteria are not prokaryotes and possess protein based bacterial micro compartments. These compartments are thought to act as primitive cellular organs, organelles, enclosed in protein shells. Some prokaryotes, such as cyanobacteria, may form large colonies.

Prokaryotes are simpler than eukaryotes, which are organisms, including humans, whose cells have a well-defined membrane bound nucleus (containing chromosomal DNA) and organelles. The first life almost certainly was less complicated and simpler than life that developed later. For this reason it is thought that prokaryotes are among the very first life forms. Some distinctive types of prokaryotes live in extreme environments such as high (or low) temperatures, acidic environments, alkaline conditions, and salt lakes. At some point in life's history, eukaryotes appeared and formed the basis of all complex cells and almost all multicellular organisms. Definitive conclusions are difficult to make because the most ancient fossil record goes back only to about 3.4 billion years ago. At that time the Earth's surface was becoming more solid so that fossil traces of life could be saved in a few locations. This leaves about 0.4 billion years with no fossil records of life.

If we could somehow move all oxygen dependent life forms from today back in time to 2.3 billion years ago and before, using a huge time machine, and release all that life onto the Earth's surface at that time, all our current life forms would quickly go extinct. At that time the Earth's atmosphere would be deadly to today's oxygen dependent life. Before 2.3 billion years ago, the Earth had no oxygen in its atmosphere. At this time oxygen first appeared and gradually increased in concentration, arriving at a stable level about 1.5 billion years ago.[4] This is because cyanobacteria first appeared at that time and learned to make sugar using the process known as photosynthesis, expelling oxygen as waste.

This process converts input sunlight energy and input atmospheric carbon dioxide into output nutrients, used by the plant, and expels oxygen

---

3. Lane, *The Vital Question*, 89–156.
4. Fairbanks, *Evolving*, 6–94.

as a waste product. This transition occurred because there was no initial competition for the cyanobacteria, and the new process was more efficient at producing the nutrients needed for life. This start of oxygen that first appeared in Earth's atmosphere is called the Great Oxygenation Event and is one of the great milestones in the development of life on our planet.

When the atmosphere became more oxygenated as it is now, the more advanced organisms, the eukaryotes that we described earlier could evolve. It appears as though the first eukaryotes evolved from two prokaryotes that lived together because their chances for survival were better than living apart. This change occurred because of one or more mutations, which is a sudden and permanent change in the genetic material of the cell. Many mutations were negative since the affected individual died before it could procreate. Fewer mutations were a positive factor, because the progeny that did survive were in less competition with other organisms for food and resources. The positive mutations spread throughout the gene pool of that species, and that species became more competitive. The environment changed from time to time so that climate, for example, influenced the competition for survival.

Table 8. Time periods for the history of the Earth. The biological evidences are generally placed into Eras that can be compared to Geological time periods.

Era	Millions of years ago	Geological time period	First appearances
Tertiary	0–2	Pleistocene	Homo Sapiens
	2–5	Pliocene	Hominids
	5–24	Miocene	Apes
	24–37	Oligocene	Monkeys
	37–58	Eocene	Horses
	58–65	Paleocene	
Mesozoic	65–144	Cretaceous	Modern mammals
	144–208	Jurassic	Birds
	208–245	Triassic	Dinosaurs

Era	Millions of years ago	Geological time period	First appearances
Paleozoic	245–286	Permian	Reptiles
	286–360	Carboniferous	
	360–408	Devonian	Sharks
	408–438	Silurian	Jawed fish
	438–505	Ordovician	Land plants
	505–570	Cambrian	Trilobites
Pre-cambrian	570–2,500	Proterozoic	Soft-bodied animals
	2,500–4,600	Archean	Origin of life at approximately 3,800

Great Extinctions

An extinction event (or mass extinction) is a swift and extensive reduction in life on Earth. Consider all the species of plants and animals that ever existed since life began. Today over 99 percent of those species are now extinct. The average time between the formation of a species and its final extinction is about two to three million years. Sometimes in the vast history of plants and animals, species die out at about the same time. This may be due to a large volcanic eruption that produced ash that blocked sunlight. It may have been an ice age when cold temperatures made it too difficult for life to survive. Another possibility is that a large meteor impacted the surface of the Earth and caused a worldwide devastation of the climate. These large scale die-offs are called mass extinctions. Six major mass extinctions are summarized in Table 9.

Table 9. Summary of six worldwide and major mass extinctions of plants and animals.

Date of occurrence, millions of years ago	Summary of major mass extinction events
650	Snowball Earth, Earth was wrapped in ice for millions of years. About 70 percent of the dominant sea plants went extinct.
443	Forty-nine percent of all life vanished.
374	Seventy percent of all marine species died out.
252	Approximately 96 percent of ocean species and about 70 percent land species were wiped out.
201	About 20 percent of all marine species vanished.
65	A meteor impact in the Yucatan, Mexico, led to the mass extinction of about 80 percent of the marine species and about 85 percent of land species. The dinosaurs vanished and, as a result, mammals became a dominant species.

Let us examine the mass extinction that occurred 252 million years ago. Approximately 96 percent of the marine life and about 70 percent of the land species were wiped out. All of life on Earth came quite close to total annihilation. If it were not for a small, but tough thread of life at that time, we would not be here. Another huge die off occurred about 65 million years ago when about eighty of the marine species and about 85 percent of land species died. These two events were really close calls. These outcomes fundamentally altered the pathway for the evolution that followed them.

In 2013, a new study concluded that the cause and origin of the enormous extinction 201 million years ago was due to volcanic eruptions, large enough to cover the entire US under 300 feet (91 meters) of lava and ash.[5] This was about the time that the supercontinent, Pangaea, started to come apart due to these same eruptions that led to the extinction 201 million years ago.

L. Billings describes the possibilities that gravitational interactions between the Earth and dark matter may have caused one or more of these mass extinctions. Dark matter was recently hypothesized to exist in order to explain why galaxies hold together by gravity from dark matter and other effects. Approximately 3 percent of the mass/energy of the universe is

5. Lee, "National Geographic," lines 1–10.

comprised of dark matter. The basic idea is that as our solar system moves in its orbit about the galactic center, the solar system comes under the gravitational influence of a thin disk of clumpy dark matter. This causes comets, originally located in the outer limits of our solar system, to move to the inner solar system and pepper the Earth with large impacts that may occasionally lead to extinctions of life. These unpredictable impacts can lead to volcanic eruptions as well, and this can lead to extinctions.

Several mass extinctions in Table 9 have no commonly accepted known cause. In the confused time after extinction, the surviving plants and animals would have newly available space and reduced competition in their new ecosystems to exploit. The survivors would likely increase in population and diversify in characteristics, such as beaks, claws, and skin coverings. Of course, many of the features of the newly extinct animals would disappear. The survivors would compete in new ways and drive each other's evolution, such as by hunting one another. These types of changes would alter life to become more modern.

Appearance of Humans

The main focus of this section will be on how chaotic and random factors in biological evolution influenced the emergence of self-conscious, self-aware, and mindful humans on this planet. The appearance of anatomically modern humans 200,000 years ago depended on long chains of unpredictable antecedent events that when considered in isolation might seem to be inconsequential. We might think that evolution gave us a smooth transition from one species to the next, from one species extinction to the next, and from one adaptation in one environment to the next. The reality is that there was a fortuitous randomness and long chain of outcomes that were linked to each other and that eventually gave rise to conscious, mindful, and self-aware humans. Yet a change in any one of those apparently minor outcomes could have put earthly evolution on a different pathway that would not have led to the emergence of modern humans.

In support of this point, we will consider just four of many possible examples. The Cambrian explosion of life occurred about 535 million years ago when an astonishing number of species first appeared. Most of the phyla, or large groups of plants or animals with shells and other hard body parts emerged at that time. Also at this time starfish, spiders, and certain insects appeared. The cause of that explosion likely involved the existence of a large land mass on our planet. The continental drift would have resulted in important changes in areas such as rainfall, solar warming, and ocean currents. Large, stable ecosystems would have been disrupted. Small and new ecosystems would have formed in the eddy currents of these major changes. A multitude of new niches would have appeared for new evolutionary forces to take effect.[6] If our few but tough fragile ancestors had not survived the radiation, earthquakes, temperature changes, and lightning strikes 535 million years ago, then no vertebrates would have survived at all.

Second, a seemingly unpromising and inconsequential group of lobe finned fishes evolved fin bones strong enough to bear their weight on land. If they remained entirely in the water, buoyant forces would have sufficiently supported them and made the bony fins unnecessary. However, because of neutral or apparently negative mutations the bones appeared, and those bones were strong enough to support their body weight on land. If such an evolutionary step had not occurred, vertebrates might never have converted to land dwelling animals and the long pathway to modern humans would have been stopped.

Third, about 65 million years ago a large asteroid crashed in what is now Mexico. It caused a fireball and sent debris and ash in the atmosphere that blocked sunlight from reaching the Earth for several months. The rain turned acidic from the effects of the impact of the asteroid and atmospheric nitrogen. Many plants withered and died as a result. Some plant eating dinosaurs died because of the absence of plant life. Ultimately, all animals depended on a food chain that starts with plant eaters or plants themselves. As a result, even the meat eating dinosaurs perished.[7]

Before this catastrophe, mammals were dominated by dinosaurs and remained small and insignificant. After the asteroid crash, many new food sources became available for the mammals, and much of the evolutionary competition disappeared. Many new ecological niches opened up and mammals flourished. If that asteroid had not randomly struck the earth, dinosaurs likely would have remained dominant, as they were for 200 million years previously, and mammals would have remained pretty insignificant.

Fourth, about 4.4 million years ago an early hominid first walked upright on two feet, called bipedalism. This became and remains one of the most distinctive features of modern humans. Other primates may walk on two legs for a short time to cross an open space or reach for a piece of fruit, but they quickly return to walking on all four limbs. Bipedalism has given humans several distinct advantages: traveling long distances is more efficient and requires less energy; body temperature in warmer climates is moderated by reducing the angle of exposure to the Sun; predators could

---

6. Horvitz, *The Complete Idiot's Guide to Evolution*, 207.
7. This scenario is favored at this time but it is not held universally.

more easily be seen with eyes higher off the ground compared to walking on all fours; the hands were freed to use tools. If an original small lineage of primates had not developed this upright posture, the long chain of events that led to modern humans probably would not have occurred.

In addition to these four examples, there are many others that might seem unimportant. However, when considered in a long chain of related occurrences, seemingly insignificant random events become an essential part of the evolutionary process that led to the emergence of *Homo sapiens* on Earth.

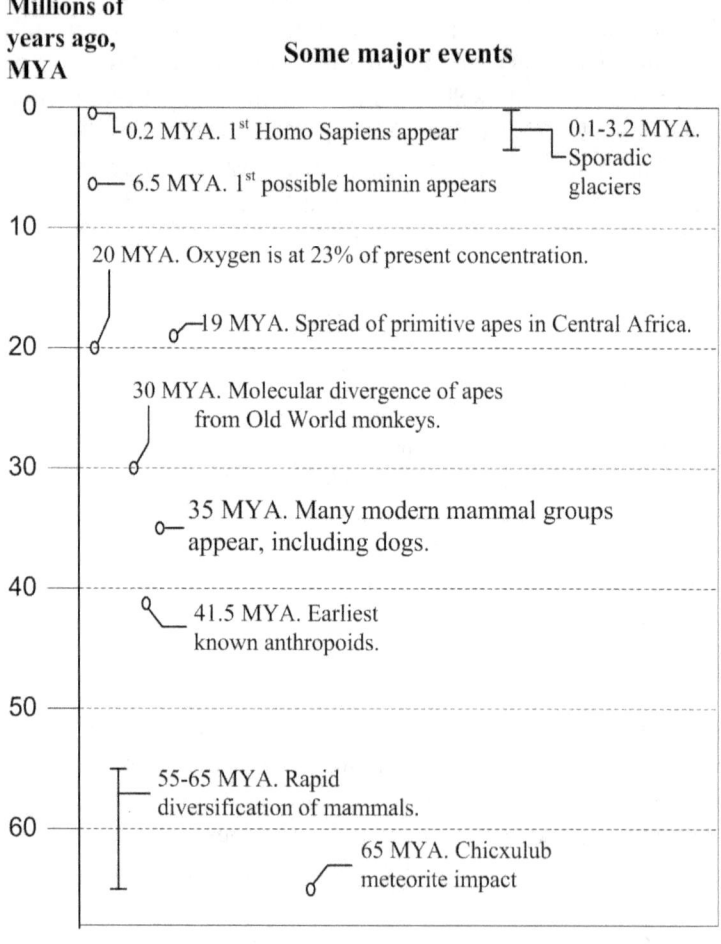

Figure 9. Summary timeline of some important events in the evolution of anthropoids (higher primate mammals, including monkeys, apes, and humans.)

In Figure 9, the word Hominin, 6.5 MYA, refers to a family of primates that includes humans and their fossil ancestors. Anthropoids, 41.5 MYA, refers to higher primate mammals, including monkeys, apes, and humans. Figure 9 also shows where the Earth stood in time relative to the great dinosaur extinction. Dinosaurs were dominant for about 200 million years, 265 to 65 million years ago, MYA. At 65 MYA, the dinosaurs and many other life forms died in a mass extinction due to an asteroid crashing into the Earth's surface. This opened up many environmental niches. Mammals took advantage of these openings and flourished, especially from 55 to 65 MYA. Anatomically modern humans, Homo sapiens, first appeared very recently on this time line, just 0.2 MYA or 200,000 years ago.

About 6.5 MYA, some unpredictable and random changes must have occurred to cause the first hominins to develop in one direction, leaving the apes to develop on their own. A successful explanation for this branching would likely support related observations about those fossils. There are at least three explanations: 1) The Savanna Hypothesis, 2) The Woodland-Mosaic Hypothesis, and 3) The Variability Hypothesis. The Savanna Hypothesis says that the homeland of the anthropoids became cooler and more arid resulting in widespread savannas or grasslands. With fewer trees to escape from danger, the anthropoids had to figure out how to acclimate to theses open savannas.

The ones that made better evolutionary changes enhanced their chances of survival. Upright walking (bipedalism) was the most efficient way to travel over these areas in search of food, caring for their offspring, and avoiding predators. Also, bipedalism freed the hands for working with tools and carrying things such as food to the rest of the family members. Survival was enhanced by socializing with others on the savannas compared to more solitary living in trees as before. As they coped with new challenges, brain size increased. Recent evidence about those environmental changes suggests that there is more to the story than just the Savanna Hypothesis.

The Woodland-Mosaic Hypothesis was proposed in response to some of the difficulties with the Savanna Hypothesis. This explanation says that the homeland of the pre-humans (hominids) was partly woodland and partly grassland or savanna, which is a patchwork (or mosaic) of woodlands and savannas. This would have given our ancestors opportunities to fill this environmental niche and to find food in both trees and savannas. Maneuvering among and between these two types of habitats would have promoted bipedalism. Survival behaviors in both regions would need to be managed. Also, these two types of habitats would have encouraged socializing and work that had to be done in the other habitat. All of this would have required extended brain functions and correspondingly larger brains.

The Variability Hypothesis takes the preceding two hypotheses one step further. Our pre-human ancestors had to contend with a wide range of environments such as forests, grasslands, and more arid regions. Hominid (such as Australopithecus) fossils have recently been found in a variety of habitats, suggesting that their skeletons and brains allowed them to be very adaptable (this is the key) so that they were able to flourish in many different kinds of environmental niches.

Recent research has shown that these homelands in Africa experienced extreme climate variations about 6.5 MYA. This would have caused large changes in vegetation types and water availability. Quick adaptability, faster than only what was allowed by anatomical variability, would have been an advantage for survival in those times. As the brain became more developed in critical thinking skills, quick lifesaving adaptations also could be made to accommodate rapidly changing habitats.

Anatomically modern humans, *Homo sapiens*, first appeared about 200,000 years ago in Africa, which takes us to the next important question. Why did humans evolve and become so successful while all the other hominins disappeared? Why did humans populate the whole Earth and how did they do it? Why were they better able to adapt to the wide range of ecosystems, climates, and changing surroundings?

The key that allowed our early ancestors to diverge from the apes and be more successful was rapid adaptation. Anatomical adaptation was much slower compared to adaptations that resulted from the use of critical thinking skills, especially as the brain became larger and more developed. For example, as an ice age advances, anatomical changes require genes to instruct a developing physique to alter its shape. Such changes occur after multiple genetic false starts. Each genetic change requires a generation (about twenty years) to play out before the next genetic iteration can begin. Now consider the brain: successful solutions to a problem require electrical and chemical signals between neurons in the brain. This involves recognizing the problem, developing a symbolic solution to it, trying out the solution, and tweaking the solution through an accumulation of experiences. All this can happen in a few hours or days, which is a more efficient form of rapid adaptation than anatomical changes that require longer periods of time to make.

About 2.8 to 2.4 MYA, the homeland climate of our ancestral hominids cooled and became drier. Food plants became less available. Finding protein sources from the vegetation, like roots and tubers, became more critical. Removing those food sources from the ground became more efficient with the use of the right tools. Also, improvements in hunting tools such as arrowheads and spears made hunting more successful during climate changes.

If the climate shifted back to a warmer and wetter environment, our ancestral hominids probably would have applied their developing critical thinking skills to adapt to these changes. Waiting around for anatomical changes would not have occurred quickly enough to take advantage of changing environmental niches. In addition, for each climate related shift, the predator situation changed along with more competition from other hominins and threats from a different set of bacterial based diseases. If pre-humans could talk, they probably would have been asking themselves questions like: How can we do this better? How can we better survive? How can we be more secure?

These efforts would have been improved greatly through cooperation and better communication with their fellow family and clan members. Happily, the larynx and vocal cords changed so that sounds and primitive speech became more accessible to our ancestors. Since human vocal anatomy is quite similar to that of apes, we can conclude that mastering speech was related less to our anatomy and more with our brains. Cooperation was enhanced through language and speech. Cooperative hunts for the big animals could be planned. During the hunt our ancestors could coordinate quick decisions as animals bolted and attempted to escape. After the kill the hunters needed to agree on how to bring the meat back to their camp. The division of meat among the family and clan members had to be determined. After a particularly successful hunt, stories would be told and songs sung about the heroes and details. There would have been laughter, smiles, and dancing. Language would have been required to do all this.

In addition to advancing language skills, the hominids that advanced their tool-making abilities likely would have important advantages compared to those who lagged behind. Arrowheads were required on the tips to arrows to improve the chances of the arrow penetrating the body of the target prey. Spear points were needed to bring down large animals such as a wooly mammoth, now extinct, probably due to over hunting by our ancestors. Superior sharp edges on knife-type tools could better butcher the meat brought back to camp from a successful hunt. Tools and methods to make fire, tools to make clothing, and tools to prepare food were all upgraded to improve chances for survival.

Not only were the tools improved, but also the methods for making them. Tool development skills became enhanced through the use of available materials. All types of advancements from making axe handles to garments became part of this learning process. The progressive evolution of modern humans required substantial abstract and critical thinking skills in the biological circuitry of a larger brain as it became better at solving problems that dealt with survival and adaptation. To improve a tool, a method for making it, and/

or a method for using it required an abstract visualization for the improvement. Not only would a larger brain have been required, but more advanced information processing would have been needed as well.

Those hominins that were better with their critical thinking skills and at passing them along to their children through language development would have had a better chance of long term survival and population growth than other groups of hominins. One illustration of the brain development is the relative size of the brain compared to the whole body (size of brain mass compared to whole body mass). For example, in *Homo erectus* who lived 1.6 to 0.03 MYA, it was 1.46%. For *Home heidelbergensis* who lived 0.6 to 0.2 MYA, it was 1.69%. For *Homo neanderthalensis* who lived 0.350 to 0.028 MYA, it was 1.98%. For *Homo sapiens* who lived 0.2 MYA until now, it is 2.75%.[8] These trends support the conclusion that there was a competitive advantage for larger brains.

About 100,000 years ago, some *Homo sapiens* began to leave central Africa where they first appeared 200,000 years ago in what is now Ethiopia (approximate location). Some of their routes took them across the Arabian Peninsula and into and across the Indian subcontinent about 80,000 years ago. From there they migrated in a southeasterly direction into what is now Indonesia and onto Australia, arriving there about 60,000 years ago. About 40,000 years ago, some early humans moved into Europe where they encountered earlier developed hominins (*Neanderthals* in and around what is now Spain).

Others colonized northern Asia about 30,000 years ago. Due to global glaciation episodes, the sea levels dropped, exposing the Bearing Land Bridge between what is now Siberia and Alaska. Some early humans crossed this bridge about 14,000 years ago, apparently following large game animals. Once in North America and without other hominin competition they spread throughout North and South America. The total worldwide population of Homo sapiens 35,000 years ago was about 3 million. At the time of this writing that number has grown to about 7.2 billion people worldwide, indicating a successful species.

Why did these worldwide migrations occur? Other primates did not migrate to this extent, only *Homo sapiens*. Today there are no other hominin species besides us. These hunter-gatherers moved to follow game and other food sources. Over many years, the average rate of movement for the more nomadic humans was about one-half mile per year. Perhaps there were other reasons for these migrations. Larger brains that were capable of developing and using language, capable to developing better tools, and

---

8. Roberts, *Evolution: The Human Story*, 32.

better at organizing the hunt must have developed the abilities for more abstract thoughts.

This would have included expressions of curiosity, such as:

> "What is over that distant mountain range? I wonder if the fishing is better near those other islands. I think we should follow those large game animals across the Bearing Land Bridge. I wonder if a fox skin blanket would be warmer than a moose skin blanket."

Some of this curiosity might not have been directly related to survival activities but to acquiring knowledge for the sake of knowledge, leading to explorations. Our ancestors must have also thought about where they came from, about the possibility of an afterlife, and about the possibility of a god.

Conclusion

To summarize, in order for life to start, it needed a way to separate its internal biochemistry from the outside world. This was done in cells, the basic unit of life that is able to reproduce and perform other functions. From one generation to the next, life evolves or changes. Those life forms that change and better adapt to their environment are more successful than competing life forms that do not adapt as well. Liquid water is particularly well suited as a solvent for all the various biochemical reactions that occur in the cell.

The solar system developed about 4.6 billion years ago, mostly from the dust and ashes of an earlier supernova explosion. During the Earth's early history, about 4.1 to about 3.8 billion years ago, the Earth sustained many impacts from other objects in the solar system. Most of these impacts sterilized the Earth so that life could not start or be sustained. Gradually, this bombardment abated and as soon as the Earth was able to sustain life, life got started. The details of how life originated are not known, but somehow lifeless molecules became alive. The first single cells of life were likely much different than they are today.

Once life began it evolved. The populations of those life forms that were able to adapt better to their environment, compared to their competitors, grew faster and began to dominate those regions. Evidences for evolution are plentiful and include evidences from genetics (DNA) and the fossil record. About 2.3 billion years ago certain life forms, cyanobacteria, started to use photosynthesis to produce life giving nutrients. This produced a waste product, oxygen. This new process was so successful that atmospheric oxygen started to be used by other subsequent life forms. This paved the way for more advances and eventually land dwelling animals.

It is commonly accepted that anatomically modern humans first appeared in Africa about 200,000 years ago. About 100,000 years ago people started to leave Africa. This was driven by survival needs to follow game animals and explore new fishing waters. Also, these relocations must have been driven by an internal curiosity and abstract thinking that would have been possible in the larger and more fully developed brains. As a result of this evolutionary process and the random events associated with it, modern humans migrated to every geographical region on the Earth's surface. They gathered in tribes and clans and created self-sustaining communities that grew in size. Thus, the changes that occurred in physical evolution stimulated advances in social evolution and historical developments.

We are now ready for the next chapter where we will focus on how randomness left its mark on one of the most important centuries in human history.

6

Twentieth Century History

IN PREVIOUS CHAPTERS, WE defined randomness as unpredictability and applied it to real life stories, micro and macro sources, the origin of our universe, solar system, and the development of conscious, mindful, and self-aware life on Earth. In this chapter, we fast forward in time and describe how randomness affected some of the most important events of the twentieth century. While we could have chosen earlier historical epochs since the start of modern human evolution, we are focusing on the twentieth century because it is the time period that is of most recent memory and has been studied thoroughly. Our current understanding of the events that shaped these one hundred years is extensive even though experts do not always agree on their causes.

As we stated in chapter 2, it is unlikely that any person living in 1900 could have predicted how the world would evolve during the next ten decades. As we will show, much of this lack of foresight was caused by randomness. No one could have predicted how the major political movements and economic changes that took place during this time period would set the stage for the dramatic developments that have occurred already at the start of the twenty-first century. As we will see, randomness played a huge role in what happened as the twentieth century unfolded and how it continues to contribute to trends that are shaping the twenty-first.

Twentieth century events were unique in one important respect when compared to previous eras. Their impact was global in scope and not limited only to local or regional changes. In particular, five major episodes stand out among the rest. In chronological order they are World War I, the Great Depression and the New Deal, World War II, the Cold War, and the rise of global terrorism. In this chapter we will examine all five in succession along with the main historical trends and some of the major unforeseen or random incidents that led to beneficial as well as disastrous worldwide consequences. It is not our intention to describe in detail the thousands of occurrences that took place during these five major developments. Instead, we will focus only on the major issues and the random changes in circumstances and unexpected events that no one could predict in advance but that influenced both the direction and outcome of all five.

World War I

We start our discussion of randomness and the twentieth century with five years of warring that changed the world forever: World War I that lasted from 1914 to 1919. Its scope and long term global impact for the next several decades and down to the present time cannot be overstated. Before the war started, the trend toward nationalism among European nations had escalated during and at the end of the nineteenth century and continued into the twentieth. Precursors such as the formation of alliances in response to Napoleon's European conquests also helped set the stage. Internal political squabbles in Morocco, Bosnia, Herzegovina, and in the Balkans left unresolved hostilities that intensified the growing polarization among Europeans.

In turn, this stimulated a trend toward militarization and a growing arms race that set the stage for the events that erupted into WWI. Furthermore, the prevailing Social Darwinist philosophy of the nineteenth century reinforced an emerging spirit of imperialism. This contributed to the perception that competition and conflict among nations was entirely natural because they would separate the strong from the weak and assure that only the fittest would survive as Darwinism assumed.

In combination, this sentiment along with the other factors mentioned above led European nations to form two major mutual defense alliances. The first was called the Triple Entente that included Britain, France, and Russia and the second the Triple Alliance that consisted of Germany, Austria-Hungary, and Italy. As hostilities escalated, the formation of these two alliances symbolized that Europe stood at the doorway of war with no signs of stepping back.

This leads to the next question. Was WWI inevitable? The answer is: not necessarily although the probability of an outbreak rose steadily as the animosities between the two factions hardened. Even though the political forces that became divided at the end of the nineteenth century increased the likelihood that Europe was fated for war early in the twentieth, this might not have occurred if growing antagonisms could have been reduced or reversed. However, this did not happen; in the midst of this intensely polarized political environment, there occurred a random event that thrust Europe and other regions around the world into half a decade of bloody warfare.

No one saw it coming, but on June 28, 1914, in Sarajevo an ethnic Serb named Gavrilo Princip assassinated Austria-Hungary's heir to the throne Archduke Franz Ferdinand and his wife Duchess Sophie. In the wake of this unpredictable event, member states of the two alliances began rallying in support of their defense partners. This forced other nations not in the alliances to either claim neutrality or join sides. One month later after the assassination of Ferdinand, on July 28 Austria-Hungary declared war on Serbia. When Russia mobilized, on August 1 Germany declared war on Russia and two days later August 3 on France. The next day, August 4, England declared war on Germany

Once alliance nations began issuing their war declarations against one another, other non-Europeans followed. This included Japan that declared war against Germany on August 23. New Zealand, Australia, and South Africa followed by committing troops as well. As the clouds of WWI settled over the European continent and around the world, the carnage of trench warfare consumed tens of thousands of lives, mostly soldiers and civilians from Europe where the battles raged back and forth without decisive military gains by either side. WWI became a stalemate that tragically cost millions of lives.

When the war started during the summer of 1914, the United States remained neutral. Most American leaders and the vast majority of civilians felt little motivation to get involved in what they saw as primarily a European problem. However, Germany's aggressive expansion into submarine warfare set the stage for a combination of volatile and intolerable situations that eventually tipped the scale in the direction of US involvement.

What sparked the shift away from US neutrality? In 1912, two years before the start of the war, Woodrow Wilson was elected as the US President. He was reelected in 1916 in part because the public supported his commitment to keep the US out of the war. Nonetheless, despite this initial position, several unexpected events occurred, two in particular that contributed to Wilson's change of mind. First, when a German U-boat unpredictably sank the British passenger liner *Lusitania* on May 7, 1915 in an unprovoked attack and 128 US citizens drowned, Wilson along with the majority of Americans were furious.

Second, more than a year and a half later on January 16, 1917 the German government telegrammed the Mexican Ambassador to create an alliance against the US. The German provocation of seeking a wartime agreement with America's southern neighbor was the final straw that broke the back of US neutrality. Germany's action was not anticipated by the Americans who could no longer sit on the sidelines. Finally, on April 6, 1917, America declared war on Germany and several months later, December 7, on Austria-Hungary. With the US entry into this First Great War of the twentieth century three years after it started, it took less than two years before Germany's head of state Kaiser Wilhelm II abdicated on November 9, 1918, and the fighting in Europe ended two days later on November 11. When the Treaty of Versailles was signed months later on June 28, 1919 it was five years to the day after the assassination of Franz Ferdinand.

WWI was followed by a comparatively calm ten year interim in the US before the start of the next great event of the twentieth century: the Great Depression. Known as the Roaring 20s, it was during this decade that the US became the world's richest nation and where a culture of mass consumerism was born. The power and presence of women grew in the wake of workforce involvement outside the home during WWI and passage of the nineteenth amendment in 1920 that gave them the right to vote. Other defining images come readily to mind, including the Flapper and Jazz Age, the Prohibition and Gangster Era, and the Scopes Monkey Trial.

It was a time when America became increasingly urban as Henry Ford and others put the nation "on wheels." The Roaring Twenties also witnessed the rise of baseball, music, and artistic heroes such as Babe Ruth, Charlie Chaplin, Louis Armstrong, Duke Ellington, George Gershwin, Ernst Hemingway, and many others. After 1927, when Charles A. Lindbergh crossed the Atlantic Ocean in the *Spirit of St. Louis*, he became a household name. To top it off, the post WWI economy prospered; most people had jobs; and at the end of the decade the unemployment rate stood around 3 percent.

In the midst of the excesses and exhilaration that exemplified the post WWI era, few were prepared for the economic eruption that lay just around the corner. No one saw it coming, but it turned out to be one of the twentieth century's most gut wrenching and unforeseen episodes: the Great Depression.

The Great Depression and the New Deal

On October 29, 1929, often called Black Tuesday, the US stock market crashed. Within months the US tumbled into a decade long period of severe economic decline and gradual recovery that reverberated around the world and helped lay the foundation for the Second World War. There was pervasive pain and suffering that the Great Depression imposed on America and around the world.

By 1932, stock prices fell by 89 percent of their original value. Between 1929 and 1933, the unemployment rate climbed to 25 percent of the workforce. Wages fell 42 percent for those who still had jobs. The cost of goods deflated by 10 percent, and the GDP (Gross Domestic Product) was cut in half from $103 to $55 billion. Soup kitchens were a common sight; in 1932 one song in particular by Harburg and Gorney captured the mood and new realities of the nation: Brother, Can You Spare a Dime?

Like all major events both before and after, the Great Depression did not appear out of the blue but instead was preceded by trends that set the stage and that are now obvious in hindsight but were mostly unpredictable at the time. Early in 1928 the US raised interest rates on money borrowed from the federal government. As a result, investors began pulling their money out of stocks and shifting it into currency markets in order to receive higher dividends. At the start of the Great Depression, the dollar was backed by gold, which made owning gold more valuable than currency.

As the economic downturn worsened, large numbers of people panicked and started withdrawing their cash deposits from banks forcing 9,000 of them eventually to fail. Surviving banks stopped giving loans to individuals and businesses. Federal legislators also panicked and passed the reactive Smoot-Hawley Tariff Act that imposed high taxes on foreign imports, which caused foreign countries to retaliate by raising tariffs on American products. In combination, these actions unexpectedly fueled a decline in factory production and a decrease in the demand for goods. As unemployment increased and workers lost their wages, the Great Depression continued its downward and unanticipated spiral.

To make matters worse, an unforeseen drought called the Dust Bowl struck the Great Plains in the thirties. This forced an unprecedented number of farm foreclosures. John Steinbeck described the devastating effect the drought had on the fictional Tom Joad (played by Henry Fonda) and his family in his 1939 Pulitzer Prize winning book *The Grapes of Wrath*. In 1940, Hollywood turned Steinbeck's book into a movie of the same title, which received widespread acclaim by critics and the public alike.

The national election of 1932 brought Franklin D. Roosevelt into the US Presidency with the hope of ending the Great Depression. Market Place purists like former President Herbert Hoover insisted that the economy would recover only after the business cycle ran it natural course. Following the principle of *laissez-faire*, he and his supporters held that government could do little to nothing to alleviate the misery of millions. Roosevelt disagreed and launched a new experiment called the New Deal that was without precedent in American history: using the federal government to manage and regulate the economy and to provide safety net support for the unfortunate. Even though no one could foresee the impact of Roosevelt's pioneering approach, alarmists predicted catastrophe. They were wrong. Slowly but surely, the economy rebounded. No doubt, WWII played a major role in ending the Great Depression. However, before we discuss this in the next section, we need to describe the groundbreaking programs that Roosevelt created.

From 1933 to 1939, he created nearly fifty new programs that covered virtually all segments of the economy. Many experts have written about Roosevelt's innovations; while lack of space does not permit us to list all of them here, one primary principle underpins them all: Government can play a major role in stimulating business growth and in protecting workers and other disadvantaged Americans from the adverse effects of economic downturns. For example, he helped increase the demand for goods and services by creating government programs that put people to work. These included public works and construction projects for building and improving parks, roads, offices, and many other facilities. Once employed, workers used their wages to buy products, which boosted demand and led private sector manufacturers to increase their supply. In 1936, national labor relations legislation gave workers the right to strike and bargain collectively for better wages and benefits.

To further safeguard workers and others, he developed a federal insurance protection plan for bank deposits, created national programs that enabled over a million home owners to refinance long term mortgages, and launched a pay as you go Social Security system for senior retirement. In order to promote production, Roosevelt abandoned the gold standard and made more money available for businesses to borrow from banks. As a consequence of this and other financial regulatory changes, his monetary policy and its long term effect on stabilizing the economy became one of the major success stories of his presidential legacy.[1]

Although experts still debate the overall impact of Roosevelt's New Deal initiative on American society, the nation began going back to work as the following summary shows. By 1934, the economy began to show signs of recovery by growing around 11 percent. In 1935, it had grown almost 9 percent and in 1936 nearly 13 percent. From 1933 to 1937, unemployment dropped from 25 percent to 14 percent. When no New Deal legislation was passed in 1938 and federal spending was cut, unemployment rose again to

---

1. Some of FDR's well known programs include the Civilian Conservation Core, Civil Works Administration, Federal Deposit Insurance Corporation, Home Owners Loan Corporation, and Public Works Administration. All were started in 1933.

19 percent. As the Dust Bowl drought wound down in 1937 and the US began spending on weapons buildup and aiding Europe militarily, unemployment began to drop again. After Roosevelt won his third term in 1940 and when Japan attacked Pearl Harbor on December 7, 1941, unemployment stood at 9.9 percent.

For ten years, the Great Depression reverberated around the world. When it ended at the start of WWII, Roosevelt's New Deal programs had left an indelible mark on the US. As has been well documented by many experts, it lessened the extremes of the business cycle and helped reduce the number of post New Deal recessions compared to those that affected society before the Great Depression. It provided pensioners with a source of retirement income, home owners with mortgage support, the needy with unemployment insurance and safety net programs, among many others. Above all, Roosevelt's New Deal redefined government's role in America's market place economy.

World War II

The third of the five major twentieth century episodes we are discussing in this chapter is the Second World War. Even though it lasted less than a decade, the War caused more deaths, both military and civilian, than any other armed conflict before or since. Although separated by the Great Depression, many writers regard WWII as an extension of WWI because the social and political conditions that produced the First World War persisted and gave rise to the Second. What is more, the unforeseen devastating effects that the Treaty of Versailles and the Great Depression had on Europe in general and Germany in particular inflamed those conditions even further.

The war guilt sections of the Versailles Treaty placed all the blame for WWI on German shoulders and forced the government to pay huge reparation for the damages that Germany inflicted on other European countries, especially France and England. The Treaty also took land away from Germany for the development of Poland and forbad union with Austria. It compelled the country to demilitarize by eliminating tanks, submarines, and the air force but permitted the maintenance of only a small army and a few naval ships.

It would not be an overstatement to say that the overall effect of the Treaty on the German people was total humiliation and anger that only deepened Germany's hostility toward its European neighbors. Furthermore, as in the case of the US, the Great Depression imposed extraordinary economic hardships on Europe as a whole and Germany in particular. During the thirties, as Europe struggled through high unemployment rates and runaway inflation, the seeds of WWII began to grow.

The appointment of Adolf Hitler as Chancellor of Germany on January 30, 1933 tipped the scale in the direction of Nazism and the emergence of the fascist totalitarian state that followed. The details of how Hitler consolidated this control over Germany and eliminated all political opposition are well known. In 1934, as soon as he declared himself the sole leader, the Fuhrer, he began rebuilding the military into the powerful and fierce war machine that fueled his expansionist visions and goal of global conquest.

In 1938, he annexed both Austria and Czechoslovakia in order to secure the German frontier and repossessed the land that the Versailles Treaty took away. Due to weak international resistance, Hitler did not stop with this takeover. A year later, he invaded and reclaimed Poland. It is September 1, 1939 that historians use as the official start date of Europe's Second World War—a mere two decades after the end of the First. On September 3, two days later, France and England declared war on Germany.

As the War gained momentum, it spiraled into such unprecedented extremes of killing that it surpassed very rapidly all other world conflicts as the bloodiest war ever. By the time it ended in 1945 only six years after it started in 1939, the bloodshed that WWII left in its wake had extinguished the lives of 66 million people.[2] In 1919, when the terms of the Versailles Treaty took effect, could anyone anywhere have foreseen the rise of Hitler to power and the carnage that WWII would produce? It is highly doubtful; it is for this reason that we view these events as random in origin.

Hitler was not alone in his goal of world domination. Before he launched his conquest of Poland in 1939 in Europe, the Japanese had invaded China in 1937 and continued their aggressive military expansion throughout Asian nations and the Pacific Islands. On September 27, 1940, Germany, Italy, and Japan joined together as Axis Powers in a mutual defense pact called the Tripartite Act that made an enemy of any one of them the enemy of all of them.

As the Japanese military continued to expand throughout Asia and the Pacific, in July 1940 its troops began to occupy the French colony of Indochina. Almost immediately, the US responded by cutting off oil supplies to Japan. As animosities between the two nations worsened, in January 1941 the Japanese started planning a surprise attack against US forces in the Pacific. In October, its army and naval officers received instructions to prepare for war. When the US demanded that Japan leave both China and Indochina in November 1941, the then Prime Minister General Tojo

---

2. Matthew White, *Atrocities: the 100 Deadliest Episodes in Human History*, 400–21.

who headed the military controlled government decided that Japan had no other choice but to launch a destructive airstrike against the US battle fleet anchored at the Hawaiian Islands.

The surprise attack on Pearl Harbor on December 7, 1941 had a devastating effect on the American naval base with the loss of nearly 2,500 military people and civilians. Numerous battleships, cruisers, and destroyers were also lost. One day later, the US declared war on Japan and on December 12 on Germany and Italy. The US joined with Britain, France, and Russia to become the four nations of the Allied Powers. Roosevelt ordered the immediate expansion of the US military in response to fighting the Axis Powers on two fronts, one in Europe and the Atlantic and the other in Asia and the Pacific. The "sleeping giant," as Japanese Naval Marshall General Isoroku Yamamoto called the US, had awakened; and the rest, as we say, is history.

Like the WWI and the Great Depression and New Deal, the story of the Axis coalition's early victories in WWII and eventual defeat by the Allied forces has been chronicled in hundreds of books, articles, movies, and other communication media. The Normandy invasion on the coast of France on June 6, 1944, popularly known as D-Day proved to be the beginning of the end for the Axis powers. Also, Hitler's invasion of Leningrad (now St. Petersburg) in the East, which lasted for 900 days from 1941 to 1944, became the bloodiest siege in the history of warfare. Millions of Russian and German soldiers and citizens lost their lives, and in the end this siege turned out to be a disastrous defeat for the German army and a major setback for Hitler's goal of global conquest.

Fighting on the Pacific front was no less fierce. Military historians often call the American naval victory in the Battle of Midway that lasted from June 3 to 7, 1942 as the turning point in the Pacific although the Allies continued their struggle to retake the chain of islands held by the Japanese in fight to the death combat. As seen below, Joe Rosenthal's iconic photo of six US marines raising the American flag at the top of Mt. Suribachi on Iwo Jima Island on February 3, 1945 epitomizes the hard fought victories that led to Japan's defeat in the Pacific.

Figure 10. Joe Rosenthal's iconic photo of six US marines raising the American flag at the top of Mt. Suribachi on Iwo Jima Island.

Starting with WWI and continuing throughout the twentieth century, the technologies of warfare grew ever more sophistical and lethal. Throughout the first half of the 1940s, the savagery and killing that the Allied and Axis powers heaped on each other on the ground, in the air, and on and under the sea escalated to unpredictable levels of brutality. The air saturation bombing by the Allies over Germany and Japan fueled fire storms that levelled entire cities such as Berlin and Tokyo. Allied and Axis troops alike visited massively destructive fire power on each other in open field tank battles. Nations launched unforeseen air raids from aircraft carriers that stalked enemies at sea. The sheer quantity, quality, and speed of weapons innovations, production, and battlefield implementation encircled the world like never before in the history of warfare.

When the US dropped two atomic bombs, called Little Boy and Fat Man, on the Japanese cities of Hiroshima and Nagasaki on August 6 and 9, 1945, warfare technology entered a hugely more lethal stage based on nuclear weaponry that laid the foundation of the Cold War. The estimates of deaths from these two bombs alone will never be known with precision, but experts place the number in excess of 200,000. Earlier in May 1945, the war in Europe ended when the Russian Army captured Berlin. Then, just three months later on August 15, 1945, warfare in Asia also stopped when Japan announced its unconditional surrender after suffering massive nuclear bomb casualties. With the downfall of the Axis powers in both Europe and Asia, WWII was over.

After examining the first three episodes that took place during the first half of the twentieth century, it is clear that randomness helped shape how the future of each unfolded. No one foresaw the assassination of Franz Ferdinand on June 28, 1914. Nor did anyone predict that the stock market would crash on October 29, 1929. When the Treaty of Versailles was signed in 1919, Hitler's rise to power and the havoc that Nazism would impose on the world was not even within eyesight. Both the attack on Pearl Harbor and the atomic bombing of Hiroshima and Nagasaki caught the US and Japan in turn by surprise.

Looking back with hindsight, we can see visibly that three of the major historical periods of the twentieth century, World War I, the Great Depression and the New Deal, and World War II, were triggered by unpredictable occurrences; once they were set in motion, there was no guarantee how they would end despite the plans and actions that leaders developed to deal with them. Can we say the same for the fourth of our five episodes, the Cold War?

The Cold War

Like the three episodes described above, the Cold War did not emerge in a vacuum but was preceded by trends that set the context for the occurrence of random events that shaped its development. When Hitler invaded Russia in 1941, Stalin immediately broke off the 1939 treaty he had made with Germany and joined the Allied coalition despite his belief that the differences between capitalism and communism were irreconcilable. Above all, Stalin's fear of European Fascism drove him to join with the Allies, although his cooperation proved to be a temporary expedient designed to defeat the Nazis and enable the Soviet Union to gain control of its western border.

In February 1945, the leaders of the US, UK, and USSR (Franklin Roosevelt, Winston Churchill, and Joseph Stalin) met at Yalta in Crimea to discuss Europe's post war reorganization. After WWII ended later that year, they met again at the Potsdam Conference in Berlin from July 17 to August 2 to hammer out a consensus on how to treat the defeated Germany and methods for putting Nazi war criminals on trial. They also began to plan for the political and economic future of Austria, Poland, and surrounding nations. Despite their three-way compact, Stalin wasted no time in maneuvering to install Communist governments throughout the region in defiance of their agreement to allow democratic elections in Poland, Czechoslovakia, Hungary, and elsewhere.

Barely six months after the Potsdam Conference Stalin proclaimed in a provocative public speech on February 9, 1946 that communism and capitalism were incompatible. As the relationship between the USSR and the West deteriorated, nearly one month later on March 5, Churchill announced that an "iron curtain" had descended on Europe. For almost fifty years, the bi-polar hostilities called the Cold War intensified and spread steadily until it encircled the entire globe. When Communists pursued their goal of aggressive world expansion, the West countered with strategies to neutralize and defeat them. As the Cold War unfolded, no one could foresee the direction it would take or if, when, or how it would end. Like many of the unpredictable events that occurred during WWI, the Great Depression and the New Deal, and WWII, randomness played a major role during the development of the Cold War.

However, before we proceed farther, it is necessary to add a word of clarification. The label Cold War can easily leave the impression that the world remained free of hot wars during the nearly fifty years that covered this time period. This is decidedly not the case as we will show below. The label Cold War refers specifically to the nuclear weapons standoff that existed between the USSR and the US. When the Soviet Union tested its first atomic bomb on August 29, 1949 the world quickly realized that humanity stood at the doorway of possible worldwide destruction if the planet's two super powers launched a nuclear war.

This anxiety soared to unprecedented heights of imagined global catastrophe when US President Truman approved on January 30, 1950 the development of a hydrogen (thermonuclear) bomb with the destructive potential 500 times greater than that of the atomic bombs the US dropped on Japan in 1945 to end WWII. The deepening distrust that the US and USSR felt against each other fueled a dreaded arms race that produced thousands of nuclear weapons so lethal that neither side would dare use them.

In effect, it was the threat of mutually assured destruction (MAD) that kept the Cold War cold as both the US and USSR recognized that a preemptive first strike by one side would be met by an equally devastating second strike by the other side. The main deterrent that prevented the Cold War from spiraling into the worst hot, and possibly last, war the world would ever witness was not the weapons per se, despite their deadly destructive power, but the reciprocal realization that both sides would destroy each other regardless of who struck first. The Cold War turned as much on instilling the psychological fear of annihilation in the "enemy" as in piling up or threatening to deploy weapons of mass destruction.

What now seems clear with hindsight is that the Cold War served as a large umbrella underneath of which several unforeseen regional hot wars and clandestine actions emerged as the Western powers led by the US countered the Soviet Communists' efforts at global expansion. This applied not only to the US's relationship to the USSR but to both the US's and the USSR's relationship to the Chinese as well after the rise of Communism. When Mao Zedong's forces defeated those of Chiang Kai-shek's during a lengthy and bloody civil war, on October 1, 1949 Mao established the Communist People's Republic of China.

From this point forward, just as the US and its Western European allies acted to counter Soviet expansion, the US and the USSR took whatever measures were necessary to stop Chinese and Communist aggression throughout Asia. As we will discuss below, two of the most deadly hot conflicts of the Cold War involved the Asian nations of Korea and Vietnam in which soldiers and civilians died by the tens of thousands. In addition, when Fidel Castro took control of Cuba on January 1, 1959 and created his Communist regime, a few years later in 1962, the world confronted again, for the first time since the end of WWII, the possible use of nuclear weapons and consequences too terrifying to contemplate.

Before the Cold War spun off its deadly hot wars in Asia and gave rise to the US and USSR standoff during the Cuban Missile Crisis, then President Truman developed the doctrine of containment to push back against Communist aggression wherever it arose around the world. Four years after the end of WWII, on April 4, 1949, more than two dozen European nations and the US created NATO (North Atlantic Treaty Organization) to guard against Soviet encroachments into Western Europe. Several years later, on May 14, 1955, the USSR and seven Eastern and Central European states controlled by the Soviet Union formed the Warsaw Pact to safeguard their security against a rearmed Germany.

As fifty years of the Cold War unfolded, both sides pursued policies intended to give them the upper hand. When Stalin launched the Berlin Blockade on June 24, 1948, the bipolar antagonisms were thrust into high relief. Designed to stop the Western Allies from entering West Berlin by rail, road, or canal, it lasted for only eleven months. After the US and Western nations organized a successful Berlin Airlift that brought food, fuel, and other supplies to the Western controlled sectors of Berlin, Stalin lifted the blockade on May 12, 1949.

As West Berlin's and West Germany's prosperity improved steadily over the next decade, it attracted a steady stream of migrants who sought to escape the growing stagnation of the East. When the US introduced the Marshall Plan in 1957 to help rebuild the European nations devastated by WWII and to combat poverty and disease, the growing economic fortunes of Western Europe served as a magnet that attracted an even larger number of East Berliners. For East Germany's State Council Chairman Walter Ulbricht, there was only one way to deal with this rising flood of out-migration. In order to stop the escalating brain drain, in 1961 he signed the order to begin construction of Communism's most blatant symbol of political oppression: the Berlin Wall.

As the Berlin Wall was being built, satellite photos revealed that the Soviet Union began conspiring covertly with Fidel Castro to install missiles in Cuba less than 100 miles off America's coastline. As apprehensions and threats over a possible nuclear confrontation between the US and USSR escalated, US President Kennedy began considering his options. After much discussion, he rejected the alternative of an air strike in favor of a naval blockade that prevented Soviet ships from delivering their missiles. The world held its breath as both sides dug in for the growing probability of nuclear war.

Then, just as the USSR and the US stood at the threshold of a nuclear Armageddon, Khrushchev made an unexpected offer. He proposed that the USSR would remove its weapons if the US consented not to invade Cuba. Kennedy accepted Khrushchev's proposal and also began negotiating secretly to remove from Turkey nuclear weapons that were aimed at the USSR. When Khrushchev agreed to remove all Soviet missiles from Cuba, the Crisis was over and a seemingly inevitable nuclear inferno was averted.

The Korean and Vietnam conflicts in Asia turned out to be two of the Cold War's hot wars that led to the death of tens of thousands. As WWII came to an end, in May, 1945, Korea was separated into two nations at the thirty-eighth parallel. The Korean War started about five year later on June 25, 1950 when the Communist regime in North Korea, which the USSR supported, invaded South Korea, which the US defended as an extension of Truman's containment policy. When the US troops reached North Korea's capital Pyongyang in October, 1950, China joined the war on the side of North Korea.

As the War ground to a stalemate, the two sides began peace talks in February, 1951. After two more years of back and forth fighting and arduous negotiations, finally on July 27, 1953, the Korean War ended with the signing of the Korean Armistice Agreement that created a 150 miles long demilitarized zone (DMZ) at the thirty-eighth parallel and that stopped Communist expansion. In early 1954, China and the US entered into discussions to unite the two Koreas but to no avail; they have remained divided into opposing and hostile enemies ever since.

Like the Korean War in East Asia, the US entered the Vietnam War in order to contain the spread of Communism throughout Southeast Asia. Compared to the Korean War that lasted for three years, the Vietnam War dragged on for well over two decades. In 1930, Ho Chi Minh helped start the Indochinese Communist Party; in 1945 he called for an independent Vietnam. France, which had ruled Vietnam as a colony since 1858, fought against Communist expansion until May 1954 when French soldiers suffered a decisive defeat at Dien Bien Phu. On July 21, 1954 the Geneva Accords divided North and South Vietnam at the seventeenth parallel in much the same way that the Korean Armistice separated the two Koreas at the thirty-eighth. From this point forward the US took over the fighting as the French exited.

When Lyndon Johnson became the US President after Kennedy's assassination in 1963, he announced his commitment to contain the spread of Communism in Vietnam. With the signing of the Gulf of Tonkin Resolution on August 7, 1964, Johnson got the authority he needed to expand military operations in Southeast Asia without a declaration of war. By December, 1968, US involvement in Vietnam reached a high point of 540,000 troops. As the war showed no sign of winding down, fierce opposition to it in the US increased. The nation stood in turmoil. As street demonstration became more tumultuous and chaotic during the late sixties, Johnson announced unexpectedly that he would not seek reelection for the Presidency.

After Nixon was elected President in 1968, it was only a matter of time before US involvement in Vietnam started to fade. He began removing troops shortly after his election victory, and on March 29, 1973 he withdrew the last American troops. The fighting between the North and South continued until April 30, 1975 when South Vietnam surrendered to the Communists. Fourteen months later on July 2, 1976, Vietnam became a unified Communist country, the Socialist Republic of Vietnam. Despite the inability of the two Koreas to reconcile their political and economic differences and the victory of Communism over non-Communist forces in Vietnam, the Truman doctrine of containment had served its purpose in preventing the Communists' goal of global conquest and the spreading of nuclear weapons to Cuba.

After Vietnam, the major hot wars of the Cold War had run their course, and the world began to change. From 1972 to 1979, the US, USSR, and numerous other nations engaged in discussions to cut back on the proliferation of nuclear weapons. When the Strategic Arms Limitation Talks II was signed in July, 1979 the world breathed a sigh of relief. Eleven years later, on October 3, 1990, Germany was reunited. In December of the same year, Czechoslovakia, Bulgaria, and Rumania threw out their Communist regimes. All these changes signaled the dawn of a new era, but the biggest surprise was yet to come.

On May 29, 1990, Boris Yeltsin was elected President of the Soviet Union; in July, 1991 the Warsaw Pact was dissolved. Then, to everyone's amazement, including top military and civilian leaders at the US Pentagon, on December 26, 1991 the USSR Supreme Court announced that the Soviet Union had ceased to exist as a separate State. Virtually no one saw it coming, but after almost half a century, with this surprise the Cold War was over.

Terrorism, Islamic Jihad, and the Caliphate

Thus far, the four episodes that we have discussed above have identifiable start and stop dates as well as the individuals and events that triggered them and brought them to a conclusion. Our fifth and final episode focuses on the emergence of global terrorism and its relationship to the late twentieth century radical jihadi movement that is attempting to re-establish a worldwide Muslim Caliphate or empire that mirrors the unified Islamic kingdom that existed from the time of Muhammad's life in the early seventh century until 1258 when it split into three separate domains. However, unlike the other four past episodes that we analyzed earlier, we do not know the future direction that this ultimately will take or the impact that random events will have.

We start by defining the word terrorism. While different writers use it in a variety of ways, for our purpose terrorism refers to the "willful targeting of civilians by a non-state actor through unconventional means."[3] This definition excludes state directed terrorism of the kind that occurred under Hitler, Stalin, Mao, and numerous other dictators throughout the course of history. Nor are we referring to individuals or groups that use terrorism to gain political power in any given nation with no desire to expand their control beyond its boundaries. Our focus will be on non-state sponsored individuals and groups who use terrorism for the purpose of global conquest.

During the past four decades, terrorism as we are defining it here has come to apply primarily to one group: the violent Islamic jihadi movement whose followers employ it systematically to destroy all opponents who resist their effort at worldwide domination. One simple saying summarizes in full what lies behind this obsession for total control: Once we had it; then we lost it; now we want it back. What is it they perceive they had, lost, and want back? The answer is the Caliphate or Muslim Kingdom. The last vestige of the Muslim empire, the Ottoman Caliphate, disappeared after World War I on March 3, 1924 when Kemal Ataturk created the modern state of Turkey.

---

3. "Modern Jihad," *Wikipedia*.

This was no small loss for devout Muslims who witnessed the end of centuries of domination from Spain to Indonesia, even though during the period of Islamic rule different political factions fought for control of the declining Caliphate. In order to describe how the struggle to restore the Caliphate became coupled with terrorism and the jihadi movement, we will focus on six main developments, each of which contributed to its evolution. They are the Wahhabi influence in Saudi Arabia (1744), the Egyptian Muslim Brotherhood (1928), the Afghanistan war against the USSR (1979 to 1989), formation of Al-Qaeda (1988), the US attack on Iraq (2003), and the rise of ISIL (sometimes referred to as ISIS), the Islamic State of Iraq and the Levant (2013).[4] The word Levant refers to the region that includes the Middle East and North Africa. All of these developments fit together into a seamless tapestry that is filled with random circumstances and events.

We will not include the Iranian Revolution of 1979 nor the Iraq and Iran war from 1980 to 1988. It is not that these events are unimportant. The contrary is true. They are very significant for developments occurring in the Middle East and around the world, especially over the fear that Iran might develop nuclear weapons. No doubt the Grand Ayatollah Khomeini's removal of the American backed Pahlavi dynasty in 1979 inspired Muslims everywhere that they too could take charge of their destiny. However, the proponents of the violent jihadi movement that seeks to recreate the worldwide Caliphate emerged out of Sunni Islam that for centuries has defined, and continues to define, the followers of the Shi'ite branch as among its main enemies.

We begin by describing the Wahhabi movement that started in Saudi Arabia in the mid-eighteenth century and became connected to the Saud family monarchy. Muhammad ibn Abd al-Wahhab (hereafter Wahhab) was a Sunni Muslim who lived in central Arabia from 1703 to 1792. Dissatisfied with what he called liberal innovations and existing forms of polytheism, he sought to purify Muslim practices by returning to the original principles or *salaf*[5] that existed during the first three generations after Muhammad's death in 632. He derived his teachings from only two sources: Islam's sacred scripture the Quran that consists of Muhammad's revelations and selected Hadiths that contain many of his other sayings and personal practices.

---

4. ISIL is also called ISIS, which stands for Islamic State of Iraq and Syria; or simply IS, Islamic State.

5. The current reference to *Salafist* Jihad is synonymous with Islamic Jihad and derives from Wahhab's ultra-conservative interpretation of Islam. At the same time, other Muslims who call themselves Salafists shun the forms of terrorist violence that Al-Qaeda and IS support.

In 1744, Wahhab and Muhammad bin Saud (hereafter Saud) made a pact that continues to this present day: Wahhab and his followers supported the Saud Monarchy, which in turn endorsed the Wahhabi view of Islam. Wahhab was an intolerant purist in both religious and legal matters. He advocated a view of Islam that is called *Sharia*,[6] which stands for watering hole in Arabic. He insisted that *Sharia* law should serve as the basis for organizing all aspects of Muslim society from individual behavior to political and military practices. Starting in the eighteenth century and continuing to today, the Quran has been the Saudi state constitution.

The Saudis did not confine their commitment to Wahhabism to the Kingdom's borders. From the start, the Monarchy began spreading *Salafist* Islam throughout Muslim societies of the Middle East and beyond. It has also supported in many countries the development of religious schools called *madrasas* that specialize in the teaching of Wahhabism. Given the intolerant nature of Wahhabi *Salafism* and its pervasive presence in the Saudi Kingdom, it is no surprise that fifteen of the nineteen hijackers in the September 11, 2001 attack on the US, along with Osama bin Laden who helped plan and carry it out, were from Saudi Arabia. In short, Saudi Wahhabism is the seedbed for modern jihadi terrorism.

Next, we turn to the development of the Muslim Brotherhood that surfaced in Egypt after Ataturk dissolved the Ottoman Caliphate in 1924. For many, Ataturk's dissolution of the Caliphate signaled a turn for the worst, because it symbolized the rejection of traditional Islamic values in favor of what they perceived to be an immoral and corrupt Western culture and its secular democratic institutions. Radical Muslims were quick to react.

In 1928, just four years after Ataturk's action, Islamic scholar and teacher Hassan al-Banna (1906–1949, hereafter Banna) established the Egyptian Muslim Brotherhood that attracted a widespread following. Although the Brotherhood was not a direct offshoot of Saudi Wahhabism, Banna espoused the same ultra-conservative and intolerant Islamic ideology that Wahhab advocated 175 years earlier.

Like Saudi *Salifism*, the Brotherhood's primary purpose was to order every area of Muslim life, from the individual to the nation, according to Islamic principles conveyed in the Quran and the Hadiths. Like Wahhab, Banna looked to the past, and specifically to the life and times of Muhammad, as the model for recreating the Caliphate. In order to do so, he set

---

6. For Sunni Muslims, there are four forms of *Sharia* that range from the most conservative to the most moderate. They are the Hanbalites, Malikites, Shafi'ites, and the Hanifites schools that different groups of Sunni Muslims developed during the first three centuries after Muhammad's death. The Wahhabi form of *Sharia* falls at the ultra-conservative end of this spectrum.

forth several main maxims that came to be shared by radical jihadists everywhere, namely, that Islam is the solution, Allah is the objective, the Quran is the Constitution, the Prophet is the leader, jihad is the way, and death for the sake of Allah is the wish.

Before his death, Banna's call to reestablish a *Salafist* form of Islam throughout the Middle East and beyond inspired one of the Brotherhood's most ardent recruits Sayyid Qutb (1906–1966) who was an Egyptian author, educator, and active in the Brotherhood during the fifties and sixties. Together, Banna and Qutb are often called the fathers of modern Islamic radicalism. Building on Banna's ideas, Qutb went one step farther. Unlike Banna who advocated applying different strategies in different locations, Qutb held that all Muslims everywhere must take up arms in the fight to reestablish the Caliphate. In 1966, after being accused of plotting to overthrow the Egyptian government, Qutb was executed by hanging. Together, Banna and Qutb left a legacy of violent *Salafism* that exerted enormous influence on Osama bin Laden.[7]

In combination, the Saudi Wahhabism and the spread of Banna's and Qutb's ideas prepared the way for the next stage of violent jihadi Islam: the Soviet invasion of Afghanistan that started in December 1979 and ended ten years later in February 1989 when Soviet forces withdrew. The link between Soviet and Afghan war and the emergence of Al-Qaeda was direct and dramatic. It served as the unexpected training ground for three of Al-Qaeda's the most prominent leaders: Osama bin Laden, Yusuf Azzam, and Ayman al-Zawahiri (hereafter Zawahiri).

In 1973, Azzam who has been called the father of global jihad was a student in Egypt where he joined the radical Muslim Brotherhood. As his commitment to Banna's and Qutb's *Salafist* ideology deepened and the government's suppression of the Brotherhood's radical views intensified, Azzam moved to Jeddah, Saudi Arabia, where he served as a lecturer at Abdul Aziz University. While there he met and taught Osama bin Laden who was a student from 1976 to 1981. Their relationship would shape the future.

---

7. In the seventies, the Muslim Brotherhood denounced the use of violence and committed itself to the ideals of peaceful rotation of power, political pluralism, freedom of the press and assembly along with other reforms consistent with democracy. In 2012, the Brotherhood's candidate Mohamed Morsi was elected as the President of Egypt. However, despite the Brotherhood's seeming commitment to democracy and pluralism, the military removed him from office in 2013 after allegations that he and his Brotherhood supporters were corrupt, intolerant, and promoted divisive Jihad views. On May 16, 2015, Morsi and 120 other members of the Brotherhood were sentenced to death. In addition, many nations have placed the Brotherhood on its list of terrorist organizations because while rejecting violence it supports radical jihadi groups around the world.

Zawahiri was born in 1951 and grew up in Egypt. When he was fourteen years old he joined the Muslim Brotherhood. When Qutb was executed in 1966, Zawahiri along with other students formed an underground cell, vowed to overthrow the government, and committed themselves to creating an Islamic state. He eventually joined with other likeminded *Salafists* and helped create the Egyptian Islamic Jihad that assassinated Anwar Sadat in 1981 and that later merged with Al-Qaeda in 1998. When the Egyptian Islamic Jihad joined with Al-Qaeda, Zawahiri became bin Laden's personal advisor and physician.

On August 11, 1988, bin Laden and Azzam along with other jihad devotees who fought in the Soviet and Afghan war formed Al-Qaeda. Together with Zawahiri, they took the jihadi movement to its next stage by moving away from national revolutions and toward international terrorism. Clearly, one of the major unforeseen consequences of ten years of Afghan warfare was the expansion of violent *Salafism*, which Azzam, the father of global jihad, had been advocating. Then, despite his key role in helping create Al-Qaeda, Azzam was killed suddenly on November 24, 1989 when an unknown assassin detonated his car over conflicts he had with other Al-Qaeda operatives, especially Zawahiri. Despite Azzam's death, Al Qaeda moved forward aggressively with multiple terrorist attacks on several international targets and inspired the formation of other radical Muslim groups in numerous countries.

Then, on February 23, 1998, bin Laden and Zawahiri issued a *fatwa* or binding declaration that it was a personal religious duty of all Muslims to kill Americans and their allies wherever and whenever possible.[8] The importance of this declaration cannot be overestimated. In less than four years, Al-Qaeda's call to indiscriminately kill any and all Americans culminated in its September 11, 2001 surprise attack on US soil. Known simply as 9/11, this assault led to the deaths of nearly 3,000 people. Despite the fact that America was caught off guard, the attack proved to be a pivotal moment for the US. In response, President George W. Bush launched a War on Terrorism that while not intending to do so moved the global jihadi movement forward to its next two stages, expansion after the invasion of Iraq and the creation of the Caliphate.

After the US invaded Iraq in 2003, jihadism mushroomed under the leadership of Abu Musab al-Zarqawi (hereafter Zarqawi) who had already established a jihadi presence in Iraq in 1999. In 2004, he pledged his allegiance to bin Laden and named the group he led as Al-Qaeda in Iraq or AQI. AQI quickly became the largest jihadi group that existed at that time. When Zarqawi and other members of AQI were killed in a US air raid in

---

8. The title of this declaration is the World Islamic Front for Combat against the Jews and Crusaders.

2006, others who took over as leaders changed the name from AQI to the Islamic State of Iraq or ISI.

In 2007, the US initiated a troop surge in Iraq that put ISI on the defensive, and by April, 2010 over 80 percent of its top forty-two leaders had been killed or captured. When ISI was in a state of disarray, on May 16 one month later, Abu Bakr al-Baghdadi (hereafter Baghdadi) was appointed its new leader. Concurrently, under an agreement signed by President Bush and later supported by US President Barack Obama, American troops began to withdraw at the request of the Shi'ite Prime Minister Nouri al-Malaki who asserted that the Iraqi government had the Sunni jihadi threat under control.

However, this proved not to be the case. As soon as Baghdadi became ISI's new leader, he began recruiting a new cadre of hard core jihadi followers. Shortly thereafter, ISI began a campaign of terror using car bombs and other lethal methods to increase the spread of violence throughout Iraq. When the Syrian Civil war erupted in 2011, ISI grabbed hold of an opportunity to expand its operations. It entered the Syrian conflict as a supportive partner to the jihadi rebels committed to overthrowing the Bashar al-Assad regime and in no time became involved directly in the fighting.

On April 8, 2013, Baghdadi announced the formation of a new ISI financed Syrian front called al-Nusra, which was headed by Zawahiri who became Al-Qaeda's new leader after bin Laden was killed on May 2, 2011. On the same day that Baghdadi announced the formation of al-Nursa, he also declared that ISI and al-Nursa would merge together under a new name: the Islamic State of Iraq and Syria (ISIS) also called the Islamic State of Iraq and the Levant (ISIL). Zawahiri opposed the merger and stated he had not been consulted. Baghdadi responded that he was going forward with the change anyway. A power struggle developed between the two leaders; after eight months of failure to reach an accord, Zawahiri disavowed any connection to ISIL, although he held out for the possibility of cooperation should future circumstances call for it.

Ever since Banna had established the Muslim Brotherhood in 1928, it had been the goal of a string of jihadi *Salafists* to reestablish the Caliphate. This objective was shared by Qutb, Azzam, bin Laden, and Zawahiri. Al-Qaeda's main strategy was to attack the far enemies away from the Middle East and then eventually replace the Muslim near enemies who ruled the Arab states, including a US partner the Saudi Monarchy that rejected Al-Qaeda's violent jihadi methods. Although Baghdadi shared the goal of restoring the *Salafist* Caliphate, he disagreed with Al-Qaeda's approach.

On June 29, 2014, Baghdadi proclaimed that the group he led, ISIL, was the long awaited Caliphate. In order to signify the absence of geographical boundaries, he dropped the IL from ISIL and renamed the group simply

Islamic State or IS. He also asserted that Muslims everywhere around the globe owed their allegiance to him and he declared that anyone who disagreed with him, including other Muslims, were apostate enemies subject to attack, subjugation, or death.

Instead of using terror to attack the far enemies as Al-Qaeda advocated, Baghdadi launched attacks on near enemies. In the process, he took control of territory in parts of both Iraq and Syria. He also established IS branches in Libya, Egypt, Saudi Arabia, Yemen, and several other regions including Europe and the US and instigated sleeper cell terrorist attacks. The extremist methods he used to expand the Caliphate include large scale slaughter of diverse religious and ethnic groups, the murder of innocent people including children, beheadings, crucifixions, immersing captives in nitric acid or burning them alive. Like his fanatical followers, Baghdadi supported using torture on enemies and the sexual enslavement of captured women.

The world did not stand idly by after Baghdadi instigated his savage strategy of "kill, conquer, and rule by terror" and by instilling extreme fear in people residing in IS's held territory. Over sixty nations, both Muslim and non-Muslim, have joined together in a counter-offensive against the Caliphate. Together, they have vowed to stay the course until it is defeated. While this coalition led by the Iraqi military has made steady progress in recapturing much of the land that IS seized, including IS's Iraqi capital of Mosul and Syria's capital of Raqqa, and in eliminating its top leaders, including Baghdadi in early 2017, the long-term results of this international struggle have yet to be determined. No doubt, as the fight to remove the Caliphate from other countries continues, like the other four major twentieth century episodes that we discussed above, we can expect that many unforeseen developments will shape the final outcome as the future unfolds.

Conclusion

We conclude briefly by reiterating that it is highly unlikely that anyone living in the year 1900 could have predicted how random occurrences led to the outbreak of WWI, the Great Depression, WWII, the Cold War, and the rise and growing demise of the Caliphate. This being said, as we advance through the remaining decades of the twenty-first century and beyond, might we develop the ability to anticipate future events with improved foresight before they happen? What role is randomness likely to play in this process? These are the questions we will address in the next chapter.

7

The Future

IN THIS CHAPTER WE will concentrate on randomness and the future. As we have shown in the past several chapters, the best available scientific evidence supports the conclusion that unpredictability plays a significant role in virtually every area of existence. This influence has affected and continues to affect the behavior of the tiniest subatomic particles, the evolution of the universe from the Big Bang forward, our personal stories, and the unforeseen events of the twentieth and twenty-first centuries. At the same time, we know that randomness does not occur in a vacuum but rather within the narrow boundaries of our highly structured cosmos.

This takes us to next question. When compared to the past, have the discoveries of modern science improved our capacity to predict the future? If we could answer this question with a yes, then our advantages going forward in time would be enormous. At a minimum, we would be able to foresee potentially harmful or tragic events before they occur and prevent them wherever possible. Given the extraordinary changes that have occurred during the past two centuries, we find ourselves wondering: how far can we go?

In our attempt to answer this question, we start with one of the most basic issues that we have discussed repeatedly throughout the preceding chapters. As modern science emerged and expanded, it progressed rapidly in the development of new knowledge and understanding. This applied especially to early discoveries of the cause and effect laws that govern nature and later findings about the origin, complexity, evolution, and size of the cosmos. As new perceptions emerged, old ones disappeared; as a result, many pundits proclaimed with utmost confidence that as science advanced, humanity would improve its ability to predict and ultimately control the future.

The origin of this confidence is well known. It is based on a deterministic or reductionist view that the universe is a closed system of natural laws that are knowable and can be used to predict outcomes. For example, we use our understanding of gravitation (natural law) to predict the location and time of a Global Positioning System (GPS) satellite. Once discovered, we can project the outcomes of cause and effect relationships with a very high level of confidence. However, what we now know is that this view of causality is overly simplistic.

While it is useful for making predictions in some areas, such as launching and directing the course of rockets and satellites into outer space, in others it is not. This is because much of what occurs in nature and human behavior is characterized by indeterminate relationships where potential effects exist as probabilities and uncertainties. Before a national election, opinion polls are taken. If a candidate polls 51 percent plus or minus 3 percent, we expect that the candidate will receive between 48 percent and 54 percent of the vote, should the vote be taken at that time. This range of probabilities could make all the difference in winning or losing, as the election of Donald Trump to the US Presidency in November, 2016 demonstrates.

The challenge in comprehending how randomness relates to the future involves knowing where determinate relationships leave off and indeterminate ones begin, as well as in identifying the phases or steps by which one transitions into the other. While it has not been for lack of effort, we will show that this has been and continues to be no easy task. For more than 200 years, researchers have been applying the methods of modern science to an increasing number of fields, such as astronomy, physics, psychology, the social sciences, and many others. Given this steady expansion, it was only a matter of time before some would begin using scientific tools to study the future. This impetus gained momentum during the sixties.

What have we learned? We begin by defining terms and then move to describing what the scientific study of the future is not. Once we have done this, we will then discuss how to think about the future using the methods of modern science.

Predictions and Forecasts

Our starting point is to distinguish prediction from forecast even though these two words are often used interchangeably. As we are using these terms, to make a prediction is to declare in advance with certainty that something will happen before it actually does. Here are some examples. We predict that when we drop a baseball off a roof, it will fall and not rise. We predict after hearing the weather report that it will not rain today. We predict that our cars will start when we activate the ignition. We predict that it will take one year for the Earth to circle around the Sun. We recognize that there is always a chance that these predictions like many others will not come to pass if something unforeseen occurs to nullify them. However, for all intents and purposes, we humans make countless predictions every day as if they were 100 percent certain to happen; we predict that we will continue to act this way in the future.

In contrast to certainty associated with a prediction, a forecast involves probability. Here are some examples. We forecast that when we are pitching the probability of striking out the next batter is 20 percent. We forecast after hearing the weather report that there is a 50 percent chance that it might rain today. We forecast that our old car has a 40 percent chance that it will break down this year. We forecast that there will be more rain this year than last year as the Earth encircles the Sun. What distinguishes these and other forecasts from predictions is that the outcomes might or might not happen. Like predictions, we make forecasts every day and then act without knowing in advance with certainty what will occur; we predict that we will continue making forecasts in the future.

As the scientific study of the future developed during the past fifty years, scholars discovered that in order to foresee events with greater clarity, it is necessary to develop ways to enhance the human capacity for foresight. Once an event has occurred, we can look back and reconstruct with hindsight the cause and effect relationships that made it happen, such as the Japanese bombing of Pearl Harbor in 1941 and al-Qaeda's attack on 9/11/2001. The parallel challenge to using hindsight to uncover the causes of events after they occur is to improve our capacity to foresee them before they occur. As we will discuss later in this chapter in the section on Scenarios, subjective biases can diminish foresight accuracy. Before doing so, however, we need to discuss what we mean by foresight.

Foresight

Modern efforts to improve foresight incorporate the methods of science, which we will describe later in this section. However, before doing so, we will identify the approaches that present day futurists do not use.

We start by recognizing that the human concern to foreknow what will happen before it actually does is as old as humanity itself, and for good reason. The future is filled with random events that lead to both joy and sorrow or, to use other contrasting images, pleasure and pain, good and evil, happiness and sadness, fortune and misfortune, or in the worst case scenario, disaster. Sooner or later everyone learns that there is no guarantee that the future will not bring harm. As we go about the daily task of pursuing as much success and satisfaction as life has to offer, we remain acutely aware that catastrophe can strike at any moment.

In order to guard against the worst and aspire for the best possible future, for thousands of years, humans invented myriad techniques to gain foreknowledge of what lies ahead. These include, but are not limited to, interpreting dreams; gazing at stars and crystal balls; analyzing hand palms; studying the shapes of animal intestines; reading tarot cards; casting bones; observing tea leaves; consulting seers, priests, prophets, and clairvoyants; visiting psychics; talking to fortune tellers; and checking astrology charts.

In addition, many diviners of the future, both past and present, have used scriptural passages to project end of the world images in their time. For example, in 44 CE, Theudas declared himself the Messiah and took 400 people into the desert to await the final catastrophe. It did not happen. Since then, the devotees of diverse religions have made over 200 such proclamations. Recently, religious enthusiast Chris McCann declared that the Earth would be incinerated on October 2, 2015. That did not happen either. With such situations, it is typical that followers of the world religions will proclaim that the "signs of the time" are consistent with descriptions that appear in a sacred scripture, which in turn points to the imminent destruction of the cosmos through some form of divine intervention. It is not our intention to describe the details of all of these end of the world predictions other than to observe that none of them came to pass.

Present day futurists do not include approaches based on sacred texts or prescientific practices. Instead, they have developed innovative methods they believe are more effective in gaining more precise foreknowledge. The new procedures build on the scientific assumption that the universe is governed by observable and measurable cause and effect relationships that we can know rationally and empirically and can apply progressively to improving foresight ability. As a general rule, this excludes all forms of magic and miracles and of occult or supernatural explanations for why things happen.

In addition, modern approaches to projecting how the future will unfold involve a perspective that differs from other fields. In most cases, researchers deal with a past or present body of knowledge such as a known historical event, social structures, behavioral patterns, scientific relationships, poetry, art, or something already existing or experienced. This is not the case when thinking about how to improve foresight, because the future has not yet happened. Images of possible futures are mental constructs that might or might not come to pass.

Furthermore, anyone who attempts to improve foresight ability must grapple with one of the most fundamental paradoxes inherent in the process through which the future takes shape. It is this: The future is not something that just happens while we wait passively for it to arrive; we humans help create it through our choices and actions. While the future that appears can be one over which we have little or no control, it can also be one for which we prepare or plan.

This means that the failure of any group to plan a future it desires opens the door for others to take the initiative. When this happens, the probability increases that the group that planned its future will get the one that it wants and the group that did not plan will get the one that it does not want. At the same time, planning for a desired future does not guarantee that it will come to pass; nor does not planning for it guarantee that it will not. This is the essence of the paradox. For example, it is a common experience that parents set money aside for their children's education; if a member of the family encounters an unexpected and severe illness, the savings might be diverted to health care.

In recognition of this paradox, current approaches to thinking about the future have gone in two directions. The first is descriptive; the second is normative. Descriptive futures are based on striving for the kind of maximum objectivity that we associate with modern science. For example, scientists like Newton made their breakthrough discoveries by observing patterns in nature and describing them using mathematics. While he and others were passionate about practicing science, the methods they employed involve detached observation, experimentation, discovery, description, and finally predictions. As a result, with this and other types of scientific knowledge and technology, we are able to predict the future velocity and trajectory of satellites once they are launched into space. This is the paradigm that many descriptive futurists use when thinking about the future: discover the laws that govern nature and society and then project them forward to foretell what will happen.

The normative approach builds on the paradox described earlier and involves our values and ethical ideals. The future that eventually comes into existence is not determined solely by the objective natural laws that govern the universe. It is also created by the subjective, free will choices that we human beings make when we plan for the future we prefer. While the desired future might not become the actual future, it is the future we or others want to happen. Thus, the future unfolds as human choices shape it against the background of natural laws and of individual and social norms and behavior. Unpredictability or randomness is an inherent part of this process. The future we plan might not be the one we get, because randomness can steer the future in unexpected directions.

Understanding the existence of this paradox leads to the next question. How is it possible to improve foresight by using both descriptive and normative approaches? We are now ready to discuss the methods that present day futurists have developed.

Foreseeing the Future

The best way to explain foresight approaches is to identify where they fit within the four cells that we summarized in Table 1 in chapter 2. To review, they are 1) determinism not involving choice (cell 1 under "Determinism" and rows labeled "Choice/No"), 2) indeterminism not involving choice (cell 2 under "Indeterminism" and rows labeled "Choice/No"), 3) determinism involving choice (cell 3 under "Determinism" and rows labeled "Choice/Yes"), and 4) indeterminism involving choice (cell 4 under "Indeterminism" and rows labeled "Choice/Yes"). In the top two cells, the future unfolds according to the repetitive laws of nature without the need for human choice of any kind. As discussed earlier, the main difference is that in cell 1 ("Determinism" and "Choice/No") the future can be known with certainty (the speed of a falling baseball) and in cell 2 ("Indeterminism" and "Choice/No") only with probability (long-term changes in weather patterns and climate).

In addition, the kinds of causal relationship that fall in cells 1 and 2 (top left and top right), whether in the form of determinism with certainty or indeterminism with probability, are extensions of modern science's commitment to discovering and describing the laws of nature as they actually exist. While we are well aware that subjective biases can influence a researcher's choice of evidence and how to interpret it, we also recognize that one of science's main goals is to strive for maximum objectivity. Newton's description of the Universal Law of Gravitation that governs the speed of a falling baseball and Lorenz's explanation of the chaotic dynamics that drive changing weather systems conform to this standard. Both are regulated by the laws of nature. The ball does not choose the speed at which it falls, and the weather does not decide to rain or not.

Cell 3 combines determinacy with choice and cell 4 indeterminacy with choice. As stated in chapter 2, we believe that the human capacity to evaluate alternative courses of action and their consequences before deciding from among them as a basis for action is not an illusion that will one day be explained away by reducing it to some form of determinism. Human choice is real. As we have shown, both determinism and indeterminism can be combined with choice as well as no choice.

Although modern futurists disavow the effectiveness of ancient approaches and scriptural interpretations to foretell the future, they have learned that improving foresight skills requires recognizing the role that values and ethical ideals play in forecasting how the future will unfold. Another way to say this is that while potential outcomes of any indeterminate situation involve varying degrees of uncertainty, this is especially so for those that include the freedom to choose alternative courses of action. Of their own volition, people everywhere make decisions after weighing options. As we discussed earlier in the previous chapter, the twentieth century was filled with choices and actions that were unforeseen until they happened; when they did, they had huge global consequences.

In light of these distinctions, we can conclude that the four cells described above represent alternative pathways for the unfolding of the future. The highest degree of non-random outcomes (predictability and certainty) is represented by Cell 1 (determinism without choice); the highest degree of randomness (probability or uncertainty) by Cell 4 (indeterminism with choice). Cell 2 (indeterminism without choice) and cell 3 (determinism with choice) fall between these two extremes. The different approaches that futurists have developed to improve foresight skills can be placed in all four of these 4 cells. They are trend extrapolation, models and simulations, the role of experts, and alternative scenarios.

Trends

We start by defining the least complex foresight method, which belongs primarily at the determinist end of the continuum. It is called trend extrapolation and rests on the assumption that the best way to foretell the future is to look for trends in the past. While this is easy to grasp, the method of trend extrapolation has limited application as a forecasting tool; applying it where it is not appropriate can lead to making many false predictions. This is because indeterminism or randomness intervenes to alter the trend. Nonetheless, practitioners of this method presuppose that we can foreknow the future by identifying events or practices that occur in a time series and then projecting whether they will increase, decrease, or remain pretty much the same as in the past.

The first step involves identifying the length of time a trend has existed. This can range from short-term trends of a year or less to longer ones that have existed for centuries. Many examples come to mind, which demonstrate the limits to this method. During the past 200 years since the onset of modern science, writers like Voltaire predicted the demise of religion. Not only has this not happened, at the start of the twenty-first century the great religions of the world, such as Hinduism, Buddhism, Judaism, Christianity, Islam, and others are as robust as ever and still growing. We cannot help but wonder how Voltaire and the others who prophesied the demise of religion would react to these current trends if they were still alive.

In addition, during the same time period, several new vibrant faiths emerged and attracted millions of followers, such as Latter Day Saints, Baha'i, Scientology, among many others. As science advanced by providing naturalistic explanations for events that were previously thought to have occurred through supernatural intervention, many perceived that this would become a long-term trend that would eradicate religion. They were wrong. The predominant pattern is this: science and religion have learned to coexist and have become increasingly compatible.[1]

Furthermore, during the twentieth century, there are many other false predictions based on shorter trend lines. The following well known quotes come from a very long list of bad forecasts. "The automobile is only a novelty—a fad." (1903, the President of the Michigan Savings Bank); "A rocket will never leave the Earth's atmosphere." (1936, The New York Times); "Television won't last; it's a flash in the pan." (1948, Mary Somerville, radio pioneer); "The iPhone won't get any significant market share." (2007), Steve Ballmer, former CEO of Microsoft).[2]

Based on these examples and many more that could be included, it is clear that predicting the future based on long-term or short-term trend extrapolation is a precarious practice. At the same time, however, this does not mean that it not a useful forecasting tool in some areas, especially when the timeline is short or where it applies to specific long-term trends. For example, in the short-run, on a daily basis most parents can predict with a high degree of accuracy that under normal circumstances their children will continue to go to school.

In terms of the long-run, the US Population Reference Bureau provides annual updates on population growth to the year 2050 for global regions and over 200 countries. In the year 2015, the world's population stood

---

1. For an extended discussion of why predictions about the demise of religion have proven false and how belief in God, science, and evolution reinforce each other, see McFaul and Brunsting, *God is Here to Stay: Science, Evolution, and Belief in God*, 101, 176.

2. For and extensive discussion of the number and causes of false extrapolations that have been made of past centuries, see Lee, *Bad Predictions: 2000 Years of the Best Minds Making the Worst Predictions*; and Schnaars, *Megamistakes: Forecasting and the Myth of Rapid Technological Change*.

at 7.3 billion. The PRB projects that by 2050, 9.8 billion people will inhabit the Earth. Even though many factors could intervene between 2015 and 2050 to alter this forecast, trend extrapolation is a valuable tool for making demographic projections.[3]

These two examples show us that there are some areas where extrapolating trends is effective in improving foresight. This is especially true, according to Peter Schwartz, where there exist driving forces that dominate and can be defined as "predetermined elements." These are already in the pipe line.[4] In the short-run, once a child starts going to school, attending classes every day is a predetermined element. This pattern will continue throughout the school year unless something intervenes to stop it. This type of situation reflects cells 3 and 4, determinism and indeterminism with choice. The parents make a decision to send the child to a particular school, and the child attends daily (determinism with choice). However, at any time, the parents might move and send their child to different school (indeterminism with choice).

The Population Reference Bureau forecasts long-term demographic changes based on predetermined regional and national populace sizes and reproduction rates that are already in the pipeline. These, too, could change with shifting circumstances. The PRB's forecasts cut across all 4 cells of determinism and indeterminism with and without choice. Both of these examples demonstrate the role that randomness or unpredictability plays in human behavior. Parents choose but later change their minds. Rates of reproduction change as people modify their attitudes toward family size. Population size can be affected by diseases or warfare that involve both no choice as well as choice. Once set in motion, trends remain stable until something comes along to alter them, which is a common occurrence.

This takes us to the next question. Why do seemingly stable trends change? The answer is simple: the circumstances that created and sustained them for whatever length of time change. While this seems like common sense and is easy to understand at one level, at another level it is complex. The main limitation of the trend extrapolation approach surfaces when two or more factors in any given situation are correlated with each other and where the outcome of their reciprocal influences cannot be known in advance. In Schwartz's view, when this condition exists, forecasting the future of any area becomes more complicated because the trend or set of interacting elements involves critical uncertainties.

---

3. www.prb.org.

4. Schwartz, *The Art of the Long View: Planning for the Future in an Uncertain World*, 113–14, 120–23, and 142–44.

Some of the most innovative methods that futurists have developed for improving foresight skills apply to situations that incorporate multiple driving forces that interact in indeterminate or random ways. As we have shown in chapter 2 and earlier in this chapter, there are some conditions of indeterminacy (cell 2) that do not involve human choice and others that do (cell 4). Both of these positions include critical uncertainties. As the number of interacting elements in any given situation increases, so does the potential for alternative outcomes.

For example, prior to the attacks on Pearl Harbor in 1941 and on New York in 2001, the US government received an array of reports, many of them contradictory, about Japan's and al-Qaeda's intentions. Only after the events was it possible with hindsight to identify the causal chain that produced them. Despite the various and confusing possibilities that existed before they occurred, we are left to wonder: could Pearl Harbor and 9/11 have been predicted in advance? If we had better foresight ability at the time, could we have seen them coming? The answer is that we will never know for sure. Compared to these and other unpredictable events that occurred in the past, have we made progress in developing new forecasting tools that enable us to foresee the future with greater accuracy?

Models and Simulations

In order to answer the last question of the previous section, we must move beyond trend extrapolation approaches and consider other methods that focus on indeterminate conditions where critical uncertainties cause unpredictable effects; which is to say, where outcomes seem to appear at random. This next step entails examining the role that models and simulations play in foreseeing the future more accurately. Models and simulations mimic our ordinary mental activity by copying how we manipulate thought processes. When we are faced with a range of choices in any given situation, we mentally rehearse what potential effects different decisions will have on us and our real world surroundings.

For example, a family saves for their child's education. During this future time, the family's net income after taxes is projected to average $60,000 per year. They project their total expenses to be $55,000 per year so that their saving rate for their child's college expenses can be $5,000 ($60,000-$55,000) per year. This simple example, which could be duplicated across a wide range of situations, demonstrates how the human mind works. Models and simulations imitate this process.

With advancements in computer technology during the past fifty years, our ability to build increasingly more sophisticated models and simulations has mushroomed as, for example, in predicting the weather five days in advance. Whereas the human mind can handle only as limited number of concepts at any one time, supercomputers can integrate and manipulate millions and even billions of parameters at incredible speeds. This gives us the ability to convert critical uncertainties related to any given situation into numerical variables that can be manipulated and modified to create alternative views of the future.

The process for developing models and simulations is easy to describe but hard to implement. The first step involves deciding on an area in which to make a forecast, which can vary from one's personal future to relationships among nations. This is followed by determining the scope of the forecast, which can be narrow or broad. The next step entails establishing the time period the forecast covers, which can range from short-term, such as a pitcher's win and loss record or the results of a pending election, to long-term, as in the case of forecasting changes in the Earth's climate. The longer the time period, the greater the uncertainty.

The fourth step centers on identifying the elements included in the model and simulation and recording the needed input data. Once these have been established, the last stage involves formulating the mathematical equations that will be manipulated to forecast the alternative futures of the specified area. In the case of predicting tomorrow's weather, the equations come from our understanding of natural processes such as the strength, location, and size of a high pressure area.

Superfast computers have given us high tech tools that open new possibilities. Given that a main goal of modern science is to discover the empirical cause and effect relationships by which nature and society operate, we are left with the issue of how successful we have been at applying this knowledge to improve our foresight ability. Stated differently, can we convert our scientific understanding of causality into complex computer simulations based on mathematical models that help us foresee the future more clearly?

In order to answer this question, we must keep in mind that the computer outperforms the human mind in processing information in terms of both speed and content. The holy grail of modern futures research is to improve human foresight by progressively reducing as many critical uncertainties as possible or even eliminating them altogether. The name of the game is control, and the underlying assumption is that the more we understand the cause and effect relationships of nature and society the more accurately we will be able to predict and shape the future.

Computer models and simulations aid in this process by calculating at very fast speeds the alternative ways in which the multiple elements that comprise a specified area can be correlated and computed. This is done by modifying the quantitative values of variables and calculating their changing multiple cross impacts. In turn, this leads to establishing the comparative probability levels of various potential outcomes. With the aid of models and simulations for which there are many different formats, researchers have forecast alternative futures in numerous areas such as global food production and distribution, renewable natural resources, energy options, innovations in biomedicine, trends in technology, changing education outcomes and literacy levels around the world, among many others.

In addition, as computer technology has advanced over the past several decades, practitioners in many fields have created models and simulations that apply directly to their specific needs and interests. For example, baseball teams use them when preparing their annual player rosters and for making midseason adjustments. Meteorologists routinely employ models and simulations to foresee pending weather changes and to track shifts in environmental conditions that give rise to tornados and hurricanes. Investors utilize them to analyze swings in the leading indicators that drive the stock market, and insurance companies rely on them to forecast modifications in public health attitudes and behavior.

After several decades of steady progress, models and simulations have found their niche in the scientific and technological landscape. Specialists of all kinds have used them as essential tools to plan the kind of short- and long-term directions they desire and to anticipate external changes that could affect them. As the trend in computer applications continued to grow, it became increasingly clear that while complex models and simulations can be used to forecast alternative futures at an advanced level of sophistication, they cannot remove all of the critical uncertainties that can steer the future in unexpected or random directions.

The reason for this is clear. It is in the nature of indeterminacy that outcomes can be known in advance only as probabilities and not with complete certainty. This situation is similar to quantum physics, discussed in chapter 3, section "Quantum Effects in Our Everyday Lives." As we have shown repeatedly in earlier chapters, this applies to both types of indeterminate relationships: those that do not involve human choice and those that do. Thus, it would appear that when it comes to the role that modern science plays in helping to improve our foresight capacity, we find ourselves on the horns of a dilemma. We can go so far and no farther.

Under conditions of determinacy, we can make predictions with certainty (see cell 1 and cell 3 in Table 1 both under "Determinism"). Under conditions of indeterminacy, we cannot (see cell 2 and cell 4 in Table 1 both under "Indeterminism"). Even with the most sophisticated models and simulations that use complex mathematical formulas to calculate the interaction effects of hundreds of variables, the best we can do is project what might or might not happen at different levels of uncertainty (probability). This is what indeterminacy or randomness means.

Thus, when we ask whether Pearl Harbor or 9/11 could have been predicted with certainty in advance, the answer is no. Under conditions of indeterminacy, especially those involving human choice and intentional deception as these two events did, many outcomes are possible. What we have learned is that while it is not possible to predict which of the many possible futures (often called the "signals" in the midst of "noise") will eventually come to pass, it is possible to prepare alternative plans on how to respond to whichever potential future becomes the actual future. We will say more about this below when we discuss the role of scenarios, surprises, and contingency planning in improving our capacity to foresee what lies ahead.

No doubt, continuing discoveries in science and advancements in computer technology will enhance our ability to calculate at increasingly sophisticated levels the interaction effects that critical uncertainties and the elements that comprise them will have on each other. At the same time, it remains to be seen whether this will lead to actual improvements in our foresight ability. This leads to the next issue. In addition to models and simulations and trend extrapolation as described above, what role do experts play in helping us improve our ability to foresee the future with greater clarity?

Experts

We define an expert as someone who possesses specialized knowledge and understanding. This does not mean that others lack understanding of any given field at different levels but only that an expert is someone whose knowledge exists in depth and in great detail. The direct contributions that human experts make to improving foresight capacity sets this approach apart from the detached mathematical manipulations of other methods like trend extrapolations and models and simulations. The assumption behind involving experts is that their depth of knowledge gives them the edge in forecasting accuracy in contrast to those who lack it, and that compared to guessing, the judgments of experts reduces the potential for errors.

The most common approach that includes the role of experts is called the Delphi method, which conjures up images of the historic Oracle of Delphi that people from ancient Greece and the surrounding regions visited to receive answers to their questions about the future. This procedure involves creating panels of experts who are given a series of questionnaires about the future of one or more designated areas. These include but are not limited to technological forecasts, economic projections, changes in consumer trends and tastes, among others. The typical time frame for projecting changes ranges from ten to fifty years although it can extend far into the future. Many Delphi experts consult with businesses to forecast trends that will affect a company's short- and long-term fortunes for good or ill.

The panels are designed deliberately to insure the anonymity of the participants by keeping them from interacting directly with each other. This is based on the assumption that in face-to-face group situations those who possess the greatest amount of charisma or are the most persuasive might bias the subjective views of others. The goal is to insure maximum objectivity by mailing questionnaires to panel members separately, collecting responses, and tabulating the results. This process is reiterated three or four times, or more if necessary, in order to arrive at a consensus among experts about when a certain change or event might occur.

Delphi projected time lines can vary from short-term to never. In one well known example, in 1968 Smith Kline and French Laboratories conducted a Delphi survey that included forecasting biomedical changes that might occur in numerous areas. These ranged from identifying new disease related enzymes to the complete chemical control of every aspect of human behavior. At the end of the study, the panel of experts projected different time lines for each area. They forecast that new enzymes would be discovered within ten years between 1971 and 1978 but that the complete chemical control of all behavior would never occur.[5]

Along with the trend extrapolation and the model and simulation procedures described earlier, the Delphi method of using experts has provided today's analysts with innovative approaches designed to improve our ability to foresee the future with greater accuracy. Despite these developments, the initial expectation remains unfulfilled that applying these new techniques would help us close the gap on critical uncertainties in many areas.

This does not mean that no real progress has been made. The contrary is true. The more we have learned about how the determinate laws of nature operate, the more we enhance our predictive ability in those areas although not necessarily in others. Futurist Peter Bishop distinguishes well-behaved mechanical systems from complex human systems:

5. Ibid.

"We learned to predict where a pendulum would be, how much ice would melt, when a lunar eclipse would occur. These kind of phenomena are 'determined' (and therefore predictable). Similar predictions are impossible, however, in the economic, social, or political systems in which individual acting with incomplete knowledge and free will have yet to exert their influence."[6]

Bishop's comment parallels our earlier observation that the alternatives of predicting with certainty to forecasting with probability fall within the 4 cells that combine determinism and indeterminism with both no choice and choice (Table 1, page 17). What seems to be a key result of developing innovative forecasting techniques during the past several decades is this: we have learned how to identify with greater accuracy the probable outcomes of any given indeterminate situation without being able to enhance our ability to predict with certainty which one will become the actual future. In addition, the longer the timeline, the more difficult it is to foresee the outcome, and the role of randomness increases.

Thus, while we can predict the future with certainty under determinate conditions like well-behaved mechanical systems, we can only forecast with probability in indeterminate ones such as complex human systems. Where does this leave us? Has all of the effort that has gone into designing innovative approaches to thinking about the future been to no avail? As we will see in the next section on scenarios, the answer is no.

Scenarios

We define a scenario as an image of the future. Before describing how to construct scenarios and why they help improve human foresight, we need to provide some background information. First, as viewed from the perspective of modern futures studies, scenarios typically include four key concepts: possible, plausible, probable, and preferable, as Figure 11 shows.

---

6. Bishop, "Thinking Like a Futurist," 40.

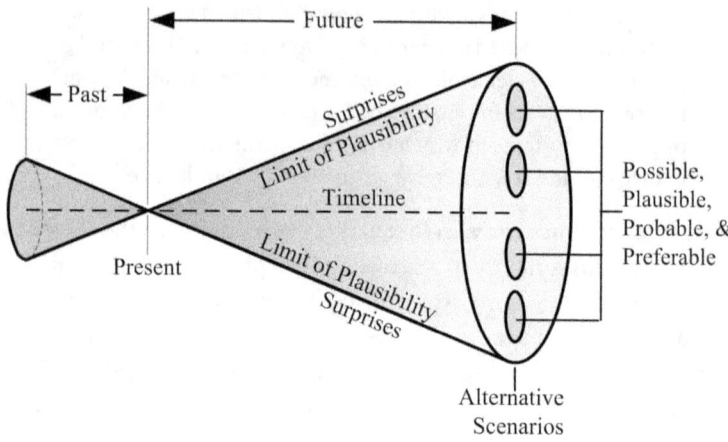

Figure 11. Alternative Scenarios and the Cone of Plausibility[7]

The assumption behind these four is that in order for an image of the future to be useful, it must be realistic. For example, while we can envision time travel as a potential future, it is not realistic or possible at this point in time. Nor is it possible to soar through space to other galaxies at warp speed as depicted in the Star Trek television and movie series. While these and other science fiction scenarios that fill the pages of hundreds of books are highly entertaining, they are currently impossible to implement. No doubt they stimulate the human imagination to stretch in new directions, but they lack plausibility. In order for a vision of the future to be useful to planners and forecasters who rely on trend extrapolation, models and simulations, and experts, scenarios must be both possible and plausible.

Next, in order to develop plausible scenarios, futurists identify current conditions and trends in several areas and then create images of different combinations. The most commonly used approach goes by the acronym STEPE that refers to Society, Technology, Economics, Politics, and the Environment. The general idea involves imagining how changes that occur in one area might affect changes in the others. While this sounds simple at one level, it is complex at another because each of the five areas and potential subdivisions within them contain countless elements that need to be integrated and correlated with those of the other areas. Because they are interwoven, projecting the ripple effects that permeate the combined interaction effects of all the elements is an enormous challenge. While models and simulations and

---

7. For similar Cone of Plausibility images see "Strategic Foresight;" and Taylor, *Alternative World Scenarios for Strategic Planning*, 4, 7.

experts can help facilitate this process, in the final analysis it is the task of the human imagination to create alternatives that help enhance foresight.

Above all, when preparing scenarios, it is necessary to remember one essential point: keep it simple. This might sound counterintuitive given the complexities associated with the development of models and simulations or multiple perspectives that might exist among experts. The best scenarios project images that can be grasped quickly and are noticeably different from each other. The next step involves assigning different degrees of probability to each scenario. While predicting the future is no simple matter, especially when it comes to complex human systems that contain many critical uncertainties, specifying probability levels to each scenario is useful to anticipating which one might become the actual future.

Yet, there is a danger in doing this, and not everyone agrees with this procedure for the following reason. When one of the scenarios is seen as the most probable, there is a tendency to make it the official future to the exclusion of the others. This can create a mindset that unintentionally blocks out the other possibilities that might actually emerge as the future unfolds. Keeping an open mind is critical to avoid being blindsided by becoming overconfident with false assumptions, which is one of the major causes of bad predictions and forecasts.

While it might appear as though one of the potential futures is more probable than the others, we need to keep in mind that establishing realistic alternatives is based on situational elements that exist at any given point in time. As circumstances change and randomness affects the relationships between the elements that comprise it, it might become necessary to reassign probability levels. This is why futurists place special importance on continually scanning the environment for changes that could affect how the future of any designated area will evolve. The future of human systems in particular has a significant unpredictable component in the midst of controlling factors.

Another way to say this is that the future of human systems is not predetermined. At any point in the present moment, many potential futures exist; the one that eventually emerges will depend on how choices affect trends and events. This is why some futurists advocate defining realistic alternatives without assigning probability levels. This helps defend against the inclination to embrace one scenario as the expected future when changing conditions begin to increase the potential that others might be gaining momentum in becoming the actual future.

As we have seen, indeterminate situations containing the highest degree of unpredictability or randomness are those that involve human choice. When confronting more than one possible course of action, individuals and groups will choose one over the others based on their perception that it is the most preferable. This means that in addition to envisioning scenarios that are possible, plausible, and probable; planning for the future always includes choosing the most preferred alternative.

While other approaches are effective in defining various visions of the future, scenarios offer an additional advantage. Extrapolating trends and forecasting alternatives based on models, simulations, and the judgments of experts fall into the category of descriptive futures. Scenario writing includes both descriptive and normative aspects. Once we have envisioned a range of alternatives based on what is realistically possible, plausible, and probable, the next step is to identify the one that is most preferable. Describing alternatives is the first step. Choosing one we prefer is the second.

The reason behind this two-step process is clear. As humans, we do not just sit around waiting for the future to happen. We take action to create the future we want as well as avoid ones we do not want. The following example illustrates why thinking about the future incorporates both descriptive and normative elements. The modern futures movement began at the height of the Cold War in the mid-twentieth century when out of fear of each other the US and the USSR were expanding their nuclear arsenals. Dark comedy movies and books such as the 1964 *Dr. Strangelove or: How I Learned to Stop Worrying and Love the Bomb* projected catastrophic visions of a future that was both possible and plausible. In preparation for what many policy leaders viewed as highly probable, both sides built fallout shelters, and grade school students were taught to hide under desks in the event of a nuclear attack.

Needless to say, this sheer horror of this scenario was hardly a preferred future. As a result, many leaders and ordinary citizens at all levels mobilized around the world to prevent this worst case scenario from occurring. This led to the creation of an international Non-Proliferation Treaty that went into effect in 1970. It was expanded in 1995 after the Soviet Union dissolved in the early 1990s; by 2003, 190 nations had joined the Treaty that aims eventually to eliminate all nuclear arsenals. While several nations still possess these and other weapons of mass destruction and others continue to develop them, the Treaty has been successful in reducing their number along with the probability that they will ever be used.

This example illustrates the importance of developing both positive (or best case) and negative (or worst case) scenarios of the future, which in turn leads to making decisions in the present that will increase the odds that a preferred future will come to pass and a not preferred one will not, even though there is no guarantee that this will happen. In short, in the final analysis, developing alternative images of the future improves the decision making process in the present.

Another way to say this is that while employing modern methods to enhance foresight does not necessarily increase our capacity to predict the future of complex human systems, especially in the long-run, the mere act of thinking systematically about options helps us make more informed judgments in the "now." Even though it might sound paradoxical, this is one of the main benefit of constructing different scenarios: after defining and foreseeing future possibilities with greater clarity, we are in a better position to choose the one we prefer and then act to make it happen. In the process of envisioning alternative futures, our imagination goes forward in order to move backwards to present circumstances and choices.

Surprises and Contingencies

The next issue involved in thinking about the future is how to deal with the element of surprise. When we envision scenarios in terms of what is possible, plausible, probable, and preferable, we assume that one of them will eventually become the actual future; this is not necessarily the case. A completely different future from any of those described in the scenarios might emerge. Why? Because the future is filled with surprises or wild cards that occur out of the blue. In all complex human systems, there exist countless critical uncertainties that could lead to many different kinds of random outcomes. Some can be foreseen, and others cannot.

When we construct scenarios, we assume at a minimum that we are rationally able to identify the most important situational elements that will coalesce to create the future even though we make forecasts only in terms of probabilities and then endeavor to bring about the future we prefer. Surprises by definition are either low probability futures that we do not expect will happen or do not foresee at all. However, when they occur, they can have huge consequences as we have shown in previous chapters.

One of the most important lessons that modern scenario planners have learned is to prepare contingency plans for each of the envisioned alternatives. As a result, they are in a better position to respond with flexibility as one of the possible futures begins to emerge as the actual future. Military strategists, for example, employ contingency planning to prepare for uncertainties and shifting circumstances related to battlefield combat. Airline pilots train constantly on ways to respond to changing weather conditions or aircraft malfunctions that could jeopardize flight safety. At its core, contingency planning for different futures exists to answer one main question:

what do we do if the future we want is not the one we get? The answer is that we have thought about this in advance, and we are prepared to react to it; as circumstances change, we will adapt by modifying our responses.

No doubt, responding to surprises that appear unexpectedly is a common every day experience in all areas of life. When something happens we have not anticipated, we adjust and respond in a way that fits the situation. The difference between our ordinary ways of reacting to surprises that suddenly appear and how futurists react to such circumstances is a matter of degree and not of kind. Many of our responses are spontaneous and occur in the moment. We do not give much forethought to how we might react and what the alternatives might be because we are not prepared to think in this way. The legacy of the modern futurism lies in developing the tools and techniques that will improve our foresight abilities to think about and plan for the future in a systematic way and to be ready to respond to it, whichever way it goes.

Conclusion

To conclude, thinking methodically in terms of alternative scenarios is a skill that we can learn. It helps us to anticipate random changes that occur in all areas of life from micro to macro, to prepare mentally for them, and to develop different ways to respond as circumstances change. In short, we can sharpen our awareness of trends, project how various factors interact with the aid of models and simulations, seek the opinions of experts, create alternative scenarios and pursue the one we prefer, and finally envision potential contingency responses regardless of which possible future becomes the actual future. While we may never be able to foresee with total clarity the real future until it happens because of life's countless indeterminacies, we can use scenarios to envision many potential futures and react flexibly should any one of them, or some unexpected future, emerge.

We are now ready for the next chapter in which we turn to the issue of randomness and justice and how to think about this connection as we move forward into the future. Can our understanding of the many methods developed by modern day futurists help clarify complex concerns that are involved in this relationship? We will also focus our attention on how randomness and justice are related to the nature and actions of God.

8

Fairness

How many times have you heard someone say: life is not fair? Why do we make such an assertion? This answer is clear. One of our most basic human traits is to seek consistency in all of our endeavors from start to finish. When dealing with the issue of fairness, we believe that individuals should get what they deserve. Ideally, when people are good, they should be rewarded; when they are bad, they should be punished. If they work hard, they should reap the benefits; when they do not, they should not. Another way to say this is that in a perfect world, all persons should get what they are due.[1]

However, sooner or later life teaches us one of its most basic lessons: from the moment we humans are born, aptitudes and abilities are not distributed evenly, and future life outcomes are not guaranteed for any of us. Some of us are born into wealth, others into poverty. Some people receive talents that empower them to succeed in life at the highest echelons of their endeavors; others are less fortunate. Only a few are gifted with the extraordinary musical skills to become a Mozart or Beethoven. The same applies to other capacities such as intelligence or athleticism that enable persons like Albert Einstein, Michael Jordan, and Hank Aaron to soar to the heights in the field of physics or the world of professional sports. People like Mother Teresa demonstrate moral achievements at the highest levels, while others such as Hitler show us the depths of savagery into which humans can plunge. Anyone who has ever participated in a state lottery knows well that based on luck alone only a few walk away with the big jackpots while the vast majority of players end up empty handed.

To even the most casual observer, these examples and many others we could cite make it clear that while we long for a world where rewards and

---

1. McFaul and Brunsting, *God Is Here to Stay: Science, Evolution, and Belief in God*, 110-32 for a discussion of the Universal Reciprocity Norm.

punishments are divvied up fairly, we discover that in many situations life does not work this way. Why should this be so? Might this change in the future? In order to answer these questions, we believe that one of the most useful approaches involves examining how randomness determines who gets what and why.

Humanity, Nature, and Free Will

We start our discussion of randomness and fairness by identifying some of the basic differences that exist between humans and non-humans. We recognize that humanity is a part of nature because like all non-human species, we have bodies. We do not exist as disembodied spirits, and we cease to survive as historical beings when our bodies die.

However, there is one crucial area that separates us from all other animals. As stated earlier, we believe we have free will. Because of mindfulness, we possess the capacity for choice, which means that before we make a decision that leads to a specific course of action, we are able to weigh alternatives before choosing the one we prefer. Choice gives us the ability to will what we want to do as well as what we do not want to do. From the moment we wake up, we make myriad choices throughout the day such as what to eat, wear, buy, where to work, whom to visit, and how to relate to other people. Seldom do we ever stop to analyze the act of choosing. In the routines of life, we just do it, because it is so commonplace in our daily experiences.

Intentional and Unintentional

Next, we distinguish intentionality from unintentionality. When we speak of intended actions, we mean those that individuals and groups choose willfully to carry out according to some deliberate purpose. Unintended actions are not based on willful choices. Nature operates by cause and effect relationships that do not involve intentionality. While non-human species are conscious of their surroundings and react to their environments in ways that enhance their survival, they do not make decisions in the same way we humans do. Non-humans survive largely through instincts that are innate from birth as in the case of bees, buffalo, worms, whales, and virtually every other species. Much of human behavior is also based on instinctive biological necessity. As long as our needs for survival, for shelter, for food, and other basic areas are met, we live primarily in culture and survive by using high levels of intelligence weighing alternatives before making willful choices.

Good and Bad Outcomes

Whether intentional or unintentional, both nature and humanity can produce outcomes that are good or bad. Outcomes from nature include earthquakes, tsunamis, and mountaintop vistas. When we speak of something being good, we see it as positive, pleasurable, constructive, meaningful, and beneficial. Goodness is associated with uplifting outcomes that advance human well-being. As the number of people who improve their life conditions expands, the greater is the total overall sum of goodness that affects individuals as well as society and nature as a whole. As good outcomes become increasingly pervasive, their benefits move away from enhancing only the status of a minority and spread steadily to encompass the majority.

Bad outcomes stand in opposition to good ones, because they are negative, downgrading, and destructive. They are harmful and benefit only a narrow minority at the expense of the broader majority. They lead to backsliding and deterioration in the conditions of life. In difficult situations where outcomes are less than ideal, we understand that tearing something down is worse than building it up even though this may be a necessary and short-term course of action in order to achieve a higher and better long-term end.

Examples of both good and bad outcomes are plentiful. When more people live longer and healthier lives because of advancements in modern medicine, we view this as a good outcome. When more people have jobs that provide financial earnings that help them improve their family conditions, the more we call the outcome good. Making voting rights available to all citizens in a democracy so that they can choose the leaders who will govern them is a step in the direction of expanding goodness. Creating a school system that promotes literacy for all children stands second to none as a good and high moral outcome.

Paralleling the examples cited above, when a population's overall health and average life expectancy declines, we recognize this shift as going from good to bad. The same applies to the loss of income that diminishes families' abilities to provide for themselves. Depriving certain groups of people the right to vote in a democracy is movement away from greater to lesser goodness. When a society provides educational opportunities for all children, it achieves a higher level of good outcomes in contrast to one that does not offer universal access.

Even in difficult circumstances where all options are less than ideal, the outcome that leads to the greatest amount of goodness is the best. The US Civil War from 1861 to 1865 led to over 600,000 deaths that included both federal and confederate soldiers and civilians. President Lincoln justified the horrendous carnage that occurred during these four years with his commitment to keeping the United States together and to eliminating slavery. By stopping the Confederacy from withdrawing from the union, he reasoned that in the long-run this would produce more goodness for the nation as a whole. As described in the previous chapter, WWII cost over 60 million people their lives; despite the massive suffering this involved, the Allied victory over the Axis powers opened the door to rejection of Nazi attempts to dominate the world and to greater global goodness.

Pain, Suffering, and Evil

The experience of pain and suffering is common to all forms of biological life, which includes humans and nonhumans alike. As *Homo sapiens*, we are bodied beings with nervous systems that respond to internal or external causes that lead to discomfort and pain, both physical and emotional. In this chapter, we are separating the ordinary sensations of pain and suffering that occur because we exist as natural biological beings from the idea of evil.

We define evil as an intentional human action that inflicts needless pain and suffering on others. While premeditated torture and killing epitomize evil in the extreme, it also occurs in less severe forms, such as deliberate psychological intimidation, when individuals and groups willfully impose harm on others. It is intentionality that makes an action evil. Our earlier references to slavery, WWI, the Great Depression, WWII and Nazi genocide, the Cold War, and the rise of the violent jihadi movement lift into high relief the sheer magnitude of pain and suffering that some human beings have willfully laid on others with horrifying consequences.

In contrast to intentional human evil, nonhumans do not make willful choices after thinking about alternative courses of action and their potential outcomes. No doubt, animal species adapt to their environments in ways that help reinforce their survival. They must kill for food, and they defend themselves under conditions of threat. However, even though they communicate through sights, sounds, and signals, they do not live in cultures that require high levels of cognitive reasoning based on symbolic linguistic systems involving written syntax and grammar. Only *Homo sapiens* possess free will to make choices that impose intentionally hurtful outcomes on one another, as well as cause pain and suffering for nonhuman species and damage to the environment. These choices are not related to survival.

Thus, when it comes to experiences of human pain and suffering, we are limiting the concept of evil to intentional human actions and not to those that are caused by nature. Although birth defects, genetic diseases, hurricanes, tornados, earthquakes, and many other natural forces can bring devastating harm to humans, they do not do so with self-consciousness and premeditated malice of forethought. They are only a part of the processes of nature in which both humans and non-human species are embedded.

This means that we do not accept the distinction that many writers make between natural and moral evil such as the following:

> "*Moral evils* are the wrongful actions of persons (such as murder, cruelty, fraud, etc.); but they also include bad intentions and vicious character traits. *Natural evils* are caused by the physical and impersonal objects and forces of our environment when they threaten or destroy human interests, health, or safety. Such evils include tuberculosis, mental disorders, famine, and many more."[2]

In this chapter, we are applying the notion of evil to intentional immoral outcomes only and not to the pain and suffering that nature perpetrates unintentionally and at random. Why this is so will become clear in the next section.

Randomness

We are now ready to move to the issue of randomness or unpredictability as described in detail in chapter 1 and elaborated throughout the other chapters. In this section, we examine how randomness relates to intended or unintended actions that can result in either good or bad outcomes. As stated above, when we speak of intentional behaviors, we mean those that individuals and groups choose willfully to carry out according to some deliberate purpose. Unintentional outcomes are not planned. Rather, they apply to results that are caused by nature and other unforeseen circumstances that lead to unexpected outcomes. Both intended and unintended actions can lead to either good or bad outcomes as we defined these two terms earlier in this chapter.

Table 10 illustrates how intentional and unintentional actions can be combined with good and bad outcomes.

---

2. Peterson et al., *Philosophy of Religion*, 309.

Table 10. Intentional and Unintentional Actions
and Good and Bad Outcomes

Intentional Actions	Intentional Actions
Good Outcomes	Bad Outcomes
CELL 1	CELL 2

Unintentional Actions	Unintentional Actions
Good Outcomes	Bad Outcomes
CELL 3	CELL 4

As Table 10 shows, in cell 1 we couple intentional actions with good outcomes. In cell 2, we connect intentional actions with the opposite of bad outcomes. In cells 3 and 4, we reverse these relationships. In cell 3 we pair unintentional actions with good outcomes; in cell 4, unintentional actions with bad outcomes.

The four cells that appear in Table 10 make it clear that intentionality can be tied to both good and bad outcomes as can unintentionality. Individuals can choose to take positive, uplifting, and constructive actions that lead consistently to good outcomes. They also can engage in evil and destructive actions that result consistently in pain and suffering. At the same time, we know that whether a person's actions are based on good or bad intentions, there is no guarantee that 100 percent of the time the outcomes will be consistent with their aims. Bad outcomes can follow good intentions, and good outcomes can flow from harmful intentions. We also recognize that many good and bad outcomes occur apart from any human intentions at all. As stated, much pain and suffering happens as a result of the forces of nature over which humans have no control. What is clear is that uncertainty plays a significant role in how intentions, actions, and outcomes can be combined. How do we explain this?

In chapter 1, we described the difference between determinate and indeterminate situations. See Table 1 (page 17). In determinate settings not involving human choice, cause and effect relationships are well known, and outcomes can be predicted in advance with certainty such as when light will appear on the eastern horizon as a result of the Earth's daily rotation around the Sun. The same applies to other determinate situations involving choice such as when parents send their children to school every day. Under stable and repetitive circumstances, the predictable outcome is that their children's learning will improve.

As situations increase in complexity, they become more indeterminate; as a result, the potential for unintended, or random, outcomes increases. This applies to circumstances involving choice as well as no choice. As we have shown in previous chapters, certain outcomes based on quantum physics as well as those associated with changing weather patterns involve indeterminate outcomes that can be known only in terms of probabilities and not certainties. Both are examples of complex situations that do not involve choice.

In addition, the following example applies to every person who ever lived, is alive now, or will live in the future. All of us are born with a specific set of genes that create physical tendencies and mental capabilities that we do not control even though starting from the moment of birth and continuing into adulthood we are influenced by many other factors. Our abilities in music, mathematics, and athletics are largely determined by our genetic heritage where randomness plays a major role.

The act of reproduction by itself illustrates the importance of randomness. Even before the moment of conception, a male produces twenty million to 1.0 billion sperm cells that the female receives during a sexual encounter. The chances are almost zero that any one of these cells will end up fertilizing the female egg. Even if a quarter billion healthy sperm cells start their journey in search of the egg, fewer than 100 might ever get close to it.

DNA, deoxyribonucleic acid, is the hereditary material in humans and is contained in each sperm cell and each egg. From sperm cell to sperm cell and from egg to egg the DNA is slightly different. We know this because fraternal twins (dizygotic) do not share the same DNA and can have different physical traits such as eye color, height, and gender. On the other hand, identical twins (monozygotic) do share the same DNA and have nearly exactly the same physical traits. This can happen only if there is a genetic variation contained in the sperm cells and egg that still originate from the same parents.

In addition, every person's DNA has its own genetic code that is made up of approximately 30,000 genes and 3 billion bits of information (each one a base pair). The genetic heritage each of us acquires, influencing who we are, is determined by the single sperm cell that successfully fertilized the egg. There are billions of possibilities for everyone's genetic makeup. In every fertilization, the tens of millions of sperm cells contains their own DNA with at least 30,000 possibilities. From the group of eggs, typically only one will be fertilized.

Multiple hormones are also involved in the conception process, and each one will have a variable effect on each sperm cell. The DNA differences in the sperm cells determine whether a person becomes male or female. Then, from the moment of conception until birth, each fertilized egg will fall under the influence of its prenatal environment and will be subject to additional random occurrences during the typical nine months gestation period.

Once we are born, other random influences begin to exert themselves. Some of us are born into families where histories of heart disease or higher cancer rates are more prevalent than in other families. Physical predispositions do not affect everyone equally for better or worse even in the same family. Rather, highly structured genetic combinations across populations contain indeterminacies that are distributed according to random-based probabilities. Much of the pain and suffering that people experience on a daily basis is not premeditated. It is not caused by the evil that some people inflict on others. Rather, it is a direct outcome of the biological inheritance that they received randomly at birth from their parents through the gene pool.[3]

In chapter 5, we demonstrated how randomness contributed in large measure to the evolution of life on Earth where permutations gave rise to entirely new species, including *Homo sapiens* along with all other plants and animals. The dissimilar genetic blueprints that all of us receive at the moment of biological conception contribute in no small measure to the myriad pleasures and pains that we will experience as our lives unfold. While we recognize that psychological and social circumstances as well as the decisions we make also influence us in substantial ways, many of the good and bad outcomes of our lives are not caused by the good or evil intentions of others. They simply happen.

This, of course, is not the whole story. Intentional actions, if they are meant to increase goodness, can lead to positive outcomes. These include deliberate actions that increase health care benefits for more people, expand family incomes, make voting rights available to all, and provide universal education for children. In these examples and many more that we could cite, good intentions lead to good outcomes. Good outcomes can result from unintended actions as well. Good outcomes occur when individuals return to normal health after suffering from viral infections that medicine cannot

---

3. Kushner, *When Bad Thinks Happen to Good People*, describes how his son Aaron died at age fourteen in 1977 from a rare and incurable genetic disease called progeria or premature aging. His book has brought comfort to many families who struggle with genetic outcomes they do not control.

cure. The outcome is good even though the body's healing processes are not controlled by human intentions or actions.

In addition, unpredictable outcomes are inherent in circumstances involving choice, such as trying to predict at the beginning of the baseball season what a pitcher's win/loss record will be or what any given hitter's end of the year batting average will be. Pitchers must choose whether to throw a fast ball, curve ball, the speed of the pitch, and its location relative to the strike zone; a batter must decide whether or not to swing the bat, when to swing, and where to swing once the ball leaves the pitcher's hand. Under conditions of fair play, both pitching and batting outcomes cannot be known in advance with certainty.

Also, the five episodes we discussed in chapter 6 (WWI, the Great Depression and the New Deal, WWII, the Cold War, and the rise of jihadi terrorism) involved willful choices that led to unpredictable evil that caused massive pain and suffering during the twentieth century and into early twenty-first.

Fairness

Given the above realization that both predictable and unpredictable outcomes are related to actions that are both intentional and unintentional, we are now ready to introduce the issue of fairness. Some of the combinations of intentions and outcomes we support as fair, and some we do not. For example, we praise people when there is consistency between their positive choices and the good outcomes they produce. On the issue of fairness, we want good people whose actions lead to good outcomes to be rewarded in some way from praise to profit. We believe that it is what they are due.

At the same time, we do not want people whose evil intentions result in bad outcomes to receive the same kind of treatment. When people intentionally inflict pain and suffering on others, despite the consistency that exists between their motives and behavior, we respond to them very differently. Bad people with evil intentions that lead to bad outcomes do not deserve to be treated in the same way as good people whose good intentions lead to good outcomes. Instead, they deserve the opposite: to be reprimanded or penalized. Thus, it is not consistency *per se* that exists between willful intentions and outcomes, but rather the kind of consistency that taps into our sense of fairness: people should get what they are due: good should be rewarded and evil should be punished.

Despite our deep sense that people should get what they deserve, we know that all too often this is not the case. While we recognize that many good things happen to good people who have good intentions and bad things happen to bad people who have evil intentions, we also know that many bad things happen to good people who have good intentions; good things happen to bad people who have evil intentions. Despite our desire for both consistency and fairness, much of what we experience is the opposite: inconsistent and unfair. This is because life is filled with randomness and unpredictability, and this applies to both fair and unfair outcomes that stem from both intentionality and unintentionality.

Thus, as shown in Table 10, intentional and unintentional actions can be coupled with both good and bad outcomes. While good things happen to good people and bad things happen to bad people, we observe all too often that bad things also happen to good people and good things happen to bad people. While much of what happens in life is predictable while much of it is not due to randomness. We recognize that fairness exists but not perfect fairness, which in turn leads us to conclude that randomness, that is, unpredictability, plays a major role as human life advances from one stage to another. Thus, when we say that life is not fair, what we really mean is that life is not consistently fair. While fairness exists in many situations where people get what they are due, in numerous others they do not.

Randomness, Fairness, and God

For centuries, theists have grappled with the question of why life's burdens and benefits are so unevenly distributed that some get what they deserve and others do not or why so much unfairness even exists at all. In this section, we will examine some of their most enduring contributions. We will start with one of the best known theological explanations for why bad things happen to a good person: the story of Job that appears in the *Old Testament* of the *Bible*.

The historical background of the *Job* narrative is the Mosaic covenant that the ancient Israelites made with Yahweh, the Hebrew name for God. Starting with Abraham, the Israelites considered themselves to be a chosen people whom God called into being for a special purpose: to be an example of righteousness for all the nations to admire and imitate and thus become obedient servants of God's will. In order to be a righteous people, God expected the Israelites to follow the 613 laws that appear in the Torah, the first five books of the *Old Testament* or *Hebrew Scripture*.

If the ancient Israelites obeyed the covenant by being faithful and righteous, God would bless them with the land of milk and honey. If they did not, God would curse them by pulling them out by their roots and casting them into darkness. When good people with good intentions take good actions, there will be good outcomes; when bad people with evil intentions take bad actions, there will be bad outcomes. God will see to it.

The book of *Job* found in the *Old Testament* challenges this simplistic notion. Job is portrayed as a good person, and bad things happen to him. This is the world as we do not want it to be. The narrative of *Job* is written in dialogue form and starts with an interchange between God and Satan. After Job is depicted as the richest man in the East, God points out to the accuser (referred to as "the Satan") that Job is also a faithful and good person who does no evil. Satan responds to God by saying that it is easy for Job to be faithful and good when he has everything he wants, wealth, good family, and worldly success. Then Satan lays down a challenge: Take away everything he has, and he will curse you. God accepts the challenge with one condition. God lets Satan take away everything Job has, but Satan cannot lay his hand against Job or hurt him. Satan then destroys Job's children and wealth.

The remaining chapters of *Job* consist of Job's complaints to God over why this is happening to a righteous man such as himself and of extended conversations with his three friends and wife over the relationship between righteousness and reward. The dialogue is both rich in imagery and probing in its search for a clear cut explanation to Job's dilemma. Despite the extended interchange, in the final analysis Job's friends and wife leave him with basically two alternatives. The first is that he is deceiving himself that he is a righteous person. He, therefore, is getting what he deserves. The second is that if he is a righteous person, he should be rewarded for it. Since he is not being rewarded, he should curse God and die.

Job responds by rejecting both of these options. He remains steadfast in his belief that he is a faithful and good person; at the same time, he refuses to curse God. In the midst of his relentless suffering, he demands that God give him an answer to the question that not only he but countless others have asked for centuries: Why me, God? This is the same question Al's parents wrestled with during their son, Danny's, terminal illness. See chapter 2.

Starting in chapter 38, God answers Job "out of the whirlwind." Rather than reply to Job's question directly about his particular circumstances, in verse four God sends a question back to Job: "Where were you when I laid the foundation of the earth?" In the next four chapters, the answer becomes clear. It is God who created and is in charge of the universe. In the final analysis, God's answer to Job's question is that God cannot be reduced to human expectations of what God should be or do.

In the last chapter (42:2) of this segment, Job responds back to God with humility and acceptance of God's sovereignty over all life. "I know that you can do all things, and that no purpose of yours can be thwarted."

Despite what is happening to Job, his task is to remain faithful and righteous regardless of his perception that he is not getting what he thinks he deserves according to the Mosaic formula of blessings and curses. In the end, God triumphs over Satan because Job remains loyal even in the midst of his misery. As a result, God once again bestows blessings on Job by restoring his former fortunes.

The story of Job is one of struggle and submission to God's will regardless of how life progresses. While Job's story ends on an optimistic note, this is all too often not the case. For countless others, life not only involves intense suffering, it also ends tragically. Thus, we cannot conclude that if individuals struggle as Job does and if they remain faithful while enduring it, God will reward them with health, wealth, and worldly success while they are still alive.

Despite Job's happy ending, this is not the core message of *Job*. The enduring theological lesson is that God's nature and activity cannot be reduced to human definitions of and demands for fairness. Ultimately, according to Job, it is God who is sovereign over all of history, and much of what happens is beyond human understanding. We will develop this theme more fully later in this chapter and in the pending last chapter. For faithful followers like Job, the challenge is to remain loyal and righteous no matter what life offers, fair or unfair.[4]

For many other writers, the theological solution to suffering that *Job* offers is less than satisfactory, because the outcome is not consistent with the experiences of too many people who do not get rewarded in this life for their steadfast commitment to live according to God's will. In plain terms, *Job* does not go deep enough in its examination of God's nature and life's injustices both now and potentially in the future.

In order to go beyond *Job*, we turn to an alternative approach that includes a different set of assumptions about God's nature. Dating from the time of the ancient Greek philosophers, it starts by defining God's attributes and actions as the "sum of all perfections." The word perfection signifies that nothing greater exists in the area where the term is applied. For example, in theological language the belief that God is perfect in three important ways denotes that God is all loving, all powerful, and all knowing and that no being, entity, spirit, substance, or essence is more loving, more powerful, or more knowing. Simply stated, perfection refers to something beyond which nothing is greater; because God is perfect in every way, nothing is greater.

---

4. Many writers have found inspiration in the story of *Job* and have offered their own views on how to deal with the issue of why bad things happen to good people. These include MacLeish, *J.B.*; and Kushner, *When Bad Things Happen to Good People*.

The contrast between this and *Job's* approach is obvious. *Job* does not seek to define God's attributes. Rather, the book grapples with the challenge to remain faithful to God and live by standards of goodness no matter what happens in life, good or bad. In the end, Job submits to God's inexplicable sovereignty over all things. The alternative of regarding God as the sum of all perfections moves beyond Job's heartfelt faith and uses reason to comprehend God's essential characteristics. God is not the mysterious "Other" whose basic attributes, in the final analysis, are beyond our grasp. Instead, we can think of God, the ultimate reality of the universe, as all knowing, all loving, and all powerful.

However, this approach is not without its complications. From the start, theologians have recognized that defining God in terms of these three perfections involves a basic contradiction that seems irresolvable. If God is all knowing, all loving, and all powerful, why would evil, pain, and suffering even exist? If God is all knowing, then God would know that evil exists. Given this assumption, it would seem that an all loving God who is also all powerful would act to eliminate evil, because God would know where it is occurring. If evil persists, this implies that God is either not all loving or not all powerful. In other words, the sum of all three perfections approach includes logical assumptions that seem to be irreconcilable. In turn, this leads to the conclusion that God cannot be perfect or that such a God does not exist.

Can this logical impasse be overcome by modifying some of the basic assumptions? What would be the implications of assuming that God is perfect in only two areas but not all three? Here are the options:

1. God is all loving and powerful but not all knowing,

    or

2. God is all powerful and knowing but not all loving,

    or

3. God is all loving and knowing but not all powerful.

Do these changes help reconcile belief in God's perfections with the existence of unfairness, evil, pain, and suffering? The answer is no as Table 11 shows.

Table 11. God's Characteristics and Evil

Is God all knowing?	Is God all loving?	Is God all powerful?	Can evil exist?	Comments
No	Yes	Yes	Yes	There might be pockets of evil God does not know about.
Yes	**No**	Yes	Yes	God' love does not cover some evil producing situations.
Yes	Yes	**No**	Yes	God cannot control some evil producing situations.

According to Table 11, assuming that God is all loving and powerful but not all knowing means that pockets of evil about which God has no knowledge could exit. Next, assuming that God is all knowing and powerful but not all loving implies that God's love in not comprehensive enough to cover some evil situations. Finally, assuming that God is all knowing and loving but not all powerful leads to the conclusion that God cannot control some evil situations.

Thus, even when we try to move beyond *Job* by supposing that God's perfections apply to only two of the three areas, we cannot reconcile this modification with life's inconsistencies. While good things will continue to happen to good people and bad things to bad people, bad things will also happen to good people and good things to bad people. In short, evil, pain, and suffering will continue to remain inherent in the human condition, and randomness or unpredictability will endure as a part of it.

Is there a way around this impasse? In the final analysis, is the position of *Job* the only viable option in reconciling belief in God with the existence of unfairness? In light of Table 11, is it even desirable to continue using the sum of all perfections approach? The answer to this question is yes: we can move beyond *Job* and still retain the sum of perfections idea. However, in order to do so we must make an additional and essential assumption.

God, Free Will, and Fairness

The assumption is this: God has given free will to humans, and this is better than not having it even if it is used for evil rather than good. From an evolutionary standpoint, starting about 200,000 years ago, we modern humans began evolving into conscious, mindful, and self-aware beings. From a theological perspective, it is precisely through this natural, evolutionary process that God gifted us with the capacity for choice. The implications of this evolutionary and theological combination are enormous, especially when we compare it to deterministic approaches that assume that free will is an illusion.

Determinism comes in both atheist and theist forms. For atheists, it is through the laws of cause and effect that nature controls how life evolves. This applies to predictable relationships that can be established with certainty in advance as well as unpredictable ones that can be known only in terms of probability. The Holy Grail for die hard reductionists in the naturalist tradition is that through scientific advancements we will one day develop a Theory of Everything that explains in total how the universe operates from the micro thoughts and emotions of individuals to the macro causal chains of the cosmos. Other atheists who stand in the tradition of indeterminacy where probabilities may never be reduced to certainties are not so confident.

The second form of determinism is called predestination, also known as divine determinism, which is associated with various schools of theism. While Christian writers such as Augustine and Calvin might disagree on details, they share a common perception that no matter how life unfolds God is in control of what will happen because God has predetermined it. This is the classic puppets on a string point of view. We might believe we have free will, but we do not, even if God allows us to think this way.

This view of predestination parallels some of the themes we described in *Job*. Since God's will is inscrutable, our only alternative is to accept what happens under the heading of God's sovereignty. For all intents and purposes, the theist's view of determinism nullifies free will or converts it into a divinely given delusion. However, if we believe we have the ability to make choices based on free will, does this negate the idea that God is all knowing? Does this imply that God cannot know in advance what choices we will make until we make them?

In other words, is belief in free will compatible with the idea that God is all knowing? If we make one modification in our understanding of God, the answer is yes. Here is the modification: While God does not predetermine our decisions, God knows what choices we will make before we make them. How so? The theological answer is this: because God knows us completely. God has perfect knowledge of how we will act even though God does not foreordain it. God is all knowing without being all controlling, which implies that we humans are responsible for the choices we make based on our free will. We retain the capacity for choice, and at the same time God knows in advance what we will choose. Thus, when viewed in this way, belief in free will is compatible with at least one of God's three perfections: all knowing.

Next, we turn to one of God's other perfections: all loving. Does the acceptance of free will invalidate this claim? As stated earlier, it would seem that an all loving God would intervene to stop the evil, pain, and suffering that we humans all too often impose on each other. However, just as it is possible to combine the notion of free will with the assertion that God is all knowing, we can combine belief in the capacity for choice with the affirmation that God is all loving.

Once we accept that free will is one of God's greatest gifts as it evolved naturally through the process of evolution, it would be inconsistent that God would suddenly nullify it for persons who use it for evil while continuing to allow it for those who choose to bring about good. This would imply that God is arbitrary by allowing some individuals to keep it while taking it away from others. Furthermore, it would mean that God gives the gift of free will and then restricts its expression to only good and not evil choices.

Also, it would mean that God would allow for the existence of some forms of evil but not others, especially horrendous evils like genocide, slavery, or the murder of innocent children. In effect, this would not be free will at all but merely another form of illusion or of defining God in terms of the human desire that God should have a cutoff point beyond which God would never permit some forms of evil to exit. However, in order for the will to be truly free, individuals must be able to use it for both good and evil purposes. God does not establish boundaries beyond which humans can use their capacity for choice for good or evil purposes. In short, mature adult autonomy requires freedom of choice. As history shows, this can result in a very high cost for free will. For example, because God allows free will, Hitler's evil choices led to the deaths of 6,000,000 Jews during the Second World War.

At this point, two other issues push to the surface. First, even when individuals use their free will for good purposes, no one is capable of perfect goodness. In theological language: All fall short of the glory of God. Since no one can be perfect as God is perfect, all persons commit acts of wrongdoing for which they stand in need of forgiveness. No one is exempt from this need even though the evil that some individuals and groups commit is greater than that of others, and in some cases vastly greater.

Second, the assumption that God is all loving implies that God is also merciful and compassionate. For those who willfully acknowledge their shortcomings in relationship to God's perfections and turn to God with an attitude of genuine contrition, God is forgiving. This does not mean, however, that God's compassion eliminates life's inconsistencies that result from the evil abuses of free will. It means merely that in theological terms individuals who humbly seek God's forgiveness for their transgressions and earnestly desire to change for the good, that is, repent, will receive it. One of the major axioms of all the world's great religions is that in the midst of life's ever changing circumstances, the one constant in the universe is God's forgiving love. Thus, belief in free will does not negate the affirmation that God is all loving and by implication caring, compassionate, merciful, and forgiving.

Can we say the same for the third of God's perfections, power? Once again, the theological answer is yes although there are greater challenges associated with this perfection than the other two. One option is to fall back on the outlook of *Job* that God is sovereign over the universe and that in the final analysis the will of God is inscrutable. However, we need to go deeper and examine other possibilities. In the area of evil, given the existence of free will and the human tendency for self-centeredness, also called sinfulness in theological terms, individuals follow their own desires and not God's. For some writers, this implies that by giving humanity the free will to make both good and evil decisions, God is a risk taker[5] who does not impose power to assure that people make only good choices at all times.

Does the idea that God is a risk taker who allows individuals to commit evil acts contradict the belief that God is all powerful? Once again, we can respond with a no; this calls for further clarification. In the final analysis, there is really only one answer to this question. If we accept that the Creator is sovereign over the creation, then sooner or later God will have God's way. At the same time, if history is any witness, from our finite human perspective there is a perplexing downside of this position. We are at a loss to comprehend why God allows evil to persist, and in some cases horrendous evil, for an unspecified period of time before stopping it, sometimes by violence if necessary, as in the case of the American Civil War that ended slavery and WWII that stopped Nazi genocide.

From a theological perspective, the major challenge is to explain why God would wait so long before ending the extremes of pain and suffering that we humans all too often impose on each other. In the midst of prolonged evil in particular, we are at a loss to know why an all loving and powerful God does not stop it sooner. From our side of the divine-human encounter, we once again find ourselves wanting God to do it our way and on our time schedule.

The only compelling counterbalance to why God allows the existence of so much evil is that God has given humanity the unconditional gift of free will and does not rescind it despite the depth and duration of pain and suffering that evil choices cause. For the devout theist who holds that God is all powerful, the most reasonable conclusion is that in specific situations, eventually

---

5. Helm, *The Providence of God*, 39–55.

God will use some humans to stop other humans from perpetuating their extreme acts of evil, even if this involves warfare; and even then, this seems to contradict the assumption that God is all loving.[6] It is at this level that we are most likely to conclude that God's ways are not necessarily our ways. This is a theme we will revisit in chapter 9. However, in light of Job's affirmation that God is sovereign over the entire cosmos, in the final analysis, it is God who decides when, where, and how to intervene, despite our desire that God should conform to how we want God to be and act.

Needless to say, claiming that God will ultimately find ways to deal with different levels and amounts of evil, including the use of warfare, is not very satisfying or persuasive for many people. This applies especially to those who suffer under the heavy hand of persistent oppression or others who feel deep sympathy for them. It is far easier to balance belief in the existence of free will and evil with God's other two perfections than it is with the third perfection of power. No doubt, the problem of persistent evil is a primary stumbling block for many people who reject belief in a God who would permit the continuation of pain and suffering when supposedly an all loving God has the power to stop it.[7] From a theist perspective, this does not mean that God is not all powerful, but it does mean that God will act to end evil on God's schedule and not ours.

God, Unfairness, and the Future

Thus, by making the above modifications, we can combine belief in free will with the assumption that God is all knowing, loving, and powerful. At the same time, there is another question that needs to be addressed. Will there ever be a time in the future when earthly life will be free of unfairness and

---

6. Cobb and Griffin, *Process Theology: An Introductory Exposition*, hold that God exercises persuasive power but not coercive power over creatures. This means that God is continually showing individuals what is the best moral choice in any given situation. However, in the process, God ceases to be all powerful. We do not accept this approach. By redefining God in this way, there is no way to answer the question of how God exercises ultimate sovereignty over creation. If God is finally not all powerful, in the final analysis, humanity is more powerful than God and can ultimately negate God's purposes.

7. In 1710, Gottfried Leibniz argued in his *Theodicy Essays* that God allows evil to exist because it contributes to a greater good. Since God is perfect in every way, God creates the best of all possible worlds that contains the least amount of evil that is compatible with free will and human sinfulness. Also, evil leads to greater goodness by building character and compassion. He also held that Christ's atonement for sin promotes goodness, and this leads to a world that contains less evil. Leibniz sparked a lively debate about God and evil that continues to this day.

inconsistency? In all likelihood, the answer is no. While good things will continue to happen to good people (fairness) and bad things to bad people (fairness), bad things will also happen to good people (unfairness), and good things to bad people (unfairness). No doubt, randomness will continue to play a major role in many of life's unpredictable outcomes.

In addition, as long as people possess free will, some will use it intentionally to harm or kill others. From a theist viewpoint, how might we think about the relationship between God, unfairness, and the future? While theologians offer several answers to this question, we can combine them into two main groups. The first centers on history, and the second on life after death.

Both groups are keenly aware of how much evil and unfairness permeate the world, but they differ in their perceptions of how God deals with it. Some authors in the history group center on evolution as the means by which God progressively removes life's imperfections. For example, Protestant minister Walter Rauschenbusch (1861–1918), one of the founders of the Social Gospel movement that started in the early twentieth century, held that the institutions of the modern society are becoming increasingly Christianized.[8] Mid-twentieth century Catholic theologian Teilhard de Chardin (1881–1955) held that the evolution of the cosmos, from matter to humanity, was evolving toward perfect union with Christ.[9]

Others in the history group reject the evolutionary approach and instead envision some kind of cataclysmic historical or end of the world event. The Millennium movement that emerged in Christianity during the past 200 years emphasizes that we are living in the end times when Christ will return soon, destroy Satan and the forces of evil, and create the new heaven and earth. The movement derives its name from Revelation 20:4–6, which refers to Christ's 1,000 year rule before the final battle of Armageddon. The Muslim parallel to Christianity's final days scenario involves the idea of the Mahdi or Guided One who will appear on Earth on Judgment Day to defeat Iblis (the devil) and the forces of evil and establish perfect Islamic justice.[10]

The life after death group does not accept the history group's view that God will remove unfairness gradually though evolution or dramatically

---

8. Rauschenbusch, *Christianizing the Social Order*; and *Theology for the Social Gospel*.

9. Chardin, *The Phenomenon of Man*.

10. The Seventh Day Adventists and Jehovah's Witnesses are two of the Christian denominations that are associated with Millennialism. The 12er branch of Shi'ite Islam holds that the Mahdi is the twelfth Imam who did not die in the ninth century but went into hiding (occultation). He will one day reappear to establish perfect Islamic justice on earth.

within or at the end of history. Instead, they focus on the afterlife when God will balance the scales of justice by rewarding or punishing everyone according to their just desserts. God is not fooled. Good people who did good things in life will be rewarded, and bad people who did bad things will be punished. Good people who experienced bad things will be rewarded. Bad people who experienced good things, especially by deceiving, exploiting, and intentionally harming others, will be punished. Inconsistency, unfairness, and evil will never disappear in history, and only God who is both merciful and just will correct this imbalance in eternity.

Conclusion

Thus, to conclude, we have shown that establishing perfect fairness on Earth is no simple possibility. For many people, fairness will prevail; for many others it will not. Life is neither 100 percent fair nor unfair but rather consists of a combination of both. The intermixing of both fairness and unfairness will continue far into the future, possibly indefinitely. Randomness will play a major role in shaping the life circumstances into which we are born and the choices that we will make during our journey through the stages of life.

Additionally, we have addressed the theological challenge of how an all knowing, loving, and powerful God who has given humankind the gift of free will confronts the harm and destruction that occurs when some use it to inflict evil, pain, and suffering on others. We have seen how it is easier to reconcile two of God's perfections, all knowing and all loving, with the persistence of evil than it is with the belief that God is also all powerful, especially in regard to persistently horrendous evil. We also described how theists differ in their views of how God deals ultimately with the continuation of evil both now and into the future. For some, this will occur within or at the end of history; for others, it will happen only in the afterlife.

We are now ready for the final chapter.

9

Randomness and God

Understanding God

IN THIS FINAL CHAPTER, we will expand on the issue of the relationship between God and randomness, which we began discussing in the previous chapter on fairness. In doing so, we will incorporate the other topics that we analyzed throughout the book. The goal is that this will help us better understand God in relation to some of the more challenging events in our lives. See chapter 2 for Al Brunsting's three stories.

We begin by reiterating the assumption that our highly structured universe came into existence and evolved under the guidance of an Intelligent Creator called God. By this, we mean that God is the Transcendent Other whose reality exceeds that of the material universe that we experience through the five senses. The main difference between ourselves as theists and others who are atheists is that the majority of atheists believe that nature is the ultimate and impersonal reality beyond which nothing superior exists.

We do not hold this view. Instead, we contend the opposite, namely, that God is a spiritual force that transcends, created, and sustains the cosmos. Furthermore, since the Big Bang 13.8 billion years ago, this divine power has intentionally guided the evolutionary process that has led to the emergence of conscious, mindful, and self-aware life on Earth that includes free will and the human capacity for choice. While there is much about God that we do not understand, this is our starting point. We also affirm that the best scientific evidence available supports this view and that the discoveries of modern science provide ample support for the assumption of a life friendly universe.[1]

Next is our perception of how humanity relates to and thinks about God. This operates at two levels. First, we believe that people everywhere need

---

1. McFaul and Brunsting, *God Is Here to Stay*, 67–88.

and seek purpose in life and that the vast majority connect their search for meaning to some view of God. We also recognize that not everyone grounds their desire to live a purpose filled life in some form of theism or spiritual reality. While atheists disavow the existence of any kind of Transcendent Other beyond nature, they are not exempt from the need for personal fulfillment that is inherent in the human search for meaning.

Second, this search always occurs within the context of different cultures. As a result, there are multiple views of God or gods as the members of dissimilar societies define and experience them. This means that no group's doctrinal beliefs are absolute, which implies that all theological views of God, whatever the culture, are finite. While many followers of different faiths perceive that they and they alone are in possession of religious truth and that the beliefs of others are either false or inferior, we do not hold to this position. Instead, we maintain that the world's diverse religions are but partial perceptions of the one God who is the Intelligent Creator of the cosmos and whose essence transcends all of them.

Regardless of the diversity of religious beliefs about the nature of God and the degree to which individuals and groups accept or reject the views of others, as we have shown repeatedly throughout this book, no one is exempt from experiencing the personal effects of unpredictability in life. Just as we exist in a highly structured universe governed by specific natural laws, we are also subject to the pervasive impact of randomness.

God and Dimensionality

Whether we focus on predictability or probability in the physical world or human behavior, all of the topics that we have discussed throughout this book occur within four dimensions. The first three deal with space that includes height, width, and length. The fourth is time. Together, these four comprise the dimensions of the physical universe within which all of our activities occur and within which modern observational science operates in its quest to discover the laws of nature. All of the determinate relationships, indeterminate relationships, and our capacity for choice operate within these specific four space and time dimensions.

Some theoretical physicists speculate that there might be more than only four.[2] In addition, recent research in neuroscience demonstrates how the brain's complex neurological webs that process thoughts and memory

---

2. Davies, "Make a Date with another Dimension."
https://cosmosmagazine.com/mathematics/how-your-brain-works-in-11 dimensions, 6/14/2017.

operate in extra dimensions. Scientists used a specialized mathematics (algebraic topology) to analyze 1) the physical structure of neurons and synapses in the brain's neocortex and 2) the function structure of how information flows in the brain.[3] They were able to establish a clear link between these two where such linkage was not made before. The neocortex is responsible for the brain's higher level activities such as sensory perception, cognition, spatial reasoning, language, and spirituality.

From this research, they concluded that information in the brain flows in temporary and not permanent configurations (topologies). For example, when an individual considers one problem, the signals in the neocortex tend to flow in one configuration. However, information for another problem may move in a different configuration within the brain. This implies that the information flowing in the neocortex (thought patterns) can exist in more than four dimensions. Whereas previously used mathematics were inadequate to accommodate additional dimensions, in this study, those extra dimensions were accounted for.

Based on the new mathematics, the results of these experiments were surprising: They show that the neocortex synthesizes information routinely in seven and sometimes up to eleven dimensions, whereas the cells in every other organ in the body work in four dimensions. As neuroscience continues, we anticipate that it will lead to a better understanding of the brain's extra dimensions and their relationship to the thinking process and how memories are stored in the neocortex. This research is consistent with our speculation that there exists a reality beyond what we can detect with our four senses, a reality beyond our comprehension, and a reality completely unavailable to us through the four dimensions that comprise our ordinary experiences.

In turn, these kinds of discoveries could lead to a clearer understanding of God's relationship to the random events and behaviors that we have described throughout this book, including but limited to the origins of our universe, evolution of our solar system, tsunamis, earthquakes, atrocities such as the Holocaust, and coauthor Al Brunsting's three stories about his sister, uncle, and brother.

If other dimensions do exist in the brain, as of this writing they are either too small to be detected or remain hidden in some way. A dimensionality beyond the four has not been proven conclusively and has not been commonly accepted by many scientists. However, experimental verification of these extra dimensions could lead to many other important breakthrough

---

3. https://cosmosmagazine.com/mathematics/how-your-brain-works-in-11-dimensions

discoveries involving subatomic particles and forces in nature such as gravity. Potential findings like these would be cause for excitement, and they would lead to a more complete understanding of our universe.

When we turn to the topic of the nature of God, whom we view as the Intelligent Creator of our highly structured universe where randomness appears throughout all micro to macro levels, we expand our thinking beyond the physical cosmos to a transcendent domain where we speculate about the existence of other dimensions beyond the four that we experience. We have no empirical, theological, or philosophical evidence that extra dimensions exist. Nonetheless, just as theoretical cosmologists and other scientists speculate about extra dimensions in the physical universe, from a theological viewpoint, we wonder whether God possesses dimensions that transcend the fourfold dimensionality of space and time and through these dimensions intervenes in ways that guide or direct our cosmic and earthly experiences.

While we cannot point to hard proofs to verify God's other dimensionality, we have some indicators that point to this possibility. Early in the twentieth century, psychologist William James conducted numerous scientific inquiries involving individuals across diverse religious traditions who claimed to have had mystical encounters with God. They were all convinced that these occurrences were real and that their deep feelings preceded any attempt to make rational sense of them.[4] In similar fashion, Walter T. Stace holds that conceptual interpretations of spiritual feelings are attempts to communicate experiences that mystics claim are non-spatial and non-temporal in nature even though they occur within the space and time dimensions of human existence.[5]

We also have numerous examples of individuals who have reported near death experiences. For example, Dr. Eben Alexander, a highly trained neurosurgeon who did not believe in any kind of life after death, fell ill with an undiagnosed infectious disease that sent him into a coma for several days. While unconscious, he underwent a series of inexplicable mental incidents including being in the presence of the divine source of the universe. When he awoke, he was convinced that God, the soul, and heaven are real.[6]

While mystical and near death experiences cannot be verified through the standard methods of modern science, their mere existence implies the possibility that other dimensions might exist. If this is so, then it is reasonable to believe that God can intervene into the natural world

---

4. James, *The Varieties of Religious Experience*.
5. Stace, *The Teachings of the Mystics*.
6. Alexander, *Proof of Heaven*.

that is limited to four space and time dimensions and at the same time transcend them through other dimensions. This implies that God does not intercede into the physical universe and human experience by violating or suspending the laws of nature but by working through them in ways we do not fully comprehend.

This leads to the next question. Assuming God possesses extra dimensionality, why do we not have direct access to it? From a physical as well as a theological or philosophical standpoint, the answer is clear. We are limited to time and space, and God is not. Or stated in a slightly different way, God is not as dimensionally limited as we are. We can visualize this in the image of a cone. See Figure 12.

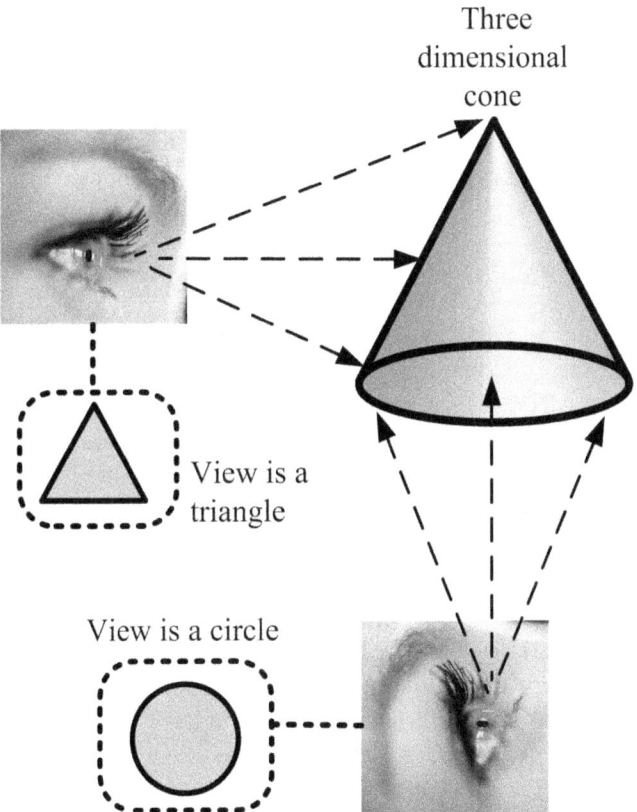

Figure 12. The cone as a three dimensional object.

When viewed from below, the cone appears to be a two dimensional circle. When it is viewed from the side, it appears to be a two dimensional triangle. Either view gives an incomplete image. This cone has a point at the top called a vertex and a circular base at the bottom. The vertex is joined to the edges of the circle by a surface. When the cone is turned over so that the circle is on top and the vertex is on the bottom, the cone looks something like an ice cream cone.

As a three dimensional object, the cone has height, width, and length. It also exists in time. When we look from the side, we see only two dimensions; when we look from the bottom, we see only two other dimensions. Viewed only from the side as a triangle or only from the bottom as a circle, our understanding is far different from what the cone actually is in all three dimensions. By analogy, we experience life in four dimensions only; from a theological point of view, we can assume that God possesses extra dimensionality that we cannot know.

Next, we turn to a brief summary of previous chapters. Our goal is to highlight only some of the key concepts and show how God relates to the type of randomness associated with each topic. At the end, we conclude by identifying five distinct areas that overlap and tie together all the diverse issues we have discussed throughout the entirety of this book.

Overview of Randomness

We begin our overview by recapping key themes that we developed in chapter 1, where we summarized how people use the term randomness in multiple ways. Despite the variations, when all is said and done, we decided to keep it simple: randomness means unpredictability. We acknowledge that we live in a highly structured universe that began with the Big Bang 13.8 billion years ago. Also, we recognize that randomness has played a major role at every stage of evolution from the start to the present and that this will continue into the future.

When we began examining the many topics that appear in the chapters of this book, we realized that we humans are much more inclined to interpret what happens to us in terms of the well-known cause and effect patterns that we start learning from the moment of birth. Why should this be so? As we stated in the Preface, we believe this tendency is tied to Darwinian survival instincts that lead us to act in structured and predictable ways that enhance our earthly adaptation and survival.

No doubt, with the emergence of modern humans on Earth starting around 200,000 years ago, our species repeated behaviors that enhanced the goal of long-term survival. In order to ensure continued existence, these early humans also used their religion to reinforce an individual's conformity to the behavior they believed supported clan cohesion. As a result, their thoughts and actions became highly structured, habitual and, to the greatest extent possible, predictable. In short, predictability led to both psychological comfort and group solidarity. This pushes our perceptions of randomness mostly out of mind, and thus we tend to consider randomness mostly unimportant.

The notion that the universe is comprised of predictable patterns does not stop here. During the last 200 years, this belief has been supported by countless scientific discoveries. In the beginning, modern science proceeded under the assumption that the cosmos consisted exclusively of a system of predictable cause and effect laws and that future scientific findings would uncover them, possibly even all of them eventually. This is the world of classical physics as exemplified by the work of Copernicus, Galileo, Newton, and innumerable others. As a result of research in areas ranging from astronomy to zoology, in the past two hundred years science has contributed an amazing amount of new knowledge to our understanding of how the universe operates.

However, this is only part of the story. In the 1930s, Heisenberg's interpretation of the behavior of subatomic particles opened the door to quantum physics. As discussed in chapter 1, this led to a fundamental insight summarized in the Uncertainty Principle where certain potential outcomes can be known only in terms of probability and not predictability. Lorenz's computer simulations on weather prediction in the 1970s parallels the Uncertainty Principle and produced novel conclusions designated as chaos theory.

What we now know is that there are many areas in the physical universe that behave according to the laws of classical physics and are very predictable (for example, gravity) and others by laws that yield results that are substantially unpredictable (subatomic particles and long-term weather patterns). When we add behaviors that occur in social, political, and economic areas along with their multi layered interactions, we become increasingly aware that our finite human existence is embedded within and surrounded by a universe of enormous complexity that includes both determinate and indeterminate (or random) relationships.

In the course of discovering indeterminate patterns that involve probability and not predictability, modern science began developing new concepts and models that help explain how randomness operates in our universe. As mentioned in chapter 1, one of the most significant is normal statistical distributions that researchers apply routinely to analyze probability distributions and their variations in many fields ranging from the physical to the social sciences. In biology, when we lack identifiable causal explanations, we rely on justifications like mutations to describe the appearance of new species of plants or animals.

After the extinction of the dinosaurs sixty-five million years ago, when a huge meteor crashed randomly into the Earth, mammals, primates, and eventually *Homo sapiens* evolved naturally as a result of unpredictable changes in the genetic code. As we humans emerged on Earth over the past 200,000 years, we developed as conscious, self-awareness beings with the capacity for choice or free will. With the ability to weigh alternatives and their consequences before deciding on a specific course of action, we introduced more complexity into the world and, thus, more indeterminism.

What 200 years of modern science has taught us is this: there are many situations where we can predict the outcomes with certainty and many others where we cannot. One of the major challenges that modern science faces as it looks forward to making new discoveries in the future is to identify where determinacies leave off and indeterminacies begin, and vice versa, and how this process happens and how to predict the results.

Where does God fit into this picture? As stated above, we understand that the universe and our place in it is limited by the four dimensions of space and time. All our existence, all our waking moments, all our history, and all our DNA point us to a world view confined by these four dimensions. Therefore, we are all strongly biased in this direction. Nonetheless, if we imagine that God transcends these dimensional restrictions, from a theological viewpoint, we can open up other possibilities. If God acts in extra dimensions beyond our four, what seems to us to be randomness, unpredictability, or even supernatural intervention would be guided by God in and through these four dimension of the natural world, although the associated causes and effects in those extra dimensions would be unknown to us.

This theological perspective is totally consistent with the view that our extraordinarily complex universe contains both determinate and indeterminate relationships. In those areas where we cannot identify with certainty the determinate causes, we have developed numerous ways to explain where indeterminacies exist, which as stated earlier include normal statistical distributions and their variations, permutations, mutations, correlations, surprises, and human choice, among others. All of these concepts apply to unpredictable changes that occur in the natural world and throughout human history.

Assuming that God possesses extra dimensionality that transcends the four space and time dimensions within which we humans exists, we can conclude that God has guided the process of evolution from the moment of Big Bang through the laws of nature that are both predictable and probable. As a result, it is not necessary to hold that God intervenes by suspending the laws of nature but instead by working within and through them. At the same time, we are keenly aware that we do not have comprehensive knowledge about how and why God intervenes.

Furthermore, we recognize that we see life only from our side of the divine-human encounter and not from God's, and that this can be confusing in the midst of our desire for consistency and fairness. As finite humans, we become especially perplexed when the outcomes of God's intervention vary so widely and seem so arbitrary and unfair. As we indicated, Rabbi Kushner addressed this question in his book, *When Bad Things Happen to Good People*,[7] which is a modern remake of Job's struggle to understand why a good and righteous person, as he perceived himself to be, should suffer. While we know that bad things can happen to good people, we also know that three other possibilities exist: good things can happen to good people, good things can happen to bad people, and bad things can happen to bad people. On the first of these four, that is, when bad things happen to good people, nowhere is this better expressed than in Al Brunsting's three personal stories.

Three Personal Stories

Chapter 2 consists of Al Brunsting's three personal stories about his sister Bernace, his Uncle Al, and his younger brother Danny. Those stories are summarized here in the context of randomness and the likelihood of God's extra dimensionality, discussed earlier in this chapter.

When Bernace was two years old and Al was four, they both contracted polio at the same time. The effects on Bernace were far worse. Bernace suffered lifelong paralysis of her right leg from hip to toes, whereas in the long-term Al was not affected. As a result of advancements in scientific knowledge, we now know that an infection of the polio virus involves that virus attaching itself to a host neuron[8] and gaining an entrance into it. Here the DNA of that neuron is confused and produces copies of the infecting polio virus. The copies break out of the host neuron, which may kill it, and infect other neurons with the polio virus.

When the growth of the number of polio viruses is finally arrested many host neurons are destroyed and usually the muscles those neurons controlled become unresponsive. Although the basic chemistry of this process is well understood and predictable, at the cellular and molecular levels

---

7. Kushner, *When Bad Things Happen to Good People*.

8. A neuron or nerve cell is transmits information through the body using electrical and chemical signals.

multiple random steps determine the severity of the disease. The outcome of this randomness was for Bernace a permanently paralyzed right leg while Al suffered no permanent damage. We are left to wonder whether the consequences would have been different if the unpredictable events that occurred at the cellular and chemical levels had deviated even slightly, and we wonder where God fits into this picture.

Al's second story involves his Uncle Al who was twenty-two years old when he was called into the military to fight in WWII. During the war, he piloted a B-17 bomber. On January 3, 1943, Uncle Al and his ten man crew had just completed a bombing run over Saint Nazaire nicknamed "Flack City." What happened during their return flight demonstrates how a chain of random events led to the tragic loss of life for Uncle Al and his team of airmen. During the bombing run, the B-17 was damaged over the target area. As a result, his slower aircraft was separated from other planes in the bomber formation. Seven German pilots of fighter aircraft spotted the slower, damaged bomber over the English Channel on return to its home air base. The German airmen shot down that B-17, and no one survived. As a result of their bravery, Uncle Al and his crew were awarded the Congressional Medal of Honor for their heroism in combat.

Al's third story is about his brother Danny who died of childhood leukemia just before his fifth birthday. He was an innocent young child. Al was fourteen years old at the time, and his parents knew one year before Danny's death that his condition was terminal. During this time, Danny acted normally, continuing to enjoy life. Al's father, an ordained minister, and Al's mother struggled to make sense of what was happening to Danny from the perspective of their Christian faith. While both parents believed that God is not cruel and that Danny's death was not senseless, they asked the inevitable question, why?

Eventually, Reverend Brunsting came to the conclusion that Danny's death served these purposes, which he expressed in his book, *He Is Not Gone*.[9] He reasoned that having gone through Danny's experience, he could be more effective in ministering to others undergoing similar circumstances. He also concluded that Danny would be in God's presence after death and that others who prayed for him would be more effective in their future prayer lives. Lastly, despite his short life, Danny's death would lead to a prelude for the adventure of eternity.

In Bernace's and Danny's stories, our contention is that God's actions and purposes transcend our understanding of the predictability of how these viruses infect the body's neurons and how the body's immune system

---

9. Brunsting, *He Is Not Gone*, 9–139.

can be altered. This size scale is especially small (about 1 micron or less, see Figure 4 page 37). While God acts in ways we do not comprehend, we affirm that there was a purpose for Bernace's polio induced paralysis and that there was a purpose for Danny's short life. Also, we draw the same conclusion in the case of Uncle Al, even though the airworthiness of his plane was so impaired that he and his crew could not return safely to their home base. We end by noting that randomness played a major role in all three of Al's personal stories, as it has and does in ours, and that God acts through extra dimensions that are inaccessible and often inexplicable to us.

Micro and Macro Sources

As in the case of Al's stories, randomness appears throughout the micro and macro sources of our experiences. The atoms and molecules that make up our bodies are implanted with randomness as are most of the physical world we live in, for example our smart phones, our GPS guidance systems, and high definition TVs. This randomness occurs in all size ranges: 1) the very small about the size of atoms and smaller and 2) all sizes larger than atoms up to and including humans, planets, solar systems, galaxies, galactic clusters, and even the whole universe. Size range number 1 occurs below about 1 nm (one meter divided by 1 billion). See Figure 4 page 37. Size range number 2 occurs above about 1 nm.

In size range number 1, particle behavior is understood in terms of quantum physics, which describes all matter in terms of fuzziness and uncertainty. In this size range, electrons (and their fields) carry signals in most of our electronic devices. A significant fraction of the US gross domestic product is due to applications of quantum physics to these kinds of commercial products. Quantum effects are tiny but very important. The reason that baseballs, houses, and aircraft do not seem fuzzy to us is because in each object of this size there are trillions and trillions of atoms and molecules each existing and moving in a fuzzy quantum state; taken together these particles average out to the non-fuzzy objects that we sense in our classical physics world. Each atom has an uncertainty (fuzziness) in its location and motion (called momentum). Our intuition about the behavior of matter and energy is not helpful in understanding quantum based behaviors, which are strange to us.

Quantum physics even helps us to understand some natural events larger than 1nm such as the Sun. The energy source for most all life in the Earth's biosphere is the Sun. Clearly, our understanding how the Sun produces all that radiant energy, falling onto the Earth is worthwhile knowledge for us.

Most of our agricultural output ultimately depends on the Sun for energy. All our fossil fuels such as gasoline and natural gas were in the end formed by the Sun. The Sun is essentially a fusion nuclear reactor that requires quantum physics to understand the release of all that solar energy that the Sun has been releasing for the last 4.5 billion years of its existence.

In the world of quantum physics we are not able to precisely predict outcomes because they are random. No matter how sophisticated and powerful our microscopes are, those outcomes are random. No technology that we have removes this randomness. The conclusion here is that at the most fundamental level randomness dominates our physical world.

At larger sizes in the classical physics domain (number 2) there are many examples of randomness that affect our lives, including tornados, tsunamis, hurricanes, volcanic explosions, famines, and the sinking of mighty ships.

We conclude from a detailed examination of the quantum physics world (smaller than about 1 nm) and also larger sizes in the classical physics world (larger than about 1 nm) that counter to our intuition, randomness plays a fundamental role. Even though our intuition and our experiences lead us to anticipate a precise chain of cause and effects for most of our experiences, the reality is that no such precise chain exists for most of what happen to us. We seem to be swimming in a great sea of randomness, even though at the deepest levels our desire is for certainty and purposefulness.

How does God play a role in all our world's fuzziness? Our contention is that God acts in other dimensions, not available to us, so that what might appear random to us is really an available space for God to exercise power and purpose. If we view the cone in only two dimensions, as depicted above in Figure 12 page 157, we cannot possibly comprehend the cone's full shape in the three dimensions. We see this as analogous to our human confinement to four dimensions and God's influence in our lives and in human history through extra dimensions.

The Universe and Our Solar System

In this summary, we took a look at the largest of all macro structures, the universe, and the role that randomness played from the start to our present time. The time scales are way, way, way beyond our own experiences with the universe being 13.8 billion years old. Likewise the space scales are way, way, way beyond our own experiences with the universe being approximately 90 billion light years across. In both time and space our own human common sense and intuitions are hopelessly limited to think about these spaces and times. We must rely on measurements and observations, simulations based on physical laws and mathematics, and our best interpretations of those observations and simulations. This requires the skills of our best scientists such as cosmologists, particle physicists, and planetary scientists. Also, it is commonly assumed that natural laws, known today, are unchanged and apply in the same way over all that time and space.

When we take this approach we conclude that just after cosmic inflation (see Figure 6 page 53) the universe was filled with a uniform brew of energy and subatomic particles (for example, electrons, quarks, pions, photons, neutrinos, and gluons) all in highly randomized motion. At about 380,000 years after the Big Bang the universe cooled enough so that these particles could start to form atoms. All mass and energy was still very random and unstructured at this time. In all this chaos, small clumps of particles emerged randomly, which later formed galaxies and stars.

Nuclear fusion was the source of light and other radiation from the stars (Figure 7 page 56). This process involves random and unstructured collisions between two atomic nuclei under high pressures and temperatures. Gravitational forces keep the nuclear fusion confined within each star's interior. Atomic elements heavier than lead, which were formed from the end of life giant star explosions, helped create our solar system. This too involved random motions and collisions at the atomic and subatomic scales. The debris from these explosions, including heavy elements, appears to be the basic building blocks for the formation of our solar system and eventually conscious, mindful, and self-aware life of Earth.

The formation of the Sun, planets, moons, and asteroids of our solar system resulted from random collisions of particles that formed in that debris. All the collisions, the beginning fusion in the proto-sun, and the distribution of the asteroids were all dominated by random processes (not counting gravity). The spatial distribution of elements in what would become our life friendly Earth was to a large extent randomly determined. Up to about 3.8 billion years ago our Earth was pounded by asteroids, meters, and other objects from the solar system. This is called the Late Heavy Bombardment. Many of these events caused much of the liquid water to vaporize and the planet's temperature to rise. During this time, life could not have existed.

As soon as the Late Heavy Bombardment ceased the first life forms appeared and evolution started to become important for the emergence of the rich variety of life. Evolution essentially depends on random mutations in an individual's genetic code and the subsequent survival of the fittest in the resulting progeny. Eventually, some 200,000 years ago, modern, self-conscious, and self-aware humans appeared. Language, tools, religions, cooperative behaviors, and languages all started to develop.

From the time of the Big Bang, some 13.8 billion years ago, to 200,000 years ago when modern humans first appeared, our understanding is that randomness dominated these processes. See Table 5 (page 68) for a summary for some of them. Our knowledge would be non-existent about all this chaos without state of the art telescopes, satellites, knowledge of the applicable natural laws, simulations, and experts to interpret all this information. Using only our intuition would be totally inadequate to appreciate the hugely important role that randomness has played to get us to where we are now.

Development of Conscious, Mindful, and Self-aware Humans

This summary extends directly from the preceding one and focuses on how conscious, mindful, and self-aware humans evolved on Earth. It appears that just after the Earth sustained the Late Heavy Bombardment (about 3.8 billion years ago) life first appeared on the surface of the Earth. We do not understand exactly how this happened, so it is called the "origin of life problem." There is no commonly accepted explanation for how life got started. We do know that randomness played important roles at various levels, such as the planetary, biochemical, and energy levels. Before we can make any progress in understanding the origin of life problem, we need to describe what life is. Table 6 (page 73) summarizes commonly accepted, basic characteristics of life: reproduction (or replication), a summary of life's dependences (such as food and energy), evolution, and containment (such as a cell membrane).

Only a few elements are needed for life (carbon, hydrogen, oxygen, nitrogen, sulfur, phosphorus, plus a few others). Carbon is used the most because many more types of bio-molecules can be formed with carbon than any other element. This in turn provides many more possibilities for cells to form and carbon supports many more potential evolutionary pathways.

Liquid water seems to be a very basic requirement for life due to its ability to support life over a wide range of temperatures and environments, which in turn opens up more evolutionary options for life. Also, liquid water is an excellent solvent for transporting biomolecules within the cell. Much of this is randomly determined at the molecular level. Our understanding is that life is self-regulating and a delicately complex set of very small machine type structures of a high order.

When life did start about 3.8 billion years ago, the atmosphere could not have supported most of the life today. At that early time there were no predators, so that environmental niches were far different than today. Life must have started as simply as possible, yet have the essential features referenced above. This means that soon after life started single cells developed to support life's functions. At some point a few of these cells learned how to attach themselves to other cells and they developed multi cellular life forms. By doing this they become better adopted to their environment. Learning originated from random mutations of the genetic code

Also, up to about 2.3 billion years ago there was no oxygen gas in the atmosphere. It first appeared at that time because cyanobacteria learned how to use sunlight, water, and carbon dioxide to make sugar with oxygen as the waste product. This is called photosynthesis. This oxygen producing bio-process was so successful that the Earth's atmosphere was eventually able to open the door to more advanced organisms that depended on atmospheric oxygen. These were major advancements: from single cells to multiple celled organisms and from carbon dioxide dependent to oxygen dependent life forms. Evolutionary changes in many of those early life forms resulted in better adaptations so that life had a better chance of survival and sustainability in those early Earth environments.

Also, there were many failures due to genetic blind alleys. Of all the species of plants and animals that ever existed on the Earth, 99 percent of them are now extinct. Sometimes a large number of species will die off simultaneously. This is called a mass extinction. Several times all life on Earth came close to total annihilation, which means that humans would never have appeared. These mass extinctions appear to be random and unpredictable. We humans have avoided several close calls. If we had not, we would not be around to go to baseball games, listen to classical music, or read books about randomness.

Very recently (on a geological time scale) modern humans first appeared (about 200,000 years ago). Our emergence on the scene depended on long chains of unpredictable antecedent events. Many of these random events, considered in isolation, seem minor and unimportant. Our species, *Homo sapiens*, became so successful that all the other hominins disappeared. We developed language and started to use tools. Religion emerged. We lived in groups and hunted together with new weapons we invented and developed. Eventually we populated the whole planet. All of this depended our new and enlarged brain that allowed for abstract thinking, self-awareness, and curiosity for how the world works.

Both this summary of chapter 5 and the preceding one for chapter 4 raise the challenging question of where God fits into this process. Once again, we are not in a position to provide an answer that includes all of the empirical details that led from one stage to another. However, this does not mean that the evolution of the universe was without God's guidance. Our view is that the contrary is true for the following reason. Even though we humans are confined by the four space and time dimensions of our finite existence, we believe that God is not. Furthermore, because we accept that God acts through extra dimensions that are unreachable to us, we contend that God has guided the process of natural and social evolution from the time of the Big Bang to the emergence of conscious, mindful, and self-aware life on Earth.

Twentieth-Century History

In the preceding chapters, both determinism and indeterminism without choice played the key role. This is clearly in evidence in the case of Al Brunsting's sister Bernace who contracted polio and his younger brother Danny who died of leukemia. The micro and many of the macro events and the evolution of the universe, solar system, and nonhuman life on Earth also involved no choice determinism and indeterminism. Randomness was pervasive. At the same time, in different situations many determinist and indeterminist events involved choice, such as the Nazi destruction of Uncle Al's airplane during WWII, the maiden voyage of the Titanic, among others.

In summarizing chapter 6, we describe the five major episodes of the twentieth century where choice dominated the development of both determinist and indeterminist events. For example, in 1914 when Gavrilo Princip chose to assassinate Archduke Franz Ferdinand, he ushered in WWI that no one saw coming. Once Princip made this choice, we understand that the follow up assassination was predetermined by his decision. As the developments of the First World War unfolded, a chain of both predictable and unpredictable events followed each other in rapid succession. Once the European nations began to form opposing alliances, it forced others to join sides or declare their neutrality as the US did.

When Germany (by choice that led to a deterministic outcome) sank the *Lusitania* in May, 1915 that cost 128 Americans their lives and then contacted the Mexican Ambassador in January, 1917, the US under then President Wilson could no longer sustain neutrality. Four months later, the US declared war on Germany (also by choice), which tipped the scale against the German led forces. In less than two years, the warring in Europe ended when Kaiser Wilhelm II surrendered in November, 1918. When the Treaty of Versailles was signed June, 1919, it was unknown to anyone at the time that this Treaty would contribute in no small way to the rise of Nazism and the Second World War (indeterminate).

The remaining four episodes also include major choices followed by unpredictable events. The second episode began on October 29, 1929, when the stock market crash (based in part on bad investment choices) plunged the planet into an unforeseen worldwide Great Depression. Through no fault of their own, thousands of workers lost their jobs and homes. Unemployment peaked at 25 percent. Banks struggled to survive, but the panicked rush of deposit withdrawals by frightened citizens forced thousands of them into insolvency. An unpredictable drought turned America's southern states into a heinous Dust Bowl that drove thousands of farmers from their land. It was a desperate time not only for the US but for virtually every other nation around the world, especially in Europe.

With the election of Franklin D. Roosevelt in 1932, conditions began to improve. From 1933 to 1939, the US, government created nearly fifty New Deal programs designed to stimulate the economy, put people back to work, protect home ownership from foreclosure, insure bank deposits, and provide income for retired seniors, among others. As the economy began to rebound, a new and unexpected threat that led to the third major episode of the twentieth century began to emerge. The harsh conditions that the Treaty of Versailles imposed on Germany along with the devastating effects of the Great Depression were important factors that contributed to the rise of German and Italian fascism.

When Hitler annexed both Austria and Czechoslovakia in 1938 and invaded Poland a year later, the US remained neutral as it had done at the outset of WWI. This came to an abrupt halt when without warning Japan struck the American fleet at Pearl Harbor on December 7, 1941. After declaring war, America and its European allies launched a massive counter offensive against both Germany and Japan. With the destruction of the German military forces and the atomic bomb obliteration of Hiroshima and Nagasaki in 1945, WWII came to an end.

However, in the midst of the exhilaration that erupted when the war ended, little did anyone know then that the seeds of the fourth major episode on the twentieth century, the Cold War, were already growing. When Stalin announced unpredictably in February, 1946 that capitalism and communism were incompatible, the US and the USSR faced each other over nuclear arsenals that threatened the world with annihilation. Under the umbrella of Truman's containment doctrine, the US and its allies stopped the worldwide spread of communism during the Korean and Vietnam wars and the Cuban nuclear missile crisis. Then in December, 1991, to everyone's surprise, the Cold War ended suddenly when the USSR Supreme Court dissolved the Soviet Union as an official nation state.

The fifth and final episode entails the rise of jihadi terrorism. Its roots can be traced back to the Wahhabi extremism that appeared in Saudi Arabia during the eighteenth century. The twentieth century form of Islamic violence began after WWI, when in 1924 Ataturk created the modern state of Turkey and dissolved the last vestiges of the Ottoman Caliphate. Four years later in 1928, by choice, the radical Egyptian al-Banna formed the Muslim Brotherhood that grew steadily and culminated in the creation of al-Qaeda in 1988 and the new Caliphate called the Islamic State in 2014.

In response, a coalition of over myriad nations has unleashed a counter offensive to destroy both al-Qaeda and the Caliphate. While the long term outcome of twentieth century jihadi terrorism has yet to be determined, if the twenty-first century is anything like the twentieth, random events will play a major role. While we make no predictions, we foresee that the Islamic State Caliphate will eventually be defeated as a distinct political entity providing that the many nations united against it continue their powerful and persistent military actions.

Where can the footprints of God be found in the random twists and turns that shaped these five episodes? Once again, we find ourselves in a position of not being able to answer this question definitively. Why? Because we live only in four space and time dimensions and do not possess nor have access to the other dimensions that we accept God has. Nonetheless, we observe how choices followed by both predictable and probable outcomes fit directly into these episodes. We believe that God has given to humanity the gift of free will that emerged through earthly evolution during the past 200,000 years. At the same time, we presume that when it is used to make choices that perpetuate evil, especially of the kind described in these five episodes, God will eventually intervene to stop it according to God's time table and in God's chosen way.

The Future

In chapter 7, our primary focus was on the future. As in the case of looking backward in chapter 6 to the five episodes that occurred during the twentieth century, we expect that as the future evolves it will also include a combination of predictable and probable outcomes that include both choice and no choice. When compared to the past, the key issue involves whether using new approaches to think more systematically about the future will improve our ability to predict forthcoming events and trends with greater accuracy before they occur.

As we noted, four of the most important modern methods include trend extrapolation, models and simulations, Delphi techniques involving panels of experts, and scenarios. We know that our universe consists of both determinate and indeterminate outcomes that involve both choice and no choice. This means that when it comes to what will happen in the future, choice will play a major role, because we humans do not sit around passively and wait for the future to arrive. Instead, we make decisions and take actions that we anticipate will lead to predictable results, but we also know that this does not always happen. There is no guarantee that the outcomes we want will occur. While many will be predictable, others will be only probable.

Since the dawn of modern science, we have gradually become more sophisticated in our knowledge of the underlying forces that govern our highly structured cosmos. As described above, classical physics, quantum physics, and free will have led us to a clearer understanding of how cause and effect relationships can be combined in four distinct ways that include determinism, indeterminism, choice, and no choice (See Table 1 page 17). We are keenly aware that the early scientific view of a completely deterministic universe is overly simplistic. We now understand that there are many situations where we can know outcomes in advance with certainty as in the case of classical physics whereas in quantum physics mostly with probability.

If we accept that the cosmos is comprised of both determinate relationships as well as some that are irreducibly indeterminate, then we will never be able to predict the future with 100 percent accuracy. This realization has led to a shift away from thinking about the future in terms of prediction and toward the development of an approach that entails envisioning alternative pathways the future might follow. The currently favored method for enhancing foresight is to think in terms of plausible scenarios any one of which could become the actual future.

Once we have created a variety of images of what might lie ahead, we can estimate different levels of probability, decide which one we prefer or do not prefer, act to bring it about or stop it, and develop contingency plans for all of them in anticipation of how we will respond depending on how the future evolves. In addition, we can mentally prepare for a future condition that may come out of the blue and is not included within the plausible scenarios we imagine.

Thus, while the modern study of the future has not necessarily improved our ability to predict the future with more accuracy than in the past, especially in the long-term, we have created methods and procedures that can help us better prepare for it. The scenario approach in particular enables us to make better decisions in the present in anticipation of taking actions that will bring about the kind of future we prefer or prevent those we do not want to occur. The lesson we have learned by looking backwards at five major episodes of the twentieth century is how much randomness shaped what happened. If the future is anything like the past, and we expect that it will be, then we can anticipate that randomness will continue to play a major role as forthcoming events in the twenty-first century and beyond take shape.

From this perspective, it is easy to take the next step in considering how God will intercede into this process. In those cases where the universe that God has created is highly structured according to no choice deterministic laws of nature, the future will develop in a highly predictable direction. However, this is not the case for unpredictable natural events and where indeterminacies due to human choices exist. It is here that probabilities will prevail and where God will intervene in ways we cannot foresee. This is because we are limited by the four dimensions of our existence. Despite this restriction, from our theist viewpoint, we assume that God transcends our finite condition.

Even though we humans choose to determine the future by our own designs, ultimately it is God who guides this process. No doubt, this will involve both good and evil choices as well as indeterminacies that entail only probable outcomes. Nonetheless, it is our contention that because God operates through dimensions beyond our four God will mold the future according to God's intentions and timetable. This will be accomplished through both the highly structured and random relationships that comprise our physical universe and human experience where the issue of fairness is of central concern.

Fairness

In chapter 8, we focused on fairness, which we understand to mean that everyone gets what they are due. In an ideal and just world, good people should be rewarded, and bad people should be punished. However, sooner or later everyone learns that we do not live in such a perfect world. From birth to death, life does not distribute its burdens and benefits equally. In addition, because we humans are creatures of nature, we experience pain and suffering in different degrees as Al Brunsting's three personal stories reveal.

When dealing with the issue of fairness, we distinguish between the pain and suffering that nature causes and the pain and suffering that some people intentionally inflict on others. Because nature operates by objective laws of cause and effect, it does not behave with intentionality. Nature does not deliberately choose to distribute varying degrees of harm to different individuals. When someone contracts a disease that causes permanent damage or death, as in the case of Al Brunsting's sister Bernace or his brother Danny, it is the result of natural processes over which we have no control at the time they occur. While the forces of nature can and do cause much pain and suffering, more so for some than others, they do not do so with malice of forethought.

Our assumption is that by comparison we humans possess God's gift of free will, and we can choose to inflict harm and destruction on others, as in the case of Uncle Al who lost his life at the hands of Nazi pilots in WWII. When individuals and groups purposefully impose harm on others, we call this evil, in contrast to the natural pain and suffering that results merely from living in the flesh. Nature is not evil, but people can be, and all too often are.

Whether we are dealing with the pain and suffering that nature causes unintentionally or that result from deliberate and evil choices, we know that randomness plays a significant role in both cases. As we show in Table 10 page 138, actions can be intentional or unintentional, and outcomes can be good or bad. This means that 1) intentional actions can result in good outcomes, but 2) intentional actions can also lead to bad outcomes. Furthermore, 3) unintentional actions can bring about good outcomes, and 4) unintentional actions can produce bad outcomes.

These four alternatives exist because in both nature and society, good or bad outcomes can result from both determinate and indeterminate causes and human choice. No one of the above four possibilities applies equally to all persons, because randomness plays a major role in how intentionality and unintentionality affect people in very different ways.

Where does God fit into this picture? In order to answer this question, we start with the one alternative that has received the greatest amount of attention: when bad things happen to good people who act with the best of intentions or who suffer because of circumstances over which they have no control. The book of *Job* in the *Bible* confronts this concern head on when Job, who perceives himself to be a good and righteous person, does not receive the rewards he believes he deserves. What he does not know is that God made a deal with the devil to test his faithfulness by depriving him of his family and fortune.

In the midst of his suffering, Job demands that God tell him why bad things should be happening to him. God's response, in a nut shell, is that God created the universe, Job did not and that God's ways are not Job's ways and by implication not our ways. After hearing God's response, Job accepts God's sovereignty over all things and that he is to remain faithful no matter what life's circumstances bring his way.

Is our assumption that God possesses extra dimensionality consistent with Job's conclusion? The answer is both yes and no. Job's image of bad things happening to a good person is only one-fourth of the story. The other three-fourths involve good things happening to good people, good things happening to bad people, and bad things happening to bad people. All four possibilities exist. While we affirm that that God has given the gift of free will for making good and evil choices and agree with Job that God's purposes will ultimately prevail, we also believe that life is not consistently fair. There is no guarantee that good intentions will lead to good outcomes, or that bad intentions will result in bad outcomes. While they might and do in many different circumstances, it many others they do not.

The second response to the issue of how God relates to unfairness as described in these four alternatives is to define God as the sum of perfections (all knowing, all loving, and all powerful) and then to reconcile the contradictions that exist between them. If God is all knowing, loving and powerful, then why does evil exist? The standard theistic answer starts with the assumption that God has given us the gift of free will that has gradually developed over the past 200,000 years of human evolution on Earth and that we can choose to use it for good or ill.

As we indicated in chapter 8, while God does not predetermine our choices, God knows us better than we know ourselves. This means that although God has advanced knowledge of the actions we will take before we take them, we are responsible for our own choices. Out of love, God permits us to use our free will to make our own choices. Since all fall short of God's perfection, God's loving mercy and forgiveness are always available for repentant hearts. Finally, despite God's all powerful nature, God allows us to commit evil but will eventually intervene to stop it. Ultimately, God's power and purposes will prevail and not ours, even though we do not know when and how this will occur according to God's timetable.

Will there ever be a time when God will eliminate evil and bring perfect fairness to Earth? While some theologians answer yes based on some form of God guided human evolution, most say no because as long as we humans possess free will, many will use it for evil purposes. The only time that perfect justice will exist will be either at the end of history or in life after death when God will give everyone what they deserve. In the meantime, randomness will remain an inherent part of our highly structured universe. In the final analysis, it is our contention that God's plans are unfolding in the midst of this process of inconsistent fairness even though we do not have access to the extra dimensions through which God's purposes are being realized.

Conclusion

First, we have underscored the tremendous impact that both classical and quantum physics have had on our understanding of how the world works. In the sixteenth and seventeenth centuries, during the period of early modern science, classical physics led to the discovery of cause and effect relationships that can be predicted in advance with certainty, such as the effects of gravity.

As the field of physics expanded during the twentieth century, investigations that focused on subatomic particles and weather systems gave rise to a different view of nature, one where the outcomes of causal relationships cannot be predicted in advance with certainty but only with probability. As a result of these discoveries, we know now that the randomness has been and continues to be a key factor in determining how our highly structured universe has evolved.

Second, we have observed that the interaction that occurs between the causal relationships that are predictable and those random events that modify them are ongoing at both the micro and macro levels. The tension between stability and change is constant, and randomness is one of the major factors that drives the development of new species and structures. We have described how normal distributions, mutations, permutations, correlations, contingencies, surprises, among others have given rise to unpredictable transformations that have appeared at virtually every stage of physical and social evolution.

Third, we have divided evolution into two distinct stages. In the first stage, and by far the longest, *Homo sapiens* did not exist. While predictability and probability were interwoven from the start, both the determinate and indeterminate events that occurred during this prolonged period did not involve the human mind and its capacity for choice. For billions of years, the expansion of the universe as a whole, the emergence of our galaxy and solar system, and the appearance of every nonhuman species on Earth occurred prior to the arrival of *Homo sapiens*. On every step on the evolutionary ladder, randomness without choice fueled the unexpected twists and turns of this process. See top left and top right cells (rows labeled "Choice/No") in Table 1 page 17.

The second stage appeared around 200,000 years ago, when anatomically modern humans started to appear. With the passage of time, they developed the ability to reason. This led them to consider the potential consequences of alternative courses of action before deciding which one to choose. Even though *Homo sapiens* like all nonhuman species continued to be subject to the determinate and indeterminate laws of nature that were a part of stage 1, in stage 2 something genuinely new began to surface on Earth: the human capacity for choice that emerged through the natural process of earthly evolution. See bottom left and bottom right cells (rows labeled "Choice/Yes") in Table 1.

Fourth, the advent of human rationality during the past 200,000 years introduced more randomness into the evolution of life on Earth. With the emergence of the human mind, also called free will, came more uncertainty. Even with the continuation of the predictable and probable cause and effect relationships that started in the first stage, the second stage introduced extra levels of complexity. In addition to there being only two alternatives of 1) determinacy without choice and 2) indeterminacy without choice, now there were two more: 3) determinacy with choice and 4) indeterminacy with choice.

Throughout all of the topics that we discussed in this book, we included either one or some combination of these four possibilities in describing the role that randomness plays in each area. Prior to the appearance of *Homo sapiens*, only the first two applied to the birth and expansion of the universe. With the arrival of modern humans on Earth, all four came into play. In the midst of our Darwinian desire for stability and consistency and in the past 13.8 billion years during every time period and at every level, randomness or unpredictability has remained pervasive and constant. As the future unfolds, both determinate and indeterminate relationships that incorporate choice as well as no choice combinations will continue to be an essential part of this process.

Fifth and last, as theists we have reflected on how God, whom we define as the Intelligent Creator who formed the cosmos and guided its evolution, relates to the randomness that is rooted in our highly structured universe. The ideas that we have introduced include the speculation that God exists and acts through the natural world and in human history in dimensions that are beyond our limitations. This assumption is consistent with the work of current scientists who are actively considering multiple dimensions beyond the space and time dimensions that limit us. Our view of God's possible actions in these extra dimensions is consistent with the research of these scientists.[10]

When we recognize that we need to consider other dimensions for a complete view of reality and not limit ourselves only to the four that confine finite human experience, we realize that some of the events that affect our lives might possibly originate from dimensions that are not available to us.

---

10. Official String Theory Web Site, "*Extra Dimensions*," and Science, Phys. Org, *Hints of extra dimensions in gravitational waves?*

Assuming this is the case, we contend that it is easy to take the next step: it is through randomness that God has guided the process of evolution from the Big Bang to the present moment. This encompasses all the micro and macro events described in previous chapters; the unexpected developments of human history; the emergence of the human mind, choice, and free will; forecasts for the future; the quest for fairness; and Al Brunsting's three personal stories as well as our own.

Thus, while there remains much we cannot explain and probably never will, we are confident in our conclusion that it is God, the Intelligent Creator, who is working actively within the randomness that is an inherent part of our highly structured universe.

Bibliography

Alexander, Eben. *Proof of Heaven*. New York: Simon & Schuster, 2012.
Al-Qaradawi, Yusuf, and K. El-Helbawy, *Lawful and the Prohibited in Islam*. New Delhi, India: Kitab Bhavan, 1985.
Bennett, Deborah. *Randomness*. Cambridge: Harvard University Press, 1999.
Bishop, Peter. "Thinking like a Futurist." *The Futurist* (1998) 40.
Brunsting, Bernard. *He Is Not Gone: The Death of a Child and the Faith of His Father*. New York: Exposition, 1961.
Cobb, John B., and David Ray Griffin. *Process Theology: An Introductory Exposition*. Philadelphia: Westminster, 1976.
Chambers, J., and Jacqueline Milton, *From Dust to Life: the Origin and Evolution of Our Solar System*. Princeton, New Jersey: Princeton University Press, 2014.
Chardin, Pierre de. *The Phenomenon of Man*. New York: Harper Perennial, 1976.
Davies, Paul. "Make a Date with another Dimension," *Cosmos* 72 Dec-Jan (2017).
Fairbanks, Daniel J. *Evolving: The Human Effect and Why It Matters*. Amherst, New York: Prometheus, 2012.
Helm, Paul. *The Providence of God*. Downers Grove, Illinois: InterVarsity, (1994) 39–55.
Horvitz, Leslie Alan. *The Complete Idiot's Guide to Evolution*. Indianapolis: Alpha, 2002.
James, William. *The Varieties of Religious Experience*. New York: Longmans, Green, and Co., 1923.
Knoll, Andrew H. *Life on a Young Planet: the First Three Billion Years of Evolution on Earth*. Princeton, New Jersey: Princeton University Press, 2003.
Kushner, Harold S. *When Bad Thinks Happen to Good People*. New York: Random House, 1981.
Lane, Nick. *The Vital Question*. London: W. W. Norton, 2015.
Laplace, Pierre-Simon. *A Philosophical Essay on Probabilities*. Chicago: Cosmo, 2007.
Lederman, L. M., and Christopher T. Hill. *Symmetry and the Beautiful Universe*. Amherst, New York: Prometheus, 2004.
———. *Quantum Physics for Poets*. Amherst, New York: Prometheus, 2011.
Lee, Jane J. "Mega-eruptions Caused Mass Extinction, Study Finds." http://news.nationalgeographic.com/news/2013/03/130321-triassic-mass-extinction-volcano-paleontology-science/.
Lee, Laura. *Bad Predictions: 2000 Years of the Best Minds Making the Worst Predictions*. Rochester: Elsewhere, 2000.

Leibniz, Gottfried Wilhelm. *Theodicy Essays: On the Goodness of God, the Freedom of Man, and the Origin of Evil*. London: Routledge & Kegan Paul, 1951.

MacLeish, Archibald. *J.B.* New York: Houghton Mifflin Harcourt, 1958.

McFallen, Johnjoe, Jim Al-Khalili. *Life on the Edge: The Coming of Age of Quantum Biology*. New York: Broadway, 2014.

McFaul, Thomas R., and Al Brunsting. *God Is Here To Stay: Science, Evolution, and Belief in God*. Eugene, Oregon: Wipf & Stock, 2014.

Mlodnow, Leonard. *The Drunkard's Walk: How Randomness Rules Our Lives*. New York: Vintage, 2009.

"Modern Jihad." *Wikipedia*.

Nagel, Thomas. *Mind and Cosmos: Why the Materialist Neo-Darwinian Conception of Nature is Almost Certainly False*. Oxford: Oxford University Press, 2012.

Official String Theory Web Site, "*Looking for extra dimensions*," 2017. http://superstringtheory.com/experm/exper5.html.

Peterson, Michael et al., *Philosophy of Religion*. Fifth Edition. New York: Oxford University Press (2014) 309.

Pjoman, Louis P. *Who Are We? Theories of Human Nature*. New York: Oxford University Press, 2006.

Rauschenbusch, Walter. *Christianizing the Social Order*. New York: Macmillan, 1907.

———. *A Theology for the Social Gospel*. New York: Abingdon, 1917.

Rescher, Nicholas. *Luck: the Brilliant Randomness of Everyday Life*. Pittsburgh: University of Pittsburgh Press, 2001.

Roberts, Alice. *Evolution: The Human Story*. Great Britain: Darling Kindersley, 2011.

Rovelli, Carlo. *Seven Brief Lessons on Physics*. New York: Riverhead, 2016.

Schnaars, Steven P. *Megamistakes: Forecasting and the Myth of Rapid Technological Change*. New York: Free Press, 1989.

Schwartz, Peter. *The Art of the Long View: Planning for the Future in an Uncertain World*. New York: Doubleday, 1991.

Science, Phys. Org, *Hints of extra dimensions in gravitational waves?* https://phys.org/news/2017-06-hints-extra-dimensions-gravitational.html.

Silver, Nate. *The Signal and the Noise: Why So Many Predictions Fail—but Some Don't*. New York: Penquin, 2012.

Skinner, B. F. *Beyond Freedom and Dignity*. Indianapolis: Hackett, 1971.

Smart, J. J. C. "Sensations and Brain Processes." *Philosophical Review* 68 (1959) 141–56.

Stace, Walter T. *The Teachings of the Mystics*. New York: The New American Library, 1960.

"Strategic Foresight." Houston, Texas: University of Houston, (2016) 4.

Taleb, Nassim Nicholas. *Fooled by Randomness*, New York: Random House, 2005.

———. *The Black Swan: The Impact of the Highly Improbable*. New York: Random House, 2010.

———. *Antifragile: Things that Gain from Disorder*. New York: Random House, 2014.

Taylor, Charles W. *Alternative World Scenarios for Strategic Planning*. Revised Edition. Carlisle Barracks, Pennsylvania: Strategic Studies Institute, U.S. Army War College (1990) 4–7.

White, Matthew. *Atrocities: the 100 Deadliest Episodes in Human History*. New York: W. W. Norton, 2013.

Index

Air Corps, 27
Al (Al Brunsting's uncle), 22, 26–30, 34, 43
anthropoids, 84–85
Aquinas, Thomas, 19
Aristotle, 19–20
atomic bombs, 10, 23, 100, 102

B-17 bomber (Flying Fortress), 22, 23, 27–29, 43, 162
Berlin Wall, 104
Bernace (Al Brunsting's sister), 22, 23–26, 34
Big Bang, xi–xiii, 3, 21, 35, 50–71, 113, 153, 158, 160, 165–66, 168
bipedalism, 83–85
Brunsting, Alice (Al Brunsting's mother), 24
Brunsting, Bernard R. (Al Brunsting's father), 23

Caliphate, 106–112, 170
causality, 1–14, 18–20, 114, 123
cause and effect, xi–xiii, 1–21, 24, 26, 36, 42, 44–48, 60, 76, 80–86, 91, 95, 113–18, 122–23, 134–41, 147, 156–60, 164, 171–76
cell phones, 3
Central College, 27
Churchill, Winston, 101–2
classical physics, 1, 5, 36–44, 48–49, 159, 163–64, 171, 175
Cold War, 101–6, 169

communism, 101–6, 169
cone, 157–58, 164
Congressional Medal of Honor, 22, 27, 162
Contract Bridge, 25–26
cosmic inflation, 51, 53–54, 60
cosmic microwave background (CMB), 55, 70, 117
Cosmic Year, 71
Cosmological argument, 19
critical thinking, 86–88
curiosity, 26, 89–90, 167

Danny (Al Brunsting's brother), 23, 30–34, 44, 161–63
Dark Ages, 93, 95–96, 110, 113
dark matter, 81–82
Darwin's theory of evolution, 19, 92, 158, 176
de Chardin, Teilhard, 151
De Moth, Arlene (Al's uncle's wife), 22, 27–28
dice, 1
dimensionality, 154–58, 160, 163–64, 170–76
dinosaurs, 39, 83–85, 160
DNA, 44, 44n4, 73–78, 89, 169

eukaryotes, 78–79
evil, 136–52, 170–74
evolution, 9, 12–13, 19–21, 44, 51–52, 69–70, 73–74, 77–80, 82–91, 146–60

INDEX

experts, 125–27
extinctions, great, 80–82

fairness, 133–52
fission, nuclear, 56–57
flak, 28–29
Flying Fortress (B-17 bomber), 22–23, 27–29
foreseeing the future, 118–22
foresight, 115–18
free will, 14–18, 134–36, 146–52
fusion, nuclear, 39, 56–64, 165
future, 113–32
galaxy (see also "stars."), 3, 41, 57–59, 62, 69, 175

Germany, 92–94, 97–105, 168–69
God as all loving, 144–52, 174
God Is Here to Stay, xi–xii, 21n10, 72n1, 120n1, 132n1, 153n1
God of the Gaps, 19–20
Great Depression, 94–97

heavy elements, 61–62, 68–70, 165
Hill, Christopher T., 35n1, 55n3
Hitler, Adolf, 98–101, 133, 148, 169
hominin, 85–88, 167
Homo sapiens, 79, 84–88, 136, 160, 167, 175–76
Hope College, 25
human migrations, 88
humanity, 134
humans, first appearance of, 82–89
hydrogen (thermonuclear) bomb, 102

intentional and unintentional, 138
intuition, 369, 50–51, 163–66
Irish Potato Famine, 46
Islamic jihad, 106–112

Japan, 98–102, 169
Job, 142–49, 173–74
Johnson, Lyndon, 105

Katrina, Tropical Storm, 45
Knoll, Andrew, 25
Korean conflict, 104

language and speech, 15, 87–88, 167
Laplace, Pierre-Simon, 5, 5n2
larynx, 87
Late Heavy Bombardment, 107, 113, 119–22, 241–44
Lederman, L. M., 35n1, 55n3
leukemia, 23, 30–32, 44, 162
life, appearance of earliest forms, 71–78,
Lusitania, 93, 168

mammals, 79–85, 160
Marshall Plan, 103
Millennium movement, 151
models and simulations, 126
Muhammad, 168
Muslim Brotherhood, 107–111, 170

Nagel, Thomas, 9n8
Nature, 147, 153–57, 160–61, 172–75
Nazism, 98, 101, 168
near death experiences, 156
neutron star merger, 62
New Deal, 94–97
Nixon, Richard M., 105
non-causality, 18–20

outcomes, 137–41

pain, 33, 136–37
Pearl Harbor, 99–101, 122, 125, 169
Perot Museum, xii
photosynthesis, 66, 69, 73, 78, 89, 167
Pjoman, Louis P., 9n7, 12n9
polio, 24–26, 42–43, 161–63
Pompeii, 46
post-polio syndrome, 26
Potsdam Conference, 101–2
predestination, 147
predictability, 6–21, 35–48
predictions and forecasts, 114–18
prokaryotes, 78–79

quantum physics, 8n5, 35–42, 35n1

randomness, 1–21, 1n1
Rauschenbusch, Walter, 151, 151n8
RNA, 42n2
Roosevelt, Franklin D., 95–101, 169

Savanna Hypothesis, 85
scenarios, 127–31
Skinner, B. F., 5n3
Smart, J. J. C., 6n4
Smoot-Hawley Tariff Act, 95
solar system, 55–70
solar system & randomness, 67–70
solar system, start of, 62–66
space, 50–57
Stalin, Joseph, 101–3, 169
stars, 55, 57–59, 62–68, 165
suffering, 136–37, 143–50, 173
Sun, 52, 61–70
surprises and contingencies, 131–32

terrorism, 106–112
time, 50–53
Titanic, 47–48

tools, 15, 84–88, 132, 166–67
tornado, 44–45
trends, 11, 119–22
tsunami, 45
Twentieth Century, 91–112

unfairness, 142, 145–46, 150–52
universe, 50–70

Variability Hypothesis, 85
Versailles Treaty, 94, 97–98, 101, 168–69
Vietnam conflict, 104–5, 169

Wahhabi, 107–8, 170
water, liquid, 62–63, 66, 74, 165–67
Woodland-Mosaic Hypothesis, 85
World War I, 92–97
World War II, 97–101